YOUTH AND TRIBAL EMPOWERMENT

YOUTH
AND
TRIBAL EMPOWERMENT

Edited by

Prof. Yerroju Bhaskaracharyulu

Professor & Former Head of the Dept.
Dept. of Adult & Continuing Education
Andhra University
Visakhapatnam (Andhra Pradesh)
(India)

&

Dr. (Smt.) Yerroju Nirmala

DPH

DISCOVERY PUBLISHING HOUSE PVT. LTD.
NEW DELHI-110 002

Published by:
Tilak Wasan
DISCOVERY PUBLISHING HOUSE PVT. LTD.
4383/4B, Ansari Road, Darya Ganj
New Delhi-110 002 (India)
Phone : +91-11-23279245, 43596064-65
Fax : +91-11-23253475
E-mail : discoverypublishinghouse@gmail.com
sales@discoverypublishinggroup.com
parul.wasan@gmail.com
web : www.discoverypublishinggroup.com

First Edition: **2014**

ISBN: 978-93-5056-468-4

Youth and Tribal Empowerment

Printed at:
Dynamic Printers
Delhi

Preface

India is one of the most populous countries with young generations and may be called as Young India. Youth are widely untapped resource for improving their house holds livelihoods and transforming their skills. Youth are generally more able and are willing to earn supplemental income to develop non traditional skills. In the hope of using youth as a dynamic resource for development, the rural and urban livelihoods team has youth strategy. The broad aim is to equip youth with necessary skills through training to provide employment opportunities and to facilitate access to financial services for those who wish to be self employed entrepreneurs.

The tribal communities in forests and mountains are different from those who migrate to cities in search of livelihood. Even today, the widely pervasive reality in respect of tribal communities in India is that most of them are geographically isolated, economically weak, socially ignorant, politically in different, culturally rich, behaviorally simple, trust worthy and leading their life in the lap of nature. They are facing problems which force them to lead a life at bare subsistence level. They are in the situation featured with poverty, deprivation, disadvantaged which are very difficulty to be tackled effectively on their own. Apart from general problems and issues, several specific causes are there. Existence of poverty and ignorance any tribal may be the root cause, but lack of interest and proper commitment on the part of the public policy makers lead to the existence of mass illiteracy among various groups of scheduled tribes in India.

Education is an integral part of empowerment process. Empowerment of the tribal community means capacitating tribal community to secure access and control of their land, forest and water resources as well as to sustain and promote viable alternatives for security of their livelihoods. Empowerment is thus an interactive process whereby tribal communities are enabled to participate actively in local governance, decision making that affects their own life situation. For us, educating tribal community in a more concrete sense means to facilitate process, which will enable tribal representatives to develop an analytical capacity for assessing their external and internal environment improving on their own communities, develop confidence and capacity to articulate their interest and perspectives thereby participating in decision making, leading to better governance, developing skills to initiate local relevant alternations to improve livelihoods and challenging external pressures, value self and community history with a critical appreciation of traditional knowledge system. We recognize that literacy contributes an important access.

In this context, an edited volume on **"Youth and Tribal Empowerment"** has brought out for wider dissemination. This book consists of some selected papers which were compiled and contributed by the distinguish scholars and academicians in this field. This book consists of 22 chapters on the following themes:

1. Youth Employment and Empowerment;
2. Youth and Health Awareness;
3. Youth and Nation Building; and
4. Tribal Education and Empowerment.

The merit of this volume lies in a contemporary relevance of the subject and a vast variety of topics covered. Distinguished academicians and scholars from all over the country have contributed their wisdom in a logically arranged sequence and explained the theoretical and practical aspects in this field.

We believe that this book will be immensely significant and useful for the researchers and academicians in the field of Youth and Tribal Empowerment and this volume would prove immensely beneficial.

We are thankful to our colleagues and all other departments' personnel who associated with this task directly or indirectly. We are very much thankful to the contributors for their significant and scholarly contributions. Their choice of theme is relevant and it is the emergent need of the present age. All contributors deserve our appreciation for their contribution in producing this book.

We are very much thankful to Mr. G. Vinay Kumar who helped us in bringing out this present volume.

Prof. Yerroju Bhaskaracharyulu
Dr. (Smt.) Yerroju Nirmala

Contents

List of Contributors

1. **T.Ananda**, Research Associate, Department of Economics, S.V. University, Tirupati.
   e-mail: anandthapai@rediffmail.com
2. **Prof. K. Sudha Rani**, Professor, Department of Adult and Continuing Education, S.V. University, Tirupati.
   e-mail: sudhasreedhar@rediffmail.com
3. **Dr. K. Devan**, Associate Professor, Centre for Adult and Continuing Education, Pondicherry University, Puducherry 605 014, *e-mail:* kdevan63@gmail.com
4. **Dr. G.Sundharavadivel**, Assistant Professor, Department of Adult and Continuing Education, University of Madras, Chennai-600005, *e-mail:* drsundara_unom@yahoo.com
5. **Dr. (Smt.) Y. Nirmala**, Andhra University, Visakhapatnam.
6. **Prof Y. Bhaskaracharyulu**, Professor, Department of Education (Merged), Andhra University, Visakhapatnam, *e-mail:* bhaskaryerroju@rediffmail.com
7. **V.Satyaseelan**, Formerly, Head-Resources Deployment & Advisor – Construction Skills Training, L & T – ECC Division – Head Quarters, Chennai.
   e-mail: vss4947@gmail.com
8. **Dr. Santosh Kumar Mishra,** Technical Assistant, Population Education Resource Centre (PERC), Department of Continuing and Adult Education and Extension Work, S. N. D. T. Women's University, Mumbai - 400020, Maharashtra, India.
   e-mail: drskmishrain@yahoo.com

9. **Dr. J.Anuradha**, Lecturer in English, Prema College of Education, Thimmapuram, Visakhapatnam.
e-mail: vanurahda_jami@yahoo.in
10. **Dr. K. Ananda Rao**, Research Scholar, Department of Sociology, Andhra University, Visakhapatnam.
11. **G.Vijayakumari**, Research Scholar, Department of Education, Periyar University, Salem District, Tamil Nadu.
12. **Dr. K.Nachimuthu**, Assistant Professor, Department of Education, Periyar University, Salem District, Tamil Nadu,
e-mail: dr_knmuthu@yahoo.com
13. **Dr. Mande Suresh**, Research Scholar, Department of Social Work, Andhra University, Visakhapatnam.
14. **R.S.Varahala Dora**, Research Scholar, Department of Education, Andhra University Visakhapatnam.
15. **Dr. N.V.S.Surynarayana**, Teaching Associate, Department of Education, Andhra University campus, Vizianagaram – 535 002.
e-mail: suryanarayana_nvs@yahoo.com
16. **Goteti Himabindu**, Vice-Principal, Sun D.Ed College, Vizianagaram – 535 002 (AP)
e-mail: gotetihimabindu@yahoo.com
17. **Dr. S.Thulasamma**, Academic Consultant, Department of Home Science, S.V. University, Tirupathi.
18. **Prof. V.Sreedevi**, Department of Home Science, S.V. University, Tirupathi, *e-mail:* profsreedevi@yahoo.com
19. **Prof. D.Usha Rani**, Director,Center for Extension Studies and Women's Studies, S.V. University, Tirupathi.
e-mail: profusharanid2006@gmail.com
20. **Dr. B.Praveena Devi**, Teaching Associate, Department of Education, AU Campus, Vizianagaram.
e-mail: bpraveenadevi@gmail.com
21. **M. Vetrichelvan**, Research Scholar, Department of Tamil, Department of Education, Gandhigram Rural University.
22. **Dr. A. Jahitha Begum**, Associate Professor & Head, Department of Education, Gandhigram Rural University, Gandhigram, (India). Mobile: 9443273174
e-mail: jahee_j@yahoo.co.in

23. **Dr. N. Sony Havilah**, Teaching Associate, IASE, Andhra University, Visakhapatnam.

24. **K. John Sudheer**, Lecturer in AMG College of Education for Women, Bheemunipatnam.
e-mail: johnsudheerhavi@gmail.com

25. **Dr. K. John Babu,** Assistant Professor, Department of Journalism and Mass Communication, Acharya Nagarjuna University, Guntur, (AP), *e-mail:* John4media@gmail.com

SECTION – I

YOUTH EMPLOYMENT AND EMPOWERMENT

1

Career Orientation in Colleges for Students Placement

– T. Ananda
– K. Sudha Rani

The process of deciding future career options can be challenging and involves careful considerations on the part of the student, the parents and the educators. All though there are many careers to choose from, individuals have traditionally been limited in there career options especially if they are unprepared for the requirements of the workplace, underestimate their capability or unaware of the range of workplace accommodations that can broaden their career options. Hence, career orientation or guidance is very important in higher educational institutions. It is at this stage that students face many obstacles as they transit from studies to work. It is the educational institutions that have to assume this important role in providing career orientation to the students at this decisive stage of their life. Recognizing this, a study was conducted to know the career orientation in colleges which enable the students to select and utilize the opportunities in the world of employment.

Objectives of the Study

- To know the steps taken for career orientation in colleges.
- To study the difference in the career orientation in Government and corporate colleges.
- To suggest measures to strengthen the career orientation services in colleges.

Methodology

A check list was prepared to collect the data from the students in order to know the career orientation given to them in their colleges. The items were given under three sub-headings namely curriculum, class-room training and infrastructure. The students were asked to put a "√"mark against the item, if there is provision of that item in their college and "×" mark if they have no such provision in their college. Two Government and two corporate colleges in Chittoor District were selected for the study. The data were collected from 10 social sciences students and 10 science students of each college. Thus the sample comprises of 40 science and 40 social science students. The percentages were calculated and presented in the following table.

Curriculum

In early days curriculum was regarded as a list of subject – material or course of study which the students were expected to read. Experiences gained out side the classroom were not regarded as a part of the curriculum. Education is a three fold process of imparting knowledge, developing skills and inculcating proper interests attitudes and life values. The traditional college curriculum generally puts a high premium on bookish knowledge and rote learning. It should provide adequate practical activities that will develop the skills, attitudes and interests of the students. Keeping this in view, the students were asked whether the existing curriculum was employment orientated.

Career Orientation in Colleges

S.No.	Item	Percentages of having the Provision					
		Government		Corporate		Total	
		Frequency	%	Frequency	%	Frequency	%
1.	**Curriculum**						
	a. Employment oriented	20	50	20	50	40	50
	b. Life skills promotion	10	25	15	37.5	25	31.25
2.	**Class-room Training**						
	a. Teaching	29	72.5	38	95	67	83.75
	b. Communication Skills	21	52.5	35	87.5	56	70
	c. Group Discussions	10	25	28	70	38	47.5
	d. Students Seminars	10	25	35	87.5	45	56.25
	c. Visits to Work	–	–	18	45	18	22.5
3.	**Infrastructure**						
	a. Equipped library	21	52.5	23	57.5	44	55
	b. Internet Facility	–	–	48	–	48	60
	c. Alumni Interactions	–	–	–	–	–	–
	d. Net working withemployers	–	–	–	–	–	–
	e. On campus recruitments	–	–	–	–	–	–
	f. Placement cell	–	–	–	–	–	–

Employment Orientation

As for as curriculum is concerned, out of 80 students the 50 per cent of respondents shows positive opinion against present curriculum including government and private colleges.

Life Skills

Training on life skills becomes all the more relevant in a country like India where the educational system does not delve into personality development. Some of them include interpersonal skills, Team spirit, Negotiation skills, Behavioural traits such as attitude, motivation, time management etc. Life skill training is essential because we do not have it in our academic curricula. Keeping this in view, the students were asked whether the existing curriculum was intended to life skills promotion among the students only 25 per cent of the government college students and 37.5 per cent of the corporate college students said that the curriculum intend to life skills promotion among them.

Classroom Training

Under the class room training, the items such as teaching, communication skills group discussion, seminars and visits to works were considered which are very important to improve the skills among the students for placements.

Teaching

The role played by the teachers in shaping young minds of future also is taken in to account. They must discharge their duties with devotion and should take teaching not only as a profession but as passion. Students in colleges will be of different backgrounds, different abilities and interests attend colleges. Further, the teachers have to manage with the vast explosion in knowledge. Students have too little time to explore the vast subject-matter included in the curriculum in depth. To meet these challenges, the teacher has to make use of new and improved communication devices in the classrooms. Keeping the importance of teaching to improve the ability of the students, their opinion on the teaching in their respective colleges was asked. 83.75 per cent of the students of government colleges expressed that the teaching is good. Majority of the students (95%) of the corporate colleges said that teaching is good.

Communication Skills

The better the communication skills, the greater are the chances of quick progress. Communicative competence is becoming increasingly important now-a-days. Oral communication, academic and professional use of the language is the three important needs of the students which enable them not only to compete for a career but also to function effectively in it. The opportunity to improve the communication skills in the class room assumes greater importance in shaping the personality. Keeping this in view, the students were asked to express there opinion on the opportunity to improve the communication skills in the class room was asked and found that 52.5 per cent of the government college students and 87.5 per cent of the corporate colleges students said that they have that opportunity.

Group Discussion and Seminars

In any academic environment, we encounter various situations involving speech, writing etc. Students have to converse with their friends, teachers, office staff to achieve various purposes. Seminars, group discussions, project reports involve speech and writing and enhance communication skills among the students. From the percentages obtained in the above table, it is clear that the opportunity for the participation of the students in seminars and group discussions in government colleges is very poor 25 per cent and the participation of the students in corporate colleges is good i.e., 70 and 87.5 per cent respectively.

Visits to Work

Students should be allowed to spend the day in the work place in a multitude of different work place settings such as industrial enterprises, banks, restaurants, airports, Police departments, Radio stations etc. This initiative provides opportunities for students to see workers in different roles and responsibilities and aims to enhance students' understanding of individual jobs in the context of the working community, while linking class room and workplace experiences directly and to create opportunities for students to see the realities of the work place. Keeping this in view the students were asked whether they have the opportunity to go to the work places in their colleges. There is no such opportunity for the students of the government colleges. Only 45 per cent of the students of the corporate colleges said that they have been taken to the work place.

Infrastructure

Under the infrastructure, library, internet facility, networking with employers' alumni interactions, on campus recruitments and placement cell were included for the present study.

Library

Libraries can contribute significantly to the creation of positive atmosphere for learning. Libraries hold an enormous range of educational materials and have the potential to deliver learning opportunities. The role of the libraries in developing advanced reading and writing skills that are basic to develop critical thinking has always been tremendous. Recognizing the importance of libraries, the students were asked about the procurement of up to date books in their libraries. 52.5 per cent of the government college students and 57.5 per cent of the corporate college students expressed that they do not have equipped libraries in their colleges.

Internet Facility

The leaps in technology have provided access to information. Internet is one of such advancement which provides lot of up to date information for all ages on all subjects. Along with that we can have the information of the reputed organisations, institutions in the world and about the careers they have, educational, training opportunities they provide. It is not possible for all the students to buy a computer and to have internet facility on their own. It will be of much use if there is such provision in the colleges for the students. Recognizing the necessity of the internet facility in making students aware of the dimensions of career options, the information was collected from the students on the provision of internet facility in their colleges and found that there is no such provision in the government colleges and corporate colleges have been providing the internet facility.

Networking with Employers

Universities should facilitate to have net working with the employers and the employers should visit the campus to participate in the career class, 'student club events', "Employers of the day" where they host a table in the lobby. It provides a kind of motivation and encouragement to the students. Strong cooperation between education and employment portfolios is particularly important to ensure that perspective is included in career guidance programme of the universities and colleges. The students of both government and corporate colleges said that there is no such type of net working with employers.

Alumni Interactions

This type of interactions enables the students to maintain a close relationship with the alumni for placements. Alumni contribute by providing information about additional jobs available in their organisations. In this study, we found that there are no such types of interactions in their colleges.

Placement Cell and on Campus Recruitments

The placement cell intends to help the students in getting employment through bridging the gaps between recruitment and career counseling. The placement cell will constantly liaise with the employers and the students with latest needs and train them for the placement thus the establishment of placement cell in the colleges gives an opportunity to the students to get access to the information of jobs, needs and requirements of that particular jobs. The students of both government and corporate colleges said that there is no placement cell and on campus recruitments in their colleges.

Findings of the study are:

1. The present curriculum is not having sound components to meet the demands of placement.
2. The government colleges are backward in providing soft skills through the curriculum when compared with corporate colleges.
3. The teaching is better in corporate colleges than government colleges.
4. Training to improve communication skills in the class room is very poor.
5. The libraries are having an average facility including books and journals.
6. Arrangement for the alumni interactions, networking with employers, establishment of placement cell and on campus recruitments is nil in all the four colleges.

Suggestions made are:

1. The curriculum should be changed according to the changing scenario of competition, global situations and market placements.
2. Life skills should be promoted among the students through proper training.
3. Participation in group discussion and seminars by the students should be encouraged to improve the communication skills.
4. Internet facility, alumni interactions on campus recruitments should be provided so that the students will have the access to career information.
5. Books on topics such as resume preparation, interviewing, careers in specific fields, employers brochures should be kept in the library so that the students can equip themselves and develop their ability to choose right career.

Conclusion

Employment is becoming complex and occupational boundaries are changing and more jobs on temporary in nature. These changes present difficulties for the students and are in need of a better understanding of the changes, the implications in terms of career prospects, the skills to adjust to the culture of new industrial working life. Five main elements characterize an education system that is likely to prepare students effectively for this new environment are:

- Emphasis on science and technology.
- Skills standards.
- Close connection between vocational and academic institutions.
- Work place learning.
- Links between employers and colleges.

2

Youth and Vocational Education and Training in India and Abroad

– K. Devan

Introduction

Vocational education or *vocational education and training* (VET) prepares trainees for jobs that are based on manual or practical activities, traditionally non-academic, and totally related to a specific trade, occupation, or *vocation.* It is sometimes referred to as *technical education* as the trainee directly develops expertise in a particular group of techniques of technology. Vocational education may be classified as teaching procedural knowledge. This can be contrasted with declarative knowledge, as used in education in a usually broader scientific field, which might concentrate on theory and abstract conceptual knowledge, characteristic of tertiary education. Vocational education can be at the secondary or post-secondary level and can interact with the apprenticeship system. Increasingly, vocational education can be recognized in terms of recognition of prior learning and partial academic credit towards tertiary education (e.g., at a university) as credit, however, it is rarely considered in its own form to fall under the traditional definition of higher education. Up until the end of the twentieth century, vocational education focused on specific trades such as, for example, those of automobile mechanic or welder, and it were therefore associated with the activities of lower social classes. As a consequence, it carries some social stigma. Vocational education is related to the age-old apprenticeship system of learning. However, as the labour market becomes more specialized and economies demand higher levels of skill, governments and businesses are increasingly investing in the future of vocational education through publicly funded training organisations and subsidized apprenticeship or traineeship initiatives for businesses. At the post-secondary level vocational education is typically provided by an institute of technology, or by a local community college. Vocational education has diversified over the 20th century and now exists in industries such as retail, tourism, information technology, funeral services and cosmetics, as well as in the traditional crafts and cottage industries.

Vocational Education and Training in India

Vocational education prepares students to build their careers in wide ranging subject-areas of manual or practical activities. Today, vocational training has emerged as an important source of employment to thousands of Indians across the country Govt. of India has taken many significant initiatives to popularize vocational education in the country. Delhi being the national capital boasts numerous quality vocational training institutions. We have compiled a list of all the important training institutes of Delhi engaged in imparting quality vocational training.

India a very Young Nation

Nearly 55 per cent of Indians (550 million people) are below 30 years of age and 70 per cent of Indians are below 35 years of age! India is a very young Nation.

India's Priority – Primary + Secondary Education + Vocational Education and Training

While India needs IIT's, IIM's and Medical colleges, (we are fairly well organised for higher education, in fact we have too much of it) the real requirement is for Primary Education & Secondary Education and Vocational Education & Training. 100 per cent of India's population needs basic or primary + secondary education while 90 per cent need to get into some sort of Vocational Education & Training after high School. Everyone cannot become an Engineer, MBBS, MBA, Accountant or a Lawyer! The Founder Trustee of our foundation is from IIT and feels that for every one IIT India needs 1000 or more Vocational Education & Training Centers!

Vocational Education and Training

If India could impart Vocational Education & Training, rather than only the conventional college education, it would benefit all and have the following additional advantages for the Nation:

- Prepare the youth for a vocation of their choice.
- Build up a formidable Work-Force of International Quality, which would have demand not only in India but in all countries of our Planet. In India only IT training is world class. See how it has and will transform India in the future. (We also produce World Class Engineers, Doctors, Accountants, etc.) In the manufacturing and service sectors there are hundreds of skills and vocations for which three is a world wide shortage. For example, TV, electrical appliance repair & service. Automobile & Motorcycle repair & service. Foreign language skills. Medical and Health services. Hospitality, Tourism, Retailing, Construction, Telecommunications, Electronic, Agriculture, General Engineering, Teaching, etc. The list is very large.
- For India we need millions of trained people in the area of services for Agriculture, Floriculture, Horticulture, Sericulture, Fishery, Heath Care, Tourism, Trading,

Services, Business and hundreds of skills for the Manufacturing Sector. We do not see World Class Vocational Education & Training Infrastructure, even after 55 years of India's independence.

- Reduce Unemployment by supplying world-class skilled people required by the Nation and for rest of the World!
- Reduce Cost & improve Productivity of Trading, Services and Manufacture by providing skilled Man Power. Run the country with a higher efficiency, lesser wastage and lower cost of operation.

Preparation

In India the scramble for College and University education is a disaster for all concerned and we require an entire spectrum of skilled man power. There is no relevance of a B.A, B.Com or B.Sc or even a M.A, M.Com or M.Sc degree in today's complex economy. Probably very little, since it may be required for hardly 3 per cent of India's population, or about 30 million people per year at the most, at this stage. We are stretching the existing higher educational facilities to a breaking point. The Faculty and infrastructure is not able to cope at the increasing number of students, after they have completed their high school education. Like "Zombies" every one wants to join some college or the other with out a road map or plan about their future. It's a National Tragedy of sorts!

Government + Industry + Trade + Services + Educational Institutions – need to work together

As you are in the think tank of India's education set up and are probably looking at ways to act as a catalyst to improve the productivity of Industry. Trade and Services as well as to make India more competitive, you may like to take up this matter of Vocational Education & Training with all the State Authorities, the Ministry of HRD and Education in New Delhi, and all the Chambers of Commerce in India as well as the All India Business Associations such as CII, FICCI & ASSOCHAM.

Our Contribution

We are working with the largest and oldest NGO Institutions in the UK, City & Guilds or C&G and can offer Vocational Education and Training Programmes, with content and certification. They are offering 600 courses in 22 major fields, bundled within 52 main or 'mother courses'. C&G is more than 124 years old, operating in more than 103 countries and certifying more then 1 million people per year! We have already initiated and enable 40 VET centers in western India, in the last 3 months.

VOCATIONAL EDUCATION AND TRAINING IN ABROAD

Australia

In Australia vocational education and training (is mostly post-Secondary and provided through the vocational education and Training (VET) system by registered training organisations. This system encompasses both public and private providers in a national training framework consisting of the Australian Quality Training Framework, Australian Qualifications Framework and Industry Training Packages which define the assessment standards for the different vocational qualifications. Australia's apprenticeship system includes both traditional apprenticeships in traditional trades and "traineeships" in other more service-oriented occupations. Both involve a legal contract between the employer and the apprentice and provide a combination of school-based and workplace training. Apprentices and trainees receive a wage which increases as they progress.

Finland

In Finland, vocational education belongs to secondary education. After the nine-year comprehensive school, almost all students choose to go to either a *lukio* (high school), which is an institution preparing students for tertiary education, or a vocational school. Both forms of secondary education last three years, and give a formal qualification to enter university or *ammattikorkoulus,* i.e. Finnish polytechnics. In certain fields (e.g. the police school, air traffic control personnel training), the entrance requirements of vocational school include completion of the *lukio,* thus causing the students to complete their secondary education twice. The education in vocational school is free, and the students from low-income families are eligible for a state student grant. The curriculum is primarily vocational, and the academic part of the curriculum is adapted to the needs of a given course. The vocational schools are mostly maintained by municipalities.

Germany

Vocational education is an important part of the education system in Austria, Germany, Liechtenstein and Switzerland (including the French and the Italian speaking parts of the country) and one element of the German model.

Hong Kong

In Hong Kong, vocational education is usually for post-secondary 3, 5 and 7 students. The Hong Kong Institute of Vocational Education (IVE) provides training in nine different vocational fields, namely: Applied Science; Business Administration; child Education and Community Services; Construction; Design; Printing, Textiles and Clothing; Hotel, Service and Tourism Studies; Construction; Information Technology; Electrical and Electronic Engineering; and Mechanical, Manufacturing and Industrial Engineering.

Hungary

Normally at the end of elementary school (at age 14) students are directed to one of three types of upper secondary education; one academic track (gymnasium) and two vocational tracks. Vocational secondary schools provide four years of general education and also prepare students for the maturity. These schools combine general education with some specific subjects, referred to as pre-vocational education and career orientation. At that point many students enroll in a post-secondary VET programme often at the same institution, to obtain a vocational qualification, although they may also seek entry to tertiary education. Vocational training schools initially provide two years of general education, combined with some pre-vocational education and carrier orientation, they then choose an occupation, and then receive two or three years of vocational education and training focusing on that occupation such as bricklayer. Students do not obtain the maturata but a vocational qualification at the end of a successfully completed programme. Demand for vocational training schools, both from the labour market and among students, has declined which it has increased for upper secondary schools delivering the maturate.

Japan

Japanese vocational schools are known as *senmon gakko.* They are part of Japan's higher education system. They are two year schools that many students study at after finishing high school (although it is not always required that students graduate from high school). Some have a wide range of majors, others only a few majors. Some examples are computer technology, fashion and English.

Korea

Vocational high schools offer programmes in five fields: agriculture, technology/engineering, commerce/business, maritime/fishery, and home economics. In principle, all students in the first year of high school (00th grade) follow a common national curriculum. In the second and third years of high school (10th grade) follow a common national curriculum, In the second and third years (11th and 12th grades) students are offered courses relevant to their spcecialisation. In some programmes, students may participate in workplace training though co-operation between school workplace training is an important part of the programme. Around half of all vocational high schools are private. Private and public schools operate according to similar rules; for example, they charge the same fees for high school education, with an exemption for poorer families. The number of students in vocational high schools has decreased, from about half of students in 1995 down to about one-quarter today. To make vocational high schools more attractive, in April 2007 the

Korean government changed the name of vocational high schools into professional high schools. With the change of the name the government also facilitated the entry of vocational high school graduates to colleges and universities.

Mexico

In Mexico, both federal and state governments are responsible for the administration of vocational education. Federal schools are funded by the federal budget, in addition to their own funding sources. The state governments are responsible for the management of decentralized institutions, such as the State Centres for Scientific and Technological Studies and Institutes of Training for Work. These institutions are funded 50 per cent from the federal budget and 50 per cent from the state budget. Compulsory education (including primary and lower secondary education) finishes at the age of 15 and about half of those aged 15-to-19 are enrolled full-time or part-time in education. All programmes at upper secondary level require the payment of a tuition fee. The upper secondary vocational education system in Mexico includes over a dozen subsystems (administrative units within the Upper Secondary Education Under secretariat of the Ministry of Public Education, responsible for vocational programmes) which differ from each other to varying degrees in content, administrative units within the Ministry of Public Education makes the institutional landscape of vocational education and training complex by international standards.

New Zealand

New Zealand is served by 39 Industry Training Organisiations (ITO). The unique element is that ITOs purchase training as well as set standards and aggregate industry opinion about skills in the labour market. Industry Training, as organized by ITOs, has expanded from apprenticeships to a more true life long learning situation with, for example, over 10 per cent of trainees aged 50 or over. Moreover much of the training is generic. This challenges the prevailing idea of vocational education and the standard layperson view that it focuses on apprenticeships.

Norway

Nearly all those leaving lower secondary school enter upper secondary education, and around half follow one of 9 vocational programmes. These programmes typically involve two years in school followed by two years of apprenticeship in a company. The first year provides general education alongside introductory knowledge of the vocational area. During the second year, courses become more trade-specific. Apprentices receive a wage negotiated in collective agreements ranging between 30 per cent and 80 per cent of the wage of a qualified worker; the percentage increasing over the apprenticeship period. Employers taking on apprentices receive a subsidy, equivalent to the cost of one year in school. After the two years vocational school programmes some students opt for a third year in the 'general' programme as an alternative to an apprenticeship. Both apprenticeship and a third year of practical training in school lead to the same vocational qualifications. Upper secondary VET graduates may go directly to Vocational Technical College, while those who wish to enter university need to take a supplementary year of education.

Sweden

Nearly all of those leaving compulsory schooling immediately enter upper secondary schools, and most complete their upper secondary education in three years, Upper secondary education is divided into 13 vocationally-oriented and 4 academic national programmes. Slightly more than half of all students follow vocational progrmmes. All programmes offer broad general education and basic eligibility to continue studies at the post-secondary level. In addition, there are local programmes specially designed to meet local needs and 'individual' programmes.

A 1992 school reform extended vocational upper secondary programmes by one year, aligning them with three years of general upper secondary education, increasing their general education content, and making core subjects compulsory in all programmes. The core subjects (which occupy around one-third of total teaching time in both vocational and academic programmes) include English, artistic activities, physical education and health, mathematics, natural science, social studies, Swedish or Swedish as a second language, and religious studies. In addition to the core subjects, students pursue optional courses, subjects which are specific to each programme and a special project.

Switzerland

Nearly two thirds of those entering upper secondary education enter the vocational education and training system. At this level, vocational education and training is mainly provided through the 'dual system'. Students spend some of their time in a vocational school; some of their time doing an apprenticeship at a host company; and for most programmes, students attend industry courses at an industry training centre to develop complementary practical skills relating to the occupation at hand. Common patterns are for students to spend one-two days per week at the vocational school and three-four days doing the apprenticeship at the host company; alternatively they alternate between some weeks attending classes at the vocational school and some weeks attending industry courses at an industry training centre. A different pattern is to begin the programme with most of the time devoted to in-school education and gradually diminishing the amount of in-school education in favour of more in-company training.

United Kingdom

The system of vocational education in the UK initially developed independently of the state, with bodies such as the RSA and City & Guilds setting examinations for technical subjects. The Education Act 1944 made provision for a Tripartite System of grammar schools, secondary technical schools and secondary modern schools, but by 1975 only. 0.5 per cent of British senior pupils were in technical schools, compared to two-thirds of the equivalent German age group.

Europe

University education does not necessarily prepare the youth for Life; also there is No guarantee of a job after a university degree. It is for this reason that 80 to 90 per cent of the youth, after the 10th, opt for Vocational Education & Training where they work part time (at minimum or lower wages), as apprentices, with Industry and Trade for 2 to 4 years and study simultaneously in a Vocational Education & Training Institute, for learning the theory and acquiring the relevant knowledge and theory. This way, the business and trade get low cost manpower, while the youth are learning a new trade, both on-the-job as well theory in the Vocational Education & Training Institute. This combination results in World Class skilled youth. There are 2500 trade options in Europe. These Vocations cover the Manufacturing, Service and Trading Sectors, including Agriculture as well as the New Economy.

Status of Vocational Training

The World Bank report of 2006 shows that among persons of age 15-29 only about 2 per cent reported to have received formal vocational training and another 8 per cent reported to have received non formal vocational training. The proportion of persons (15-29 years) who received formal vocational training was the highest among the unemployed. The proportion was around 3 per cent for the employed, 11 per cent for the unemployed and 2 per cent for persons not in the labour force. The activity of persons receiving vocational education is as shown.

Comparison with Other Countries

There is little capacity in vocational education in India and even that is under-utilized. World Bank Report suggests that the enrolment figure is less than three per cent of the students attending Grades 11-12. This implies that between 350,000 to 400,000 students are enrolled in vocational education, which works out to less than three per cent of the 14 million students or more in Grades 11 and 12, implying

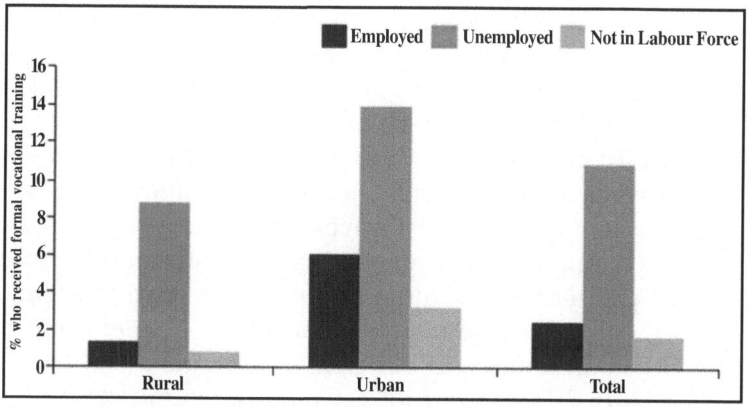

Source: Status of Education and Vocational Training in India, 2004-05, NSS 61st Round

that less than one per cent of students who had entered Grade 1 over the last decade or so would have eventually participated in vocational education. In comparison the status in various other countries is as shown below:

Country	Secondary Enrolment Ratio	Number of Students (Thousands)	Vocational-technical Share (Per cent of Total Secondary Enrolments)
Russia	88	6277	60
China	52	15300	55
Chile	70	652	40
Indonesia	43	4109	33
Korea	93	2060	31
Mexico	58	–	12
Malaysia	59	533	11
South Africa	77	–	1

Source: World Bank, 2006.

Thrust Areas

- The training courses lack focus on the changing job market. As a result it was seen from various reports that the number of students is declining for long term vocational courses, mainly in ITIs. The training policy should be focused on the changing job market in order to attract young people. More autonomy needs to be provided to institutes and they should have market linked infrastructure. For publicly funded training, equity distribution is also a problem. But job creation must be done regionally, not centrally; otherwise it will create regional imbalances of trained manpower. According to NSSO report (No. 470, 55th round) about 27 per cent of the Indian populations were migrants. The proportion of migrants was higher (33 per cent) in urban areas than (24 per cent) in the rural areas. It was mainly in search of jobs. Creating job opportunities regionally can help maintain the equilibrium in future days.

- Funding for the public ITIs is very low compared to other countries like China and USA which have restructuring-funds, whose share goes for improvement of vocational training systems in order to achieve international quality. Although things have changed for the better in the 11th five year plan with the introduction of the National Skill Development Mission. But it is also desirable to have mechanisms to raise funds privately for up gradation of ITIs.
- ITIs must focus on low-literate youth and provide new vocational qualifications/training programmes and also on unorganised sector, otherwise it will cause long term losses. To take an example automobile industry is a technology intensive industry but most of the workshops are running without formally trained staff (we have currently no database of that). Sometimes, lack of training skills may harm the delicate instrument of vehicles. A vital challenge is to formally train workers for the crafts industry where a considerable number of informally trained craftsman work together.
- Lack of accountability and training/supply management are also major problems for ITI institutes.

- In our country different institutes impart vocational training but they do not have coordination among themselves. Information about this sector is not available from a single source. In fact we need to create a central database from where one can get full access on vocational training system right from school level to ITI/ITC institutes.
- In rural sector, radiographer and other trained para-medical persons are very less in comparison to the large number of the rural population. Policy makers should focus on the paramedical vocational studies, so that incremental change in number of trained paramedical worker can benefit rural masses.
- A central vocational training standardization system, accredited nationally and globally, for maintaining the quality of the vocational education can enhance credibility of vocationally trained persons in the industry.
- To attract more students from school level, reorientation of vocational courses is needed.
- There should be a bridge organisation to relate R&D institutes and vocational education system. It would help the vocationally trained person to get the benefits of R&D.

Conclusion

The industrial and labour market trends clearly indicate the necessity of strengthening of vocational education in India. The introduction of vocational education at secondary level through bivalent schools and SSC (vocational) will enable us to broaden the vocational education base at secondary level of education. A clear pathway for vocational students to enter higher education streams is the way to move forward. Through this concept note we have made an endeavour to provide some of the possible solutions to address these issues. Framing of vocational qualification framework, introduction of vocational degrees and setting up of a Vocational University with polytechnics, community colleges, CPs and other VEPs as affiliated colleges are some of the recommendations which require further deliberation at National and State level. Vocational Education and Training (VET) is an important element of the nation's education initiative. In order for Vocational Education to play its part effectively in the changing national context and for India to enjoy the fruits of the demographic dividend, there is an urgent need to redefine the critical elements of imparting vocational education and training to make them flexible, contemporary, relevant, inclusive and creative. The Government is well aware of the important role of Vocational education and has already taken a number of important initiatives in this area.

REFERENCES

Gandhi Smriti & Darshan Samiti (1997).

James A Draper (1989), Adult Education: A Focus for the Social Sciences.

Journal of Knowledge Society (2004), Science and Technology for Knowledge Society.

Swati Mujumdar, Director, Symbiosis Centre for Distance Learning.

Sam Pitroda Lecture at the PanIIT 2010 Higher Education Round Table at IIT Delhi

Werner Mauch, Renuka Narang (1998), Lifelong Learning and Institutions of Higher Education in the 21st Century.

World Education Fellowship, 42nd International Conference (2004), VISION - The Youth Speak.

3

Employability and Skill Development Among Youth in India

– G.Sundharavadivel

> There are two educations. One should teach us how to make a living and the other how to live
>
> – *John Adams*

Introduction

Skills and knowledge are the engines of economic growth and social development of any country. Countries with higher and better levels of knowledge and skills respond more effectively and promptly to challenges and opportunities of globalisation. India is in transition to a knowledge based economy and its competitive edge will be determined by the abilities of its people to create, share and use knowledge more effectively. This transition will require India to develop workers into knowledge workers who will be more flexible, analytical, adaptable and multi skilled. In the new knowledge economy, the skill sets will include professional, managerial, operational, and behavioural, inter personal and inter functional skills. To achieve these goals, India needs flexible education and training system that will provide the foundation for learning, secondary and tertiary education and to develop required competencies as means of achieving lifelong learning.

As per the 2001 Census of India, population age 15-24 years accounts for 195 million of the 1,029 million of India's population. By 2011, this age group grown to 240 million (Office of the Registrar General, 2006) and account for a slightly higher proportion of the total population than in 2001.

Who They Are

- Many youth are illiterate or have very low educational attainment.
- Most youth are exposed to some form of media.
- Female youth are more likely than male youth to belong to the lowest wealth quintile and less likely to be in the higher wealth quintiles.
- The majority of unmarried youth live in nuclear households, whereas the majority of married youth live in non-nuclear households.
- Many youth are married.
- Many youth are economically active.

What They Think

- Most youth desire a small family and
- Most young men have a positive attitude toward contraception, but some are misinformed about it

How They Behave

- Early childbearing define India's fertility pattern
- Tobacco use and alcohol consumption by youth are matters of concern and
- Both traditional and modern methods of contraception are popular among youth

Literacy and Educational Attainment

Literacy levels increase from 63 per cent and 84 per cent among women and men age 24 to 77 per cent and 92 per cent among women and men age 15.The change in literacy rates has been more rapid for women, who started from a lower base, than for men. However, as many persons age 15-19 have yet to complete secondary schooling, there is some drop in the proportion of persons who have completed 10 or more years of schooling from age 20-24 to age 15-19.

Countries with higher and better levels of skills adjust more effectively to the challenges and opportunities of globalisation. The Indian economy has shown a remarkable acceleration in economic growth in recent years. As Indian industry and services grow and compete internationally, they are faced with the realisation that the availability of the requisite skills – in terms of relevance, quality and quantity has become an urgent need. Lack of access to employment, that is decent and remunerative, lowers self-esteem and leads to denial of basic needs of the individual and the family, and can lead to social instability. It is, therefore, important to work towards the goal of decent and remunerative work for all women and men seeking such work, in conditions of freedom, equity, security and human dignity.

Current Scenario

As Figure 3.1 shows, at least 50 per cent of young men in every state except Himachal Pradesh and Jammu and Kashmir are employed. The proportion of men employed exceeds 75 per cent in Chhattisgarh and Gujarat. In Delhi and Kerala, not even one-fifth of women are employed, whereas in Jharkhand and Chhattisgarh, more than half are employed.

The educational attainment of a population, particularly of the young population, is an important indicator of the society's stock of human capital and its level of socioeconomic development. The educational attainment of youth in the age group 15-24 also reflects the achievement of the educational sector in the past 20 years. In this section, differentials in educational attainment of women and men are discussed by selected background characteristics. In NFHS-3, each respondent who had not completed standard six was given a card with four pre-printed sentences and asked to read one of the sentences. Respondents who have either completed six

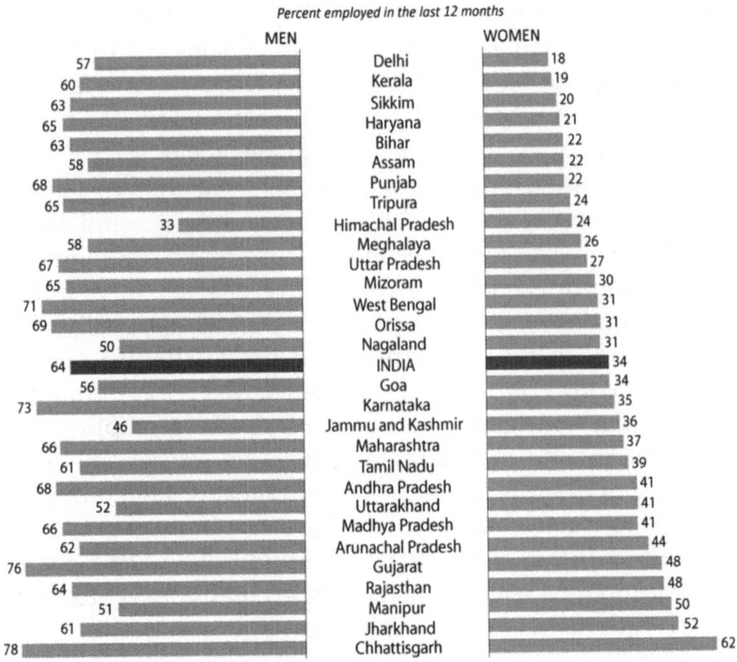

Fig. 3.1: **Employment of Youth by State**

years of education or passed the literacy test by being able to read all or part of a sentence on the card are defined as literate. The proportion of literate youth by single year of age shows the increasing level of literacy among younger respondents. Literacy levels increase from 63 per cent and 84 per cent among women and men age 24 to 77 per cent and 92 per cent among women and men age 15 (fig). The increasing trend in the literacy rates indicates progress toward achieving universal literacy in recent years.

Urban youth are less likely than rural youth to be employed mainly due to the higher school/college attendance of urban youth. The proportion of employed men and women decreases sharply with increases in education and wealth. For example, practically all young men (94%) with no education were employed at the time of survey, whereas a majority of young men with 10 or more years of education were not employed. A large proportion of ever-married men (93%) are employed, whereas only 58 per cent of never married men are employed.

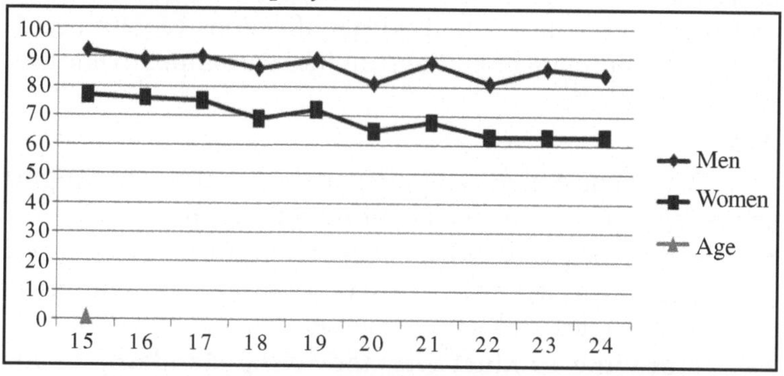

***Fig. 3.2:* Literacy Rates Among Youth by Age**

National Policy on Skill Development

A National Policy on Skill Development has been formulated by the Ministry of Labour & Employment. The objective is to create a workforce empowered with improved skills, knowledge and internationally recognized qualifications to gain access to decent employment and ensure India's competitiveness in the dynamic Global Labour market. It aims at increase in productivity of workforce both in the organised and the unorganised sectors, seeking increased participation of youth, women, disabled and other disadvantaged sections and to synergize efforts of various sectors and reform the present system. At present the capacity of skill development in India is around 3.1 million persons per year. The XI Five Year Plan envisions an increase in that capacity to 15 million annually. India has target of creating 500 million skilled workers by 2022. Thus, there is a need for increasing capacity and capability of skill development programmes. A framework for better coordination between various stakeholders – Ministries, States, Industry etc. will be established. It will promote excellence and will meet the requirements of knowledge economy.

Mission

National Skill Development Initiative will empower all individuals through improved skills, knowledge, nationally and internationally recognised qualifications to gain access to decent employment and ensure India's competitiveness in the global market.

AIMS

The aim of skill development in the country is to support achieving rapid and Inclusive growth through:

- Enhancing individuals' employability (wage/self employment) and ability to adapt to changing technologies and labour market demands.
- Improving productivity and living standards of the people.
- Strengthening competitiveness of the country and
- Attracting investment in skill development.

Objectives

The objectives of the national policy on skill development are to:

- Create opportunities for all to acquire skills throughout life, and especially for youth, women and disadvantaged groups.
- Promote commitment by all stakeholders to own skill development initiatives.
- Develop a high-quality skilled workforce/ entrepreneur relevant to current and emerging employment market needs.
- Enable the establishment of flexible delivery mechanisms that respond to the characteristics of a wide range of needs of stakeholders.
- Enable effective coordination between different ministries, the centre and the states and public and private providers.

Scope

The coverage of the national policy on skill development includes the following:

- Institution-based skill development including ITIs/ITCs/ Vocational schools/technical schools/polytechnics/ professional colleges etc.
- Learning initiatives of sectoral skill development organised by different ministries/departments.
- Formal and informal apprenticeships and other types of training enterprises.
- Training for self employment/entrepreneurial development.
- Adult learning, retraining of retired or retiring employees and lifelong learning
- Non-formal training including training by civic society organisations.
- E-learning, web-based learning and distance learning.

Major challenges and issues in skill development programme

Some reasons for low performance are:

- Low priority for vocational education
- Shortage of trained teachers and trainers
- Inadequate linkages with industries
- Absence of a National Competency Testing and Accreditation system
- Lack of infrastructure – building, modern equipment and raw materials.
- Inadequate or non-coverage of trades in service sector which has higher employment potential.
- Lack of equivalence for employment purposes
- Lack of vertical mobility.
- Inflexible curriculum.
- Lack of convergence between various agencies and
- Lack of overall social recognition.

Some Issues on Vocational Education are:

- Employability and Demand and Supply matching
- Informal Sector's requirement
- Multiple skills

- Flexibility of Course design, modularity
- Out of School Children
- Open and distance learning
- Use of Technology
- Linkage to local demand
- Career guidance
- Teacher's Training and Retention
- National Vocational qualification system Skill requirement in – Curriculum, Assessment and Certification
- Emerging Sectors
- Involvement of Industry and Civil Society
- Horizontal and Vertical Mobility
- Equity (Girls, rural population, SC, ST, Minority and Disabled)
- Financing
- State Government's Role

These challenges are immense and in order to achieve the goals there has to be substantial expansion of quality technical/vocational education and training for raising employability and productivity.

Conclusion

There is a considerable optimism about India's recent economic development. Basic education has become an important aspect of social policy for achieving growth. However the story of India's achievement in attaining the Education For All goals related to youth and adult literacy and lifelong learning since 2000 is one of the mixed successes. Progress of adult literacy has remained uneven across the regions and lopsided with wide disparities in terms of gender, social and religious groups. It is imperative, therefore, for India to move up the skill-ladder and produce a larger number of people with higher education and generic training for new types of knowledge work, both in high skill services and high technology industrial production. Knowledge professionals will need support from middle-skilled workers in new knowledge and technology areas. The skill development system will need to meet this challenge. The response time is limited as the rate of change is high and accelerating.

The country is poised at a moment in history when a much brighter future for its entire people is within its reach. Skill development will help actualize this potential. Development and articulation of a national policy on skill development is a matter of priority. A task of skill development has many challenges which include:

- Increasing capacity and capability of existing system to ensure equitable access to all.
- Promoting lifelong learning, maintaining quality and relevance, according to changing requirement particularly of emerging knowledge economy.
- Creating effective convergence between school education, various skill development efforts of government and between government and Private Sector initiative.
- Capacity building of institutions for planning, quality assurance and involvement of stake holders.
- Creating institutional mechanism for research development quality assurance, examinations and certification, affiliations and accreditation and
- Increasing participation of stakeholders, mobilizing adequate investment for financing skill development, attaining sustainability by strengthening physical and intellectual resources.

REFERENCES

A Profile of Youth in India, National Family Health Survey (NFHS-3) India 2005-06-By International Institute for Population Sciences, Deonar, Mumbai – 400 008.

Adult Literacy and Lifelong Learning by Lla Patel, National University of National Planning and Administration, New Delhi.

Annual Report : (2008) Ministry of Human Resource Development, Department of Education, India.

India Country Paper – UNESCO.

National skill Development Policy (March 2009), Govt. of India, New Delhi.

National Development Council Document (2008): Planning Commission India.

National Policy on Education 1986 (1998): Ministry of Human Resource Development, Department of Education, India.

National Conference on Technical Vocational Education, Training and Skills Development: A Roadmap for Empowerment (Dec. 2008): Ministry of Human Resource Development, Department of Education, India.

Skill Formation and Employment Assurance in the Unorganized Sector (2009): National Commission for Enterprises in the Unorganized Sector.

Technical and Vocational Education and Training in India (Nov.2008): Report compiled by Perya Short, Education Counselor (South Asia).

4

Employability Among Women Youth

– Y. Nirmala
– Y. Bhaskaracharyulu

Introduction

India is one of the most populous countries with younger generations and may be called as young India. Among the total population, women constitute half of the total population and their working hours ranges between 17-19 hours a day. The returns in terms of economy are nearly half but, they could be realized with only one tenth of the total returns. Further, they are being treated as secondary even though they play a vital role in both productive and reproductive spheres of life. They also meekly submit the condition and become victims of male atrocities added to their low/no literacy with low wages and low status. Keeping their plight in view, the Government of India has launched several programmes for their upliftment especially for the women in productive age group i.e., youth belonging to 15-35 years. Sakshar Bharath is one such programmes implemented and initiated by the Government for uplifting the illiterates and particularly women. Sakshar Bharath programme is the programme that intended not only to promote traditional education, but also the vocational training that will promote their occupational skills and life skills which will help them to gain the potentialities for national building and productivity. Further, the target group of the programme are vulnerable groups such as weaker sections, miniorities, school drop-outs and pass outs, neo literates with a special stress on women youth. Hence, an attempt was made in this paper to discuss about the Sakshar Baharath Programme in promoting the employability among the women youth.

Saakshar Bharat, a centrally sponsored scheme of Department of School Education and Literacy (DSEL), Ministry of Human Resource Development (MHRD), Government of India (GOI) was launched by the Prime Minister on the International Literacy Day, 8th September, 2009. It aims to promote and strengthen Adult Education, especially among women, by extending educational options to those who lost the opportunity of accessing to formal education and crossed the standard age for receiving such education, now feel a need for learning literacy, basic education (equivalency to formal education), vocational education (skill development), physical and emotional development, practical arts, applied science, sports, and recreation.

To impart functional literacy to non-literates in the age group of 15-35 years in a time bound manner, the National Literacy Mission (NLM) was launched in 1988 and it continued through Ninth and Tenth Five Year Plans. By the end of the Tenth Five Year Plan (March 2007), NLM had covered 597 districts under Total Literacy Campaign (TLC), 485 districts under Post Literacy Programme (PLP) and 328 districts under Continuing Education Programme (CEP). As a cumulative outcome of these efforts, 127.45 million persons became literate, of which, 60 per cent learners were females, while 23 per cent learners belonged to scheduled Castes (SCs) and 12 per cent to Scheduled Tribes (STs).

Despite significant accomplishments, illiteracy continues to be an area of national concern. Though precise number of non- literates at this stage is not available and will be known only after 2011 census, 2001 census had revealed that there were still 259.52 million illiterate adults (in the age group of 15 +) in the country. Keeping in view the government's decision that literacy would be its key programme instrument for emancipation and empowerment of women, efforts to give impetus to school education, health, nutrition, skill development and women empowerment in general are impeded by the continuance of female illiteracy. It also expects the increase in female literacy to become a force multiplier for all other social development programmes. However, this is only the instrumental value of female literacy. Its intrinsic value is in emancipating the Indian woman through the creation of critical consciousness to take charge of her environment where she faces multiple deprivations and disabilities on the basis of class, caste and gender.

In the context of Government's overall policy aimed at empowerment of women and in recognition of the fact that literacy, especially female literacy, is a pre-requisite to socio-economic development, it was considered imperative that the National Literacy Mission (NLM), as a programme instrument, be recast with an enhanced focus on female literacy. It is also felt that such a repositioning of the mission would have a very positive impact on re-energising the literacy movement that, after an initial decade of spirited social mobilization, had waned over two decades of its operation.

To recast the mission, a protracted process of countrywide consultation with stakeholders was gone through. A series of consultative meetings were held across the country with representatives of the government of States, NGOs, literacy practitioners, managers, administrators, State Resource Centres, universities, social activists and other stakeholders. The broad strategy was also discussed with Education Secretaries of all States, The Council of National Literacy Mission Authority (NLMA) has considered and approved the strategy of Saksshar Bharath as an instrument for promoting functional literacy among the target particularly among women. The general opinion of the stakeholders, expressed during the consultations, was that the new mission ought to take note of considerable demand for female literacy generated on account of large scale changes at the grassroot level and the new opportunities that have been created over the past several years, most notably, the increasing vibrancy of Panchayati Raj Institutions (PRIs), post 73rd Constitution Amendment, the shift to the model of Self-help Groups (SHGs) that operate through collectivities for self-employment programmes, the massive new organisational capital being forged again through work collectives such as National Rural Employment Guarantee Act (NREGA) , Joint Forest Management Groups etc.

It is in this background that Saakshar Bharat has been devised as the new variant of National Literacy Mission. Saakshar Bharat will cover all adults in the age group of 15 and beyond though its primary focus will be on women. The scheme has not only been relieved of the shortcomings noted in its preceding editions, but also, several new features added to it. Basic Literacy, Post literacy and Continuing Education programmes, will now form a continuum, rather than sequential segments. Besides, the volunteer based mass campaign approach, provision has been made for alternative approaches to adult education. Jan Shiksha Kendras (Adult Education Centres) (AECs), will be set up to coordinate and manage all programmes, within their territorial jurisdiction. State Government, as against the districts in the earlier versions, and Panchyati Raj institutions, along with communities, will be valued stakeholders. Vigorous monitoring and evaluation systems will be installed. Last, but not the least, budgetary support has been enhanced substantially.

Saakshar Bharat is in operation from 1-10-2009. Though duration of the scheme, National Literacy Mission, was valid only till the end of the Tenth Five Year Plan, residual activities under the Mission were allowed to continue till 30-09-2009, as a special dispensation, so that the ongoing activities could be completed during the extended period with the following objectives.

Objectives of the Programme

The Mission has four broad objectives, namely:

- Impart functional literacy and numeracy to non-literate and non-numerate adults
- Enable the neo-literate adults to continue their learning beyond basic literacy and acquire equivalency to formal educational system
- Impart non and neo-literates relevant skill development programmes to improve their earning and living conditions
- Promote a learning society by providing opportunities to neo literate adults for continuing education

Targets

The principal target of the mission is to impart functional literacy to 70 million adults in the age group of 15 years and beyond. Auxiliary target of the mission is to cover 1.5 million adults under basic education programme and equal number under vocational (skill development) programme. Within these targets, the Mission will primarily focus on, but not limited to, women. Schedules Castes (SCs), Scheduled Tribes (STs) Minorities, other disadvantaged groups and adolescents in rural areas in low literacy States will be other focused groups. For each focused group and area, there will be a specific target and for each target, an explicit approach and strategy.

Target Specific Approach

Women

Women being the prime focus and predominant participants, the entire programme was given gender treatment. The gender, social and cultural barriers that women face were taken into consideration while designing teaching learning programmes. Gender should not be seen in isolation but in conjunction with other social categories like caste, ethnicity, religion, disability, etc. Gender perspective will permeate all components of the programme, including the approach, strategies, planning, management structures, teaching-learning materials and monitoring and evaluation.

Special priority was given to women belonging to SC, ST, Minority and other disadvantaged groups in rural areas.

This approach was built on women's existing knowledge and levels of their literacy and numeracy in order to ensure that in the long run the existing levels are substantially upgraded and they are able to use the skills acquired in their own contexts. Innovative, tried and tested programmes related to women's literacy, including interventions related to thematic or issue-based literacy was up scaled. Women were engaged in large numbers as volunteers and instructors to encourage women learners to participate in the programme. Further, they will be trained in skill promotion programmes so as to equip them with the necessary vocational training programmes and to promote employability among them for furtherance of their living standards.

Scheduled Castes, Scheduled Tribes and Minorities

The SCs (15%), STs (8%) and Minorities (20%) together constitute more than 40 per cent of India's population. In terms of illiterate population, SCs constitute 20.5 per cent and STs 12 per cent. Minorities, especially Muslims, constitute another large block of illiterate population. Targets have been fixed taking into account not only the share of their total population, but also their share of the non-literate population and commensurate resources should be invested for raising their literacy level. SLMAs and other sub-State level implementing agencies must draw special strategies taking into account their socio-cultural background and sensitivities and share these strategies with NLMA. Larger roles for their respective communities need to be conceived in planning and implementation structures and processes. Monitoring mechanism will have an inbuilt feature to maintain a constant watch and highlight the progress made by the learners belonging to these groups while simultaneously taking timely corrective measures to prevent relapse to illiteracy.

Adolescents

The dominant aspect of the design interventions of the prevalent educational programmes for non/semi-literate adolescents is fertility, sexual behaviour, planned parenthood, etc. To address the real life needs of these adolescents, innovative design interventions will be conceived that would lead to acquisition of marketable qualifications, supported by certification. These programmes will be a combination of basic education and practical training in a skill or vocation. Camp based instruction has been found more suitable for the needs of the adolescents. The Mission will have a flexi approach to provide room for such innovations.

Geographical Area Coverage

Another goal of the Mission is to minimize inter and intra regional/state disparities. Inter state disparities range between 33 per cent and 88 per cent. Intra state disparities are equally stunning. To minimize regional disparities, the programme, in its first phase, that is during the 11th Plan period (31-03-2012) will remain confined to districts with adult female literacy rate of 50 per cent or less as per 2001 Census. Nearly 18 crore non-literate adults live in these districts. Besides, 33 districts affected with left wing extremism will also be covered under the Mission irrespective of the existing literacy rate.

Rural and other Special Areas

According to 2001 Census, 84 per cent of India's non-literates live in rural India. Since illiteracy is far more widespread in rural areas as compared to urban India, and for the reason that urban areas are better endowed with educational infrastructure leading to better access to opportunities, the Mission would concentrate on and deploy public resources in rural areas. An all out effort may be made to saturate rural areas first before expanding to non-rural areas. In these areas, the focus will be on women and adolescents belonging to SC, ST, Minorities and other disadvantaged groups.

Strategy for Urban Areas

In the urban areas, Mission objectives may be achieved innovatively, using new actors. The programme may be handled through Jan Shikshan Sansthans, State Resource Centres, NGOs, social groups and any other institution identified by NLMA through Public Private Partnership (PPP) or any other mode. Linkages with Ministry of Housing and Urban Poverty Alleviation under Jawaharlal Nehru National Urban Renewal Mission (JNNURM) could also be developed for synergy and augmentation of resources.

Basic Education Programme

This programme is designed to achieve the second objective of the scheme, namely, 'Enable the neo-literates to continue their learning beyond basic literacy and acquire equivalency to formal educational system'. Arrangements will be made to enable young adults to continue their learning till they are able to achieve equivalence levels with Grade III, IV, V, VI, VII and VIII and beyond in the formal school system or through the Open Learning System. The Open Basic Education (OBE) programme initiated by the National Institute of Open Schooling (NIOS) and other Open Schools will be taken as the starting point. While formulating equivalency programmes, the life experience and local knowledge systems of the adult learners will be taken into consideration.

Vocational Education (Skill Development) Programme

For furtherance of the third objective of the scheme, that is, 'Equip non and neo-literates with vocational skills to improve their living and earning conditions', suitable skill development training will be imparted to those having rudimentary levels of education or no education. Jan Shikshan Sansthans (JSS), set up under the Scheme for Assistance to Voluntary Agencies for Adult Education and Skill Development of DSEL, will be institutionally networked with the Adult Education Centres so that they could impart skill development training, as well as literacy linked vocational training. JSS, in coordination with the District Implementing Agency, will enlist neo-literates for appropriate skill development training. Besides specific activities for which a specific budgetary provision is available under the Mission, JSSs will utilise their programme budget to impart vocational skill training. Parallel efforts will be made by the SLMA and District Implementation Agencies for developing synergies with other agencies in the public as well as private sector for enhanced opportunities of skill development training at the gram panchayat level.

Continuing Education Programme

Continuing Education Programme (CEP) is aimed at achieving the fourth objective of the Scheme that is, 'Establishing a learning society by providing opportunities to neo literates and other targeted beneficiaries for lifelong learning'. The programme recognizes increased demand for learning generated by Basic and Post Literacy Programmes and the potential need of adult learners to further enhance their skills on their own terms and at their convenience. CEP, as the very name suggests, will not have a fixed time frame as in the case of the other three programmes, but will be organised on a continuous basis. The approach is to create a sustainable learning environment so that learners are encouraged to continue with their literary aspirations and take advantage of the programme facilities to satiate their learning appetite.

The Programme will provide facility of a library and reading room, which would be gradually provided with other contemporary ICT devices. Short-term thematic courses like Health awareness/care, Food and nutrition, Water conservation/drinking water/sanitation, Population development education issues – AIDS/STD, Sex education, Consumer awareness/Consumer rights, Legal literacy, RTI or any other topic of interest and relevance to the lives of the learners will also be offered under this programme.

To implement the programme, 1.70 lakh Lok Shiksha Kendras (Adult Education Centers) will be established in Panchayat grams of the districts covered under the programme. It will subsume the already sanctioned Continuing Education Centers (CECs) in a particular district. Existing CECs and the nodal CECs in the districts not covered under the programme will have to be closed down, unless the Government of States wish to run them at their own cost through Public Private Partnership or otherwise. Gram Panchayats may as well be given this offer. Specific approval of NLMA will be required to continue an existing CEC under this programme.

A Lok Shiksha Kendra will act as a centre for registration of learners for all teaching learning activities in their jurisdiction; Nerve center for literacy campaign including identification of the learners and volunteers, batching and matching of the learners with suitable Volunteers as well as their training, providing literacy kits to learners and volunteers, keeping track of the progress made by each learner-volunteer group; Nodal centre for mass mobilization activities; Technology center; Center for thematic courses on behalf of other departments such as Agriculture, Animal Husbandry and Veterinary, Fisheries, Horticulture, Sericulture, Handloom, Handicrafts, Health, Education, Rural Development, Urban Development, Women and Child Development, SCs, STs, OBC welfare, Panchayatiraj, Science & Technology etc. or based on local demand; Library and reading room; Venue for group discussion; Vocational and skill development and extension facility for other departments; Center for promoting sports and adventure and recreational and cultural activities; A composite information window and Data center for Adult education besides any other activity related to the mission.

Resource Support

In order to provide academic resource support to literacy and adult education programmes, State Resource Centres (SRCs) have been established throughout the country. Not only their number will be increased but also their capacities enhanced so that they could extend adequate academic and technical resource support to adult and continuing education programme specially in the realm of development of teaching learning material and training of literacy practitioners and managers. Besides SRCs, Resource Support Groups with due representation of educationists, social activists, experienced and committed volunteers/functionaries, representative of local training institutions etc., will be constituted at national, state, district, block and Gram Panchayat level.

Convergence and Partnerships

Public Public Partnerships

NLMA and SLMAs will work towards actively promoting convergence of the Mission's programs and activities with other development strategies specially in education, rural development, health, child and women development, poverty alleviation, agriculture, Panchayati Raj and social welfare sectors. The Mission would take the unified energies of the Departments of School Education and Literacy and higher education down to the village level. Teachers would be encouraged to motivate non-literate parents of their students to enrol as learners and motivate educated youth in the village to volunteer as teachers for the campaign. They could also act as teachers of the literacy classes. Physical infrastructure created under Sarva shiksha Abhiyan may be used for the literacy programme during non-school hours.

Non-Government Organisations

Alliance between GOs and NGOs would be further strengthened. NGOs and other groups that have demonstrated long-term commitment to issues of adult education and which have an established and unsullied track record of performance in this area will be drawn in as resource groups at all levels. Voluntary Sector will be encouraged to take up activities under any programme of the Mission as well as innovative programmes aimed at achieving its objectives for which they may be provided grant-in-aid at the approved cost norms. Selection of the NGO will be the responsibility of the SLMA or the sub-state implementation agency as decided by the SLMA. However, NLMA may select any NGO to assist it in any aspect of the Mission.

Public Private Partnerships

Adult education in India has always been predominantly a government responsibility with some degree of involvement of NGOs. In contrast to very prominent collaboration in the case of formal school system, the contribution of private and corporate sector in adult education has been miniscule. Private and corporate sector can play a momentous role in promoting objectives of the Mission. As in the case of NGOs, institutions in private sector that have the urge, inclination and commitment to adult education programmes, may be encouraged to undertake any activity for which they could be provided grant-in-aid at the approved cost norms. Selection of such agencies will be the responsibility of the SLMA or the sub-state implementation agency as decided by the SLMA. However, NLMA may select any agency to assist it in any aspect of the Mission. NLMA is authorized to develop Public Private Partnerships and other models of partnership to generate funds and also to obtain donations. Alike in selection of NGOs as also institutions in the private sector, there would be total openness and transparency in the process. Fiscal incentives like income tax exemptions may be considered to encourage larger role of private sector in adult education.

International Partnerships

To gain from international experiences, NLMA will strive to establish an international network and work closely with UNESCO, UNICEF, and other international bodies engaged in adult education and arrive at bilateral and multilateral arrangements for mutually beneficial partnerships.

Conclusion

No doubt, the Sakshar Bharath is designed to promote not only the literacy skills among its clientele especially among women, but also to promote basic vocational skills so as to equip them with the required employable skills with potentialities. Further, for achieving this target, it has also adopted the strategy of convergence with the other partners such as public- public, non-governmental, private-public and other international organisations etc., Let us hope that the objectives of the programme will be fulfilled and the women who constitute half of the total population will be equipped with adequate skills and potentialities to suit to the global requirements and also claim their rightful share in the development.

REFERENCES

Seminar proceedings of the National Seminar on "Employability of the Youth, Department of Adult & Continuing Education, S.V. Univerisity, Tirupathi, 28th February – 1st March, 2011.

5

Skills Learning Opportunities to Rural Youth and Challenges

– V.Satyaseelan

ABSTRACT

In the present scenario of country's development, rural youth who continue in rural areas are only those who are school drop-outs, economically poor or who want to remain in their own villages for the reasons like compulsion of parents, not having ambition and self-confidence, want to continue with their peer group in their village etc. Such youth, in the threshold of late-adolescence and early-adulthood are imposed with variety of economic, social and psychological problems. This phase of life is vulnerable to high-risk tendencies and behaviour due to rapid changes (physical, mental and psychological) occurring at this stage, coupled with lack of proper information and education from parents, teachers, service providers and peers. Such rural youth do not possess any job skills or hands-on skills to engage themselves in some form of gainful employment venture to make their livelihood. For employability and sustainable livelihood, they need to acquire skills through "*vocational training*" which is also a "*Lifelong Learning Opportunity*".

This chapter briefly describes the Vocational Training System under the constitution, brings out the key features of Skill Development Initiative Scheme under Ministry of Labour and Employment and touches upon the Swarnjayanti Gram Swarozgar Yojana (SGSY) Scheme under Ministry of Rural Development, which provide excellent opportunities to rural youth for Lifelong Learning of Skills for their employability in Industries and livelihood.

The Construction Industry in India is the second largest economic sector next to Agriculture and it is suffering from huge skill shortage. The Industry has high potential growth due to high demand for Infrastructure Development in our country and also it provides vast scope for enormous opportunities to impart Skills training to rural youth and employ them. But the Construction Industry's experience reveals the reluctance of rural youth to opt for a career in construction field due to various reasons attributing to nature of hardship in work, conditions of employment, locations of employment and the wages.

Government's strategies, goals and plans of expenditure are focusing towards development of Industries as well as Rural Development. But the trend of rural youth is not matching the Learning and Earning opportunities in Industries which are normally located in urban and semi-urban areas. At the same time, there is no attraction to rural youth in Agriculture sector, which also continues to suffer. Such mismatching is the major cause for the challenges at national level.

Introduction: Rural Youth and Employability

In the present scenario of country's development, there are vast educational opportunities for the rural youth in their own villages or in the nearby towns. Those who are passing out, move out of their villages to the urban or semi-urban areas for higher studies and better employment opportunities. Some of the youth who are not good in academic studies but belong to rich families, also move out of their villages to the urban or semi-urban areas either for 'paying hectic amount and getting admission for higher education' or for getting some employment.

Ultimately, youth who continue in rural areas, are only those who are school drop-outs, economically poor, or who want to remain in their own villages (for the reasons like: either compulsion of parents, or they do not have ambition and self-confidence, or they themselves want to continue with their peer group in their village etc.). Such youth, in the threshold of late adolescence and early adulthood are imposed with variety of economic, social and psychological problems. This phase of life is vulnerable to high-risk tendencies and behaviour, due to rapid changes (physical, mental and psychological) occurring at this age, coupled with lack of proper information and education from parents, teachers, service providers and peers.

Employment needs and futuristic financial requirements to sustain their livelihood impose a great deal of predicament among the youth. Considering the relationship between educational level and employment prospects, both move hand-in-hand. If the education level is high, the employment prospects are more and if the education level is low, the employment prospects are less. In urban areas, a fairly good percentage of youth are able to get their education and employment to make their livelihood. In rural areas, the educational drop-out rate is more and therefore, unemployment percentage among the rural youth is high. Such drop-out rural youth do not possess any job skills or hands-on-skills to engage themselves in some form of gainful employment venture to make their livelihood. Thus the potential and aspiring youth become stagnated without gainful employment and therefore their creativity and energy are not being utilised in any form. For their employability and sustainable livelihood, they need to acquire job skills or hands-on skills through vocational training.

Vocational Training System

Vocational Training is a concurrent subject under the constitution and the Central and State Governments share responsibility for effective implementation of vocational training system in the country. At the national level, the Directorate General of Employment and Training, Ministry of Labour and Employment, is the nodal body for formulating policies, laying down norms, standards, conducting trade test and certification of vocational training. The State Governments through Industrial Training Institutes/Industrial Training Centres (ITIs/ITCs) impart institutionalised vocational training under Craftsman Training Scheme, one of the flagship programmes run by the DGE&T.

The vocational training system under the Ministry of Labour and Employment is one of the most comprehensive systems in the country. The craftsman training is provided to youth with the objective to prepare semi-skilled workers for the industry and after they get more work-experience in their employment, they become skilled workers in the industry. The craftsmen training is implemented through a network of Govt ITIs and Private ITCs located in various parts of the country. The educational qualification varies from class VIII pass to class XII pass depending upon the trades. The duration of training varies from six months to three years. The trainees, after completion of craftsmen training, appear in the All India Trade Test to obtain National Trade Certificate awarded by National Council of Vocational Training (NCVT), which is recognised for the purpose of recruitment to the subordinate technical posts at the shop floor level within the country as well as abroad.

Training under Apprenticeship scheme is also imparted under the Apprentices Act 1961, in industrial establishments, to school-leavers and ITI graduates with the objective to prepare skilled workers for the industry. The educational qualification varies from class VIII pass to class XII pass, depending upon the trades. The duration of training varies from one year to four years. All India Trade Tests for Apprentices are conducted under the aegis of NCVT. Successful Apprentices are awarded National Apprenticeship Certificate, which is a recognised qualification for recruitment to the shop floor level subordinate technical posts within the country as well as abroad.

Skill Development Initiative Scheme (SDIS) under DGE & T

Need for Launch of the Scheme

The skill level and educational attainment of the workforce determines the productivity as well as the ability to adapt to the changing industrial environment. A majority of Indian workforce does not possess marketable skills which is an impediment in getting decent employment and improving their economic condition. While India has large young population, only 5 per cent of the Indian labour force in the age group of 20-24 years has acquired vocational skills through formal means whereas the percentage in industrialised countries varies between 60 per cent and 96 per cent. About 63 per cent of the school students drop out at different stages before reaching Class-X. Only about 2.5 million vocational training seats are available in our country whereas about 12.8 million persons enter the labour market every year. Among the existing vocational training centres, only very few are available for admission of early school dropouts. This signifies that a large number of school dropouts do not have access to skill development for improving their employability. The educational entry requirements and long duration of courses under formal training system are some of the impediments for a person with low educational attainment, to acquire skills for his livelihood and development. Further, the largest share of new jobs in India is likely to exist in the unorganised sector that employs up to 93 per cent of the national workforce, but most of the training programmes cater to the needs of the organised sector.

Government of India implemented a strategy in 2005-06 to strengthen Public-Private Partnership between Government and Industry to promote skills development programme under the name "Skill Development Initiative Scheme". Accordingly, Ministry of Labour and Employment undertook development of a new strategic framework for skill development for early school leavers as well as existing workers, especially in the unorganised sector, in close consultation with Industry, micro enterprises in the unorganised sector, State Governments, Experts and Academia which was essential considering their educational, social and economic background. Under this scheme, priority has to be given to cover those above the age of 14 years who have been or withdrawn as child labour to enable them to learn employable skills in order to get gainful employment. Cluster approach has to be adopted with a view to further reducing the incidence of child labour and their parents also could be enrolled on a preferential basis to provide them skills, so as to improve their employability.

Objective of the SDI Scheme

- To provide vocational training to school leavers, existing workers, ITI graduates etc, to improve their employability by optimally utilising the infrastructure available in Govt, private institutions and the Industry. Existing skills of the persons can also be tested and certified under this scheme.
- To build capacity in the area of development of competency standards, course curricula, learning material and assessment standards in the country.

Key Features of SDI Scheme are:

- Demand driven short term training courses based on Modular Employable Skills (MES) decided in consultation with Industry. MES is the 'minimum skills set' which is sufficient for gainful employment.
- Central Government will facilitate and promote training while industry, private sector and State Governments will train the persons.

- Optimum utilisation of existing infrastructure to make training cost effective.
- Flexible delivery mechanism (part time, weekends, full time, and onsite/offsite) to suit needs of various target groups.
- Different levels of programmes (Basic level as well as skill upgradation) to meet demands of various target groups.
- The services of existing or retired faculty or guest faculty to be utilised.
- Courses would also be available for persons having completed 5th standard.
- Testing and Certification of skills acquired formally.
- Testing of skills of trainees by independent assessing bodies, which would not be involved in training delivery to ensure that it is done impartially.
- The essence of the scheme is in the certification that will be nationally and internationally recognised.

SDIS-MES Target Group

SDI Scheme based on Modular Employable Skills, would benefit different target groups like:

- Workers seeking certification of their skills acquired informally.
- Workers and ITI graduates seeking skill upgradation.
- Early school drop-outs and unemployed.
- Those who had been child labour and their families.

Expected Project Output of SDIS

As per Central Governments plans, one million persons would be trained or their skills tested and certified, over a period of five years. More than 200 modules for Employable Skills as per Industry and labour market demands would be identified and course curriculum developed.

Age of Participants

The minimum age limit for persons to take part in the scheme is 14 years and there is no upper age limit.

Vocational Training Providers - Concept

The training under SDI scheme will be provided by various VTPs under Central Govt, State Govts, Public and Private Sector and Industrial establishments. VTPs will provide counselling & vocational guidance, training facilities as per norms, impart good quality training, post training support to trainees in getting employment, maintain data base on trainees trained and the outcome of training. They will track the trainees for three years or till they get gainfully employed. VTP will also be required to have close networking with the industry for immediate placement of the trainees. They will also maintain accounts, ensure proper utilisation of funds and submit reports and utilisation certificates as per prescribed schedule. Training cost @ Rs 15/- per person per hour will be reimbursed to VTPs in respect of those successful persons who got training from the VTPs approved by DGE&T. Selection of VTPs as per criteria, process of approval, monitoring the functions of VTP, periodical check measures, quality audit, testing & certification by approved independent bodies, and reimbursement of training cost etc will be controlled by committees formed by respective Regional Directors under DGE & T.

Swarnjayanti Gram Swarozgar Yojana (SGSY) Scheme & MHRD

The Ministry of Rural Development has been and is funding to promote several special projects under SGSY scheme, for demand driven short term skill development programmes to rural population in Below Poverty Line (BPL) category, leading to their skills-learning and placement in entry level jobs in emerging manufacturing and service sectors. These projects are for meeting the aspirations of the vast segment of rural unemployed youth from BPL families, unable to enter the job market due to their low levels of education and skills, but looking for life-long skills learning opportunities to meet the skill requirements in the Industry for their gainful employment. The projects are ideally backed and driven by the Industry with assured employment/placement to beneficiaries after skills-training. The training cost is predominantly funded by the Ministry of Rural Development and partly borne by the potential employers and Industries. The primary objective of the SGSY scheme is to encourage Industry's participation to promote skills development programmes to rural population in BPL category and to provide them gainful employment. While benefiting the rural youth, the Industry itself is able to get trained manpower and the Government is also able to address the unemployment problem of rural youth, to some extent for country's growth.

Excellent Opportunities for Life-Long Skills-Learning and Earning

As described above, both the schemes (SDI Scheme under Ministry of Employment and Training and SGSY scheme under Ministry of Rural Development) are highly potential and they provide excellent opportunities to rural youth for life-long skills-learning and earning.

Skills-Learning Opportunities in Construction Industry; Live-Situation

The Construction sector in India is the second largest economic activity next to Agriculture and it provides employment to about 36 million people. As an Industry, it has grown at a Compounded Annual Growth Rate (CAGR) of about 11.1 per cent over the last eight years and the investment in Construction Industry accounts for around 52.4 per cent of the Gross Fixed Capital Formation in India. While it serves as a demand booster in a short term, it contributes towards boosting infrastructure capacity in a long term. Among the total manpower in the Industry, 81 per cent constitutes unskilled workers, 14 per cent skilled workers trained through ITIs & other vocational courses and the remaining 5 per cent consists of managerial staff, executives, engineers, supervisors, foremen, accounts & administration staff. The incremental requirement of skilled manpower at workers level alone is expected to go up from the recent strength of 5 million in the year 2009 to 7 million in 2022. The strength of unskilled workers which was 29 million in the year 2009 is expected to go up to 38 million in 2002. That means, there is a vast scope in the Construction Industry for training 38 million untrained workers and rural youth over a period of 13 years from 2009 to 2022, to make them employable in 'skilled' category.

Trend of Rural Youth Towards the Available Opportunities in Construction Industry

The Industry's experience and the data reveals that most of the rural youth are not at all interested to opt for skills learning and employment in Construction Industry. Table 5.1 indicates the summary of number of job melas/campaigns held in different locations in Tamil Nadu, Pondicherry, Kerala and Andhra Pradesh during the period April 2005 to Sep 2009 to select eligible youth for free training (with a stipend of Rs. 2000 per month and free accommodation) in Construction Skills Training Institute (of L & T) located in Chennai, number of candidates shown willingness & got selected as per eligibility criteria and number of candidates joined the different trade-training courses ranging from 45 days to 3 months. 81 job melas/campaigns were conducted, 3367 candidates were selected and only 313 of them (9.3%) joined the training courses.

Findings/Challenges

On studying the trend of rural youth with such a low response for construction skills training, the following findings/facts do emerge as challenges:

- Rural youth who are habituated to be in their villages are comfortable with seasonal plantation jobs for about 6 months in a year and remaining idle for the rest of the year.
- Their parents do not want to send them to far-off urban and semi-urban areas for livelihood.
- They are aware that construction work demands migration of workers from one project to the other project and the nature of work also is very difficult, when compared to the shop floor work in manufacturing industry.

Table 5.1: Sourcing of Candidates through Job Melas for Construction Skills Training at Chennai (April 2005 to September 2009)

Fin. Year	State or UT	No. of Melas Conducted in Different Locations	No. of Candidates Appeared	No. of Candidates Selected as per Eligibility Criteria	Joined in the Institute for training
Apr'05 to Mar'06	AP	1	42	25	20
	TN	1	60	22	2
Apr'06 to Mar'07	AP	1	65	27	13
	TN	3	204	94	22
	Pondicherry	1	34	6	4
Apr'07 to Mar'08	AP	1	Data Not Available	25	0
	TN	11		740	65
Apr'08 to Mar'09	AP	3	Data Not Available	104	26
	TN	47		2132	117
	Kerala	1		14	0
Apr'09 to Sep'09	AP	1	Data Not Available	1	1
	TN	8		105	0
	MP	2		72	43
Total		81		3367	313
Percentage joined for training				9.3% of 3367	

- Even if a few of them are interested, they are influenced by their peer group to change their mind.

• They strongly believe that instead of moving away from their villages to far-off locations to do the difficult construction work for an initial salary of Rs 3000 to 4000 per month, they can have "easy going" in their villages and earn the same amount in seasonal plantation jobs.

- Construction Industry's workers are in unorganised sector and most of them are employed only thro' labour sub- contractors and not under direct rolls of primary employer. Sub-contractors prefer to bring workers of their choice thro' their known sources, rather than employing institutionally-trained tradesmen. They treat them like bonded labour and exploit them by paying less wages and getting signature in the pay sheet for more amount than what is really being paid. They focus their attention towards making more money in the business by exploiting the workers. Workers brought by sub-contractors thro' their own sources are very loyal to them and maintain integrity.
- Primary employers do not want to employ the workers in their direct rolls and if they do so, the workers will unite together, demand more wages, benefits and facilities and go on strike. They also do not interfere with the sub-contractors on the payment terms with their workers as long as the signed pay-sheets produced by the sub-contractors, show the wages not less than what is stipulated for different skill levels of workers as per Minimum Wages Act in the particular State.
- The statutory authority for enforcement of Labour Laws/ Minimum Wages Act in the State is the Labour Commissioner. During the regular inspection of officials from Labour Commissioner's office, they check the pay-sheets produced by the sub-contractors and certified by the principal employer. As long as the wages recorded in the pay sheets are complying with the Act and if there is no specific complaint or incidence of labour unrest/

agitation brought to their attention, they are satisfied with unlawful and person-oriented satisfying measures adopted by the principal employer.

- Some of the rural youth show interest in Apprenticeship Training Schemes in manufacturing or automobile industry and they accept Technician's work in shop-floor/workshop. They believe that after completing the apprenticeship training, some of them will get selected and be absorbed in permanent cadre in the same company.
- Business Process Outsourcing (BPO) Agencies, call centres, retail chain outlets/super markets and ready-made garment manufacturing units attract the youth for a decent in-door job with less hardship. Star Hotels offer them employment as waiters or room-attendants and in house-keeping services. Corporate Hospitals also attract them to work as ward boys and in house-keeping services. Although there is no career progression opportunities in such jobs to the rural youth unless they qualify themselves with more education, they feel more happy in these in-door jobs as they can do easy work in air-conditioned comfort and get subsidised food facilities. In many of such jobs, they get free accommodation also.

Conclusion

All the excellent initiatives by Government to promote Vocational Training under PPP scheme are meant for skill development of unemployed rural youth but they are industry-oriented. Despite Govt's strategies and policies towards development of Industrial growth, many unemployed youth are getting attracted towards easy jobs in commercial establishments and service sectors involving lesser hardship rather than hard work in industries. As a result, Industries continue to suffer due to severe shortage of skilled workers and the growth of Agriculture/Food production sector is also further getting neglected.

Another fact is that in all Government-funding schemes, huge amount is promptly budgeted and truly spent by Govt as per records. But, in real terms, the ruling politicians, implementing public servants/officers/employees and the implementation agencies/NGOs derive maximum benefit (by means of corruption and misappropriation of funds) and very little benefit practically reaches the target population for whom the schemes are really launched. Tsunami Rehabilitation schemes and the National Rural Employment Guarantee Scheme (NREGS) are the examples.

Re-orientation in Government Policies and Strategies, tightening the implementation mechanism to ensure that 100 per cent benefit reaches the targeted population and elimination of corruption and misappropriation of funds at all levels is the need of the

REFERENCES

Ministry of Youth Affairs & Sports, Govt of India: The National Youth Policy.

Rajiv Gandhi National Institute of Youth Development: Policies & Development Programmes.

Ministry of Rural Development, Govt of India: Various schemes for development of Youth.

Planning Commission, Govt of India: Approach to 11th Five-Year Plan, 2006.

Ministry of Labour & Employment, Govt of India: Skill Development Initiative Scheme – Implementation Manual, 2007.

ICRA Management Consulting Services Limited (IMaCS): Skill Gap Report for Construction Industry, Submitted to National Skill Development Corporation, 2009.

AICMED, West Bengal Committee to Eradicate Illiteracy, Kolkata: Adult Education and Development Journals 2005/2006.

6

Youth and Employment Scenario in Latin America and The Caribbean

– Santosh Kumar Mishra

Key Words: Youth, employment, Latin America and the Caribbean, society, formal education, professional training, vocational skills development, and low-income entrepreneurs.

Introduction

The employment situation of young people in Latin America and the Caribbean is critical. It is critical because average unemployment among young people is, in all countries of the region, much higher than average unemployment overall. In fact, in Latin America and the Caribbean the youth unemployment rate is twice the overall unemployment rate and three times the rate for adults; in some countries it is as high as five times the rate for adults over age 45. What is more, young people account for about 50 per cent of all unemployed workers in nearly every country in the region. The situation is especially critical in certain countries, where unemployment among 15- to 24-year-olds circa 1999 reached levels of 29.5 per cent (Panama) and 27.9 per cent (Uruguay and Venezuela), according to ILO data.

The same source indicated that the situation was particularly serious among 15- to 19-year-olds, whose unemployment rates were 37 per cent in Colombia, 35.9 per cent in Argentina and 29.2 per cent in Chile. While open urban unemployment in 1998 was 7.2 per cent in Chile and 10.2 per cent in Uruguay, youth unemployment was 20.8 per cent (15- to 19-year-olds) and 15.1 per cent (20- to 24-year-olds) in Chile and 25.1 per cent (15- to 24-year-olds) in Uruguay. These gaps were also observed circa 1997 in the OECD countries, where youth unemployment was about 13.4 per cent, compared to 5.9 per cent for adults.

This is aggravated by the fact that over the past decade (1990-1999), 7 out of every 10 jobs created in Latin America were in the informal sector, while average unemployment is now higher than it was 10 years ago (to an extreme degree in countries such as Colombia and Argentina). All of this means that employment has become harder to find and that most new jobs are of lower quality and are more unstable, more insecure and lower-paying. Lastly, a young person, on average, requires a longer period of time to find a job than an unemployed adult. If we consider all these issues together, we find ourselves facing a critical youth employment situation in Latin America.

Who are Youth?

One of the most common definitions of youth in quantitative terms comprises persons between the age of 15 and 24. It is used by both the United Nations and the World Bank and is applied in many statistics and indicators. Young people are grouped together to form a statistical entity, making it possible to compare data across time and countries. However, this crude definition must be qualified somewhat, when youth is defined in qualitative terms.

Different scholars have provided different ways of defining youth. Curtain (2002), quoted in the U.N. World Youth Report 2003, defines it as a phase when a person moves from a time of dependence (childhood) to independence (adulthood) and identifies four distinct aspects of this move:

- Leaving the parental home and establishing new living arrangements;
- Completing full-time education;
- Forming close, stable personal relationships outside of the family, often resulting in marriage and children; and
- Testing the labor market, finding work and possibly settling into a career, and achieving a more or less sustainable livelihood.

These transitions are interconnected, i.e. leaving home and setting up one's own personal economy require an independent source of income, and to reach this stage a young person generally has to acquire qualifications and to have succeeded in demonstrating his or her skill in the labor market. Young people, when faced with uncertain employment prospects and financial insecurity, are likely to avoid establishing stable personal relationships, postpone marriage, and/or put off having or accepting the responsibility for children. In the absence the prospects for a sustainable livelihood, more extreme social behavior may occur, e.g. engagement in illegal activities such as drug trafficking, violent crime or gang activities. Poor economic prospects may also contribute to antisocial behavior, including exposing others to HIV/AIDS through the practice of unsafe sex.

This transition model exposes the problems of moving from one developmental phase to another. The role of youth policy in this context is to create favorable conditions for success by preparing young people for the roles and responsibilities of adulthood. It also entails the idea that childhood and youth are in themselves valuable stages of life, more than just necessary stops on the way to adulthood. Youth policy, therefore, becomes not only a source of guidance towards adulthood, but a means of providing and ensuring the requirements for a safe and productive live for children and youth. This means viewing children and young people as subjects (not objects) in every respect – not only at the personal level, but in society as a whole, participating in decision-making and the debates that surround it.

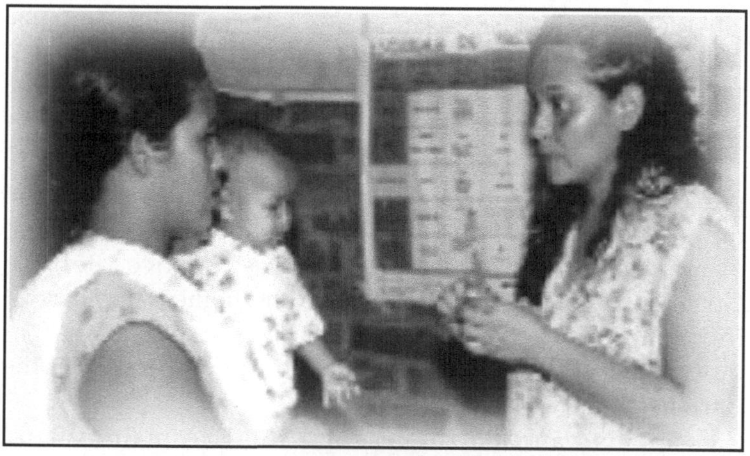

Employment Opportunities for Youth in Latin America and the Caribbean

The Regional Scenario: A Specific and Highly Heterogeneous Region

Latin America and the Caribbean is a highly heterogeneous and specific region in all aspects – historical, political, economic, social, cultural, linguistic, and also in educational terms – thus making it difficult to generalize diagnoses, conclusions and recommendations for the region as a whole. On the contrary, acknowledging such heterogeneity reinforces the need for diversified and context-sensitive policies and programmes.

The region consists of two sub-regions – Latin America, and the Caribbean – each of them also internally heterogeneous. They constitute different worlds in many respects and have little contact due to geographical as well as historical, cultural and linguistic barriers. Latin American countries are organised geographically into North, Central and South America. There are also sub-groupings according to various specific supranational coordination and trade agreements, such as the Andean Community (CAN), the Southern Common Market (MERCOSUR), the Union of South American Nations (UNASUR), the Caribbean Community

(CARICOM), the Organisation of Eastern Caribbean States (OECS) and the Association of Caribbean States (ASC). Moreover, there are different geopolitical groupings organised around different international bodies.

In a region inhabited by 577 million people (less than 10 per cent of the world population – UN, 2004 data), the indigenous population is estimated at around 40 million, organised in over 400 ethnic groups. Mexico, Bolivia, Guatemala, Ecuador and Peru have the highest numbers of indigenous people. There is also an important Afro-descendant population in several countries, especially in the Caribbean and in Brazil.

Spanish and Portuguese are the two main official languages in Latin America, and English and French in the Caribbean, but some 600 languages are spoken throughout the region as well as standard and non-standard variants of many of them. Beneath the few main official languages, associated to their respective colonial pasts, the region has a highly complex linguistic reality often hidden in regional diagnoses and studies and not properly acknowledged in education policies and programmes. Multilingual and multicultural contexts are common in Latin America. The Caribbean has also a varied linguistic situation. In the majority of English- and French-speaking countries in the Caribbean the first language of the population is a Creole, related to the official language (such as in Guyana, Jamaica or Haiti) or to a non-official one (as in Dominica and St. Lucia where English is the official language but the main spoken language is Kwéyòl, a French-based Creole, or in Suriname where the official language is Dutch but the language spoken is Sranan Tongo, an English-based.

However, in all these countries, except for Haiti, education – including literacy classes for adults – is conducted in the official language. Latin America and the Caribbean is the most urbanized region in the South. Between 1950 and 2005, the proportion of the population living in urban areas grew from 41.9 per cent to 77.6 per cent. There are important and systematic rural/urban gaps in most countries, the education gap being just one of them. This is also the most unequal region in the world, with the biggest difference between rich and poor. The region has the highest concentration of the *'ultra-rich'* (those with over $30 million in cash, besides properties and art collections). Their fortunes are growing faster than those of their counterparts in other regions in the world, and they are the least generous. *On the other hand,* by 2007 34.1 per cent of the population were living in poverty and 12.6 per cent in extreme poverty. Youth and adults participating in ALE programmes generally belong to these segments of the population. This is why adult education has traditionally been associated with social transformation and political action. In modern neo-liberal times, however, it appears to be associated with plans and strategies aimed at *'poverty alleviation'*, *'social inclusion'* and *'social cohesion'* – the new terminologies and trends.

There was a slight reduction in poverty in the 2002-2007 periods. *However,* this trend stopped in 2008, due fundamentally to the world increase in the prices of food and of oil. Three million people moved back from poor to extremely poor. According to Food and Agricultural Organisation (FAO (2008), between 2006 and 2008 the fight against hunger in the region practically lost all the advances that had been made during the previous two decades. Between 1990 and 2005 malnutrition in the region had been reduced from 12 per cent to 8 per cent; in 2007, however, scarcity of food resulted in an increase in the number of hungry people to 51 million, a figure similar to the 52.6 million in 1990. Following the eruption of the international financial crisis at the end of 2008, initiated in the United States and rapidly expanded throughout the world, it is estimated that the situation of the poor will further deteriorate in 2009 and many of the gains of previous years may be lost once again.

ALE faces many major economic, social and political challenges in this region, including illiteracy still concentrated in a few countries, in rural areas, among women and among indigenous peoples; limited access to and completion of compulsory education (of generally poor quality) for out-of-school youth and adults; unemployment; social exclusion; increased urban segregation; internal and international migration; violence; racism; and sexism. As in the rest of the world, there is a growing ageing segment of the population.

In many countries there is concern with the increasing number of *'unattached'* youth – youth who do not study and do not work (in Spanish, *No Estudia ni Trabaja* has become an acronym – NET). In 2004 in Paraguay, 65 per cent of urban youth and 78 per cent of those living in rural areas were in this situation. In Argentina, in 2005, it was one out of every 20 youth. In Brazil, in 2006, this figure was 27.1 per cent. In Mexico, in 2007, 30 per cent of students completing secondary education continued studying, 25 per cent found a job, while the remaining 45 per cent had no activity (Rivas, 2007). In Jamaica, in the period 1998-2001 between 24 per cent and 34 per cent of youths were 'unattached', over half of them in rural areas, one quarter of them living below the poverty line and having attained education to grade 9 level or lower, and half of them living in female-headed households (Jamaica CONFINTEA VI report, 2008). Cuba is at this point the only country that has systematic government policies to deal with youth who drop out of school; they are incorporated to public vocational education and training institutions that offer students the possibility of completing formal secondary education while they are provided on-the-job training opportunities. Cuba is in fact the only country in the region that has a lifelong learning policy – *'from cradle to grave'* – without calling it such.

Existing Scenario

In Latin America, young people today are more educated than their parents were. They have greater knowledge and higher consumer expectations as a result of their exposure to the cultural industry, and they have taken in the promises of development propagated by political figures, the family and the schools. On the other hand, the rate of youth unemployment is two or three times higher than the rate for the rest of the population. Young people have assimilated implicit promises of social mobility and a place in society, given the fact that they are more educated than their parents, but at the same time they come up against a situation in which their real work opportunities are more limited and do not correspond to the fund of knowledge they have accumulated during childhood and adolescence. They are treated as children by adults (politicians, entrepreneurs and the media), and a cultural bias often stigmatizes them as potentially violent, drug-consuming and morally weak – to the extent that this bias often becomes a self-fulfilling prophecy. Faced with difficulties in assuming a role in production, young people become more likely to operate on the fringes of, or even against, the existing_institutional structure. It is no coincidence that young people have headed the increase in urban violence over the last decade. In some countries, including Mexico, Venezuela, Colombia and Brazil, the media industry developed vigorously and both the coverage and the achievements of the school system soared over that period, but trends in youth employment and quality of life for new generations were radically different. Steeply rising levels of violence in Latin American cities in the 1980s and early 1990s (with these very countries - Mexico, Venezuela, Colombia and Brazil - heading the list) were symptomatic of these problems.

Key Issues

The employment situation of young people in Latin America and the Caribbean is dynamic and segmented because of following reasons.

It is dynamic because the relationship between educational achievements and requirements in the work environment is changing rapidly as those requirements shift in response to changes in technology and in national economies' areas of specialization and linkages with the global system; because the ratio of young women to men in the economically active population is changing; because the reforms being made to increase labour flexibility are increasing the vulnerability of workers, especially those who are first entering this new institutional framework; because young people's expectations are very dynamic and easily influenced by cultural changes; and because, for the young people now joining the economically active population, the new production patterns have moved away from the concept of stability and long-term employment.

It is segmented because more highly educated young people have a better employment outlook in terms of income, working conditions, social status and mobility, technological competitiveness and job satisfaction. In all the countries of Latin America, except Cuba and to a lesser degree Uruguay, there is a very strong correlation between educational achievement and the income level of students' families, which reproduces existing disparities in the future. This situation is compounded by the fact that in the "new economy", access to employment for young people tends to be polarized. On the one hand, there is a privileged group of computer-literate young people who become professionals on a "fast track" career path or successful entrepreneurs who have a greater command than adults of the new skills required in the information society (the use of virtual networks and adaptation to deregulated flexible markets); while on the other hand, there is a large number of young people who hold insecure, low-level jobs in the informal sector or who are employed in the formal sector in low-skill positions where wage levels are declining in comparative terms. Lastly, there is segmentation by gender (Latin American women continue to have lower incomes than men with the same level of education and skills), by area (rural youths in Latin America have far fewer opportunities than urban youths for the simple reason that they do not live near modernized enclaves) and by network (young people from middle- and high-income urban families have greater access to good jobs through family contacts, classmates and friends in business or in the State technocracy).

The segmentation of unemployment is clearly biased by income group and educational level. By analysing youth unemployment according to household income level, ECLAC has shown that, between 1990 and 1997, the ratio between typical unemployment rates in the poorest and the richest quartiles steadily increased in 8 of the 12 Latin American countries studied. In Honduras in 1997, the unemployment rate for the first income quartile was 13.1 times higher than the rate for the fourth quartile (the highest income level); this gap was also very wide in Argentina (9.5) and Bolivia (8.3). In Brazil, circa 1997, youth unemployment was 10.1 per cent in the fourth quartile, compared to 22.7 per cent in the first quartile. In Chile the rates were 5.8 per cent and 25.8 per cent, respectively, and in Bolivia they were 2.0 per cent and 16.5 per cent, respectively. In Argentina, the open unemployment rate for young people from poor households in urban areas rose from 40.0 per cent to 55.4 per cent between 1990 and 1997, while the rate for the country's youth population as a whole was 24.3 per cent in 1997. Similar gaps were observed in Colombia and Panama.

At the same time, unemployment among young people not attending school is more severe among those from low-income households. According to ECLAC sources, in Brazil unemployment among young people not in school rose by 8 percentage points between 1990 and 1997, owing primarily to the lack of growth in young women's employment, while in Argentina, unemployment among young people not in school and belonging to poor households rose by more than 15 points over the same period. In Mexico this group saw a 3 per cent rise in unemployment during that time.

Lastly, the segmentation resulting from the correlation between education levels and working conditions also reveals three problematic groups in the Latin American countries. First, there are adolescents and young people who work and who cannot continue their education (representing about two thirds of those who have managed to find jobs), most of whom work to contribute to household income. The second group consists of young people who neither work nor attend school. While this group has shrunk since the early 1990s, it continues to account for 12 per cent to 40 per cent of young people in poor households, and 2 per cent to 10 per cent of those in higher-income households. The third group consists of young people who have left school with less than 10 years of education (meaning that they have very little chance of earning incomes that represent upward social mobility). This group has also become smaller, but young people in this category continue to represent between 20 per cent and 50 per cent of the total -in the lowest-income quartile, this proportion ranges from 38 per cent to 82 per cent in different countries.

The Uncertain Outlook for the Coming Decade

The Political and Socio-economic Prospects of Latin American and Caribbean Society

Political stability: Virtually all the Latin American and Caribbean countries have democratic Governments elected by popular vote and are consolidating democratic institutions. As a result of the hard lessons of the political violence of earlier decades, they attach great value to social peace and their domestic political forces are strongly committed to democratic legitimacy. Although political conflicts have been generated by the social conflicts stemming from poor income distribution, unemployment, lack of opportunities for young people and economic instability, political democracy and the rule of law seem to be surviving such difficulties. The region can therefore expect to witness, at least for the coming decade, a trend towards the continuance of democratic regimes and the further development of mechanisms for improving accountability, reducing government corruption and broadening the participation of social actors in decision-making processes. While a tendency towards political authoritarianism and populism is still apparent in some countries, it should not preclude respect for the rules governing democratic institutions.

Economic growth: The growth potential of the Latin American and Caribbean economies is unclear because it is highly dependent on external factors that are currently volatile or adverse, such as financial capital flows, foreign direct investment, trade barriers in industrialized countries, the uncertain economic outlook in the region's export markets and competitiveness in comparison to other regions. In addition, increasingly sustained investments in human capital are needed to maintain high levels of economic growth over the long term and to generate high-quality jobs for future generations. Thus far, however, the education reforms of the 1990s have not had a positive impact on the quality of human resources in the countries of the region. Accordingly, so long as growth continues to depend on trade and financial cycles instead of reflecting a strong increase in the capacity of human resources for productive innovation, development will be precarious and its impact on job creation will not necessarily be positive.

Social problems: Today, income is very poorly distributed in most of the countries of the region, and in some of them (Venezuela and Argentina), distribution patterns have deteriorated significantly. The liberalization and privatization model being imposed in nearly all the countries has not had a positive impact on income distribution, has generated new vulnerabilities in social groups that are not closely linked to the modern sector of the economy and has created a serious gap between included and excluded groups. This gap has been widened by the digital divide, since only 6 per cent of the Latin American population has access to electronic networks, and most of this group is in the high-income or higher-middle-income category. Lastly, the pattern of economic modernization has tended to reinforce long-standing negative trends in the region such as residential segregation, the loss of a sense of solidarity between different income groups and tremendous disparities in productive capacity.

The Impact of Youth Unemployment on Society

Sustained high rates of youth unemployment have multiple effects on society. First, they mean that the countries are failing to take advantage of the human resources they need to increase their productive potential, at a time of transition to a globalized world that inexorably demands such leaps in productive capacity. Second, they reinforce the intergenerational transmission of poverty. Third, owing to the discrepancy between more education and exposure to the mass media and fewer employment opportunities, they may encourage the spread of disruptive behaviours, recourse to illegal alternatives for generating income and the loss of basic societal values, all of which erode public safety and social capital. Fourth, they may trigger violent and intractable political conflicts. Fifth, they may exacerbate intergenerational conflicts when young people perceive a lack of opportunity and meritocracy in a system that favours adults who have less formal education and training but more wealth, power and job stability.

Tackling the Problem of Youth Unemployment

Promoting youth employment and employability requires an integrated effort that includes action in the areas of education, skills development, the job supply and support for young, low-income entrepreneurs. These initiatives must provide for participation by various stakeholders, from the State to private entrepreneurs, including non-governmental organisations, local authorities, youth leaders, the media, parents' associations, etc.

With *regard to formal education*, regional data show that, on average, a minimum of 12 years of formal schooling are now required for access to employment opportunities that will prevent poverty or offer a way out of it. The data also indicate that the highest returns on education go to those who complete their secondary and university education.

Although the countries of the region continue to make progress towards expanding the coverage of secondary education with a view to promoting a better future for young people by enabling them to take part in production, in most countries the gap between high-income and low-income groups in terms of secondary and higher education coverage has also tended to widen in recent decades. Consequently, efforts in the area of education should focus on achieving universal coverage, preferably up to the end of secondary school, and on reducing differences in the quality of the education provided to different socio-economic groups.

Strenuous efforts are therefore needed to ensure that current education reforms give priority to keeping adolescents from vulnerable groups in secondary school and to encourage more low-income students to enter higher education in order to provide more democratic access to productive employment in the future. In view of the changes taking place in employment styles and career paths, it is essential to promote the use of computers and information technologies (mainly networking) in schools in order to narrow the digital divide. It is equally important, in conjunction with these new tools, to develop higher cognitive functions by orienting the learning process towards problem identification and problem solving, increasing the capacity for reflection and creativity, enhancing the ability to distinguish between what is relevant and what is not and developing planning and research skills, since these functions are vital in an information-saturated world.

Professional training, vocational skills development and support for young, low-income entrepreneurs are essential and require greater investment in the quality and coverage of the relevant programmes, a qualitative leap in adapting training and skills development to new employment demands and technological change and the involvement of multiple stakeholders, including universities, entrepreneurs' and employers' associations, financial agents and others.

The biggest challenge in this regard should continue to be vocational training coupled with the provision of initial work experiences. This approach addresses two of the primary causes of youth unemployment: lack of experience and lack of training. The impact of vocational training should be maximized through the use of strategies for targeting (aimed at the most vulnerable youth sectors), decentralization (assigning a more active role to the municipal level) and *inter-agency cooperation* (with the widest possible range of training institutions, both public and private), taking a *comprehensive approach* (by combining training with internships and support for job placement) based on *labour market agreements* (basically between training entities and firms) and supported by stringent *monitoring and evaluation* mechanisms.

A national training and skills development system which provides internships in businesses and links with employers, is technically up to date and stays abreast of changes in the job supply could substantially improve the options for young people who do not have a university education. Another important field of endeavour is the provision of support in the form of access to financing, information and networks for young entrepreneurs wishing to establish viable microenterprises and small businesses, as a large proportion of the jobs now being created in the region are in small businesses. Young entrepreneurs should receive particular support in the use of and access to new information and communication technologies, since incorporation into contact and information networks is, and will increasingly be, the most effective and efficient way to generate value added in microenterprises and small businesses. To the extent that young people are enthusiastic and quick to learn about these new technologies and about the use of electronic networks, this asset gives them great autonomy in acquiring productive knowledge, using market information, advertising their skills, generating alliances and contacts and finding better areas of specialization.

Vocational training and education should take a less rigid approach, given the increasingly profound changes taking place in labour markets. They should focus on developing *cross-cutting competencies*, providing skills for occupational "families" rather than for a specific occupation, promoting an entrepreneurial spirit and teaching the basic principles and techniques of management. All these efforts should aim at providing training in a wide range of substantive areas and processes under the governing concept of *transition training*. They should form *training chains* designed to meet young people's needs at four different stages:

- *when* they are still in the education system;
- *when* they leave the system and enter the labour market in search of their first job;
- *when* they are engaged in very low-productivity informal activities or are chronically unemployed; and
- *when* they have found an occupation and need to become integrated into ongoing training chains to improve their assets and their labour-market participation.

Action at the macro level is needed, both in relation to employment policy (and its coordination with economic policy) and in the regulation of labour markets. Many of the efforts made in these areas may end in failure, however, so long as most countries in the region continue to promote a liberalization-privatization-deregulation dynamic which restricts employment, widens the gap between the formal and informal sectors and between specialized and non-specialized activities, deprives people of social protection if they lose their jobs, makes employment more precarious and discontinuous and is indifferent to the dangerous and increasing correlation between being "young" and being "excluded".

Proactive labour policies must be based on an awareness that job creation is sustainable only when the economic activities concerned are competitive in the long term. In Latin America, employment has grown much more rapidly in Mexico and the countries of Central America and the Caribbean (3.7% per year during the 1990s as a whole), which have been specializing in exports of manufactures, than in the South American countries (2.9% per year over the same period), where natural-resource-based exports have been relatively more important. The retooling of production activities and increased labour mobility make it necessary to implement aggressive vocational training policies.

Public investment, productive innovation and macroeconomic stabilization policies should place greater emphasis on job creation. This is not only a matter of expanding job opportunities for young people. It is also a means of incorporating new generations into the production system, which is important because it is they who have the assets best suited to the new production requirements that have arisen in open markets: more years of education, which make it possible to increase the intellectual value added of production; more familiarity with the new information and communication technologies; and more flexibility in adapting to new types of work.

Special programmes to improve the job prospects of particularly vulnerable groups should be implemented and/ or expanded. Not all young people are affected to the same extent by unemployment and problems with employment. Rates of unemployment and underemployment are much higher among young people who belong to ethnic minorities, who have low levels of education, who live in far-flung rural communities, who have some level of disability or who have a history of violent crime. To break the vicious circle of unemployment and exclusion, it is necessary to take specific actions in relation to these groups. These actions may include State subsidies for private firms that hire young people in such situations, quotas in public-sector employment for young people in these groups, various indirect forms of affirmative action, special job training programmes focusing on specific vulnerabilities and vocational guidance and placement programmes for these groups. In general, these actions require concerted efforts by the State (especially ministries of labour and training services), the private sector and civil-society support associations.

Best Practices

One clear model of best practices is the *"Chile Joven" vocational training programme*, which was launched in 1990 and has already been adapted to conditions in other Latin American countries that are replicating it. The programme is unusual in that it provides training within relatively short time periods using innovative operational methods, and emphasizes the relevance of the occupations selected and the effective job placement of young people instead of focusing exclusively on technical training. The programme's implementation involves numerous actors, both public and private, ranging from the Ministry of Labour to entrepreneurs with a commitment to the training and employability of young people. The applicable rules of the game are competitive, so that even applying to the programme requires young people to exert their own efforts and initiative from the outset. The programme targets young people with medium and low levels of education, and assessments are made of the subsequent labour market participation of the beneficiaries. The *"Chile Joven"* programme includes various complementary, flexible sub-programmes that expand the options available to young people: an on-the-job training and work experience sub-programme, a two-track learning sub-programme and a self-employed workers' sub-programme.

The first of these sub-programmes includes a technical training phase that partially qualifies participants for an occupation (200 hours) and a job training phase that develops social skills to facilitate young people's job placement (50 hours). The beneficiaries then take part in a three-month work experience performing the job learned in a firm, either as interns or with job contracts. The executing agencies include private training firms and corporations, which offer nearly 2,000 courses that benefit some 35,000 young people.

The two-track learning sub-programme has a pre-training component that provides remedial instruction in basic subjects (60-120 hours), a training component to complement on-the-job training and develop an understanding of the technology used in the occupation (180-300 hours) and an on-the-job training component in a firm with a teacher-mentor, in parallel with the training component in the technical agency. In this case the beneficiary is a regular worker in the firm and the State provides the firm with a subsidy equivalent to

40 per cent of the minimum wage for the duration of the course. Some 140 such courses are being given, for the benefit of about 3,000 participants.

Lastly, the sub-programme for self-employed workers includes occupational training (80 hours) and management training (at least 100 hours); upon completion of the second component, the student must prepare a project to be financed by the programme's credit assistance network. The network, in turn, makes two assessments: one prior to the provision of financing, which includes a pre-feasibility study of the project and formalizes the support to be provided with a letter of commitment; and another, once the course has begun, that evaluates the feasibility of the student's project. At least 50 hours of technical assistance are provided for the projects, and the beneficiaries receive a monthly subsidy of US$ 54 for the duration of the technical assistance phase, up to a maximum of three months.

Another prime example of a State-led initiative is the PROJOVEN Programme in Uruguay. This is a cross-sectoral vocational training programme for low-income young people between the ages of 17 and 24. It was launched six years ago and involves the National Employment Board, the National Employment Office of the Ministry of Labour and Social Security and the National Youth Institute. The Programme is financed with the resources contributed by private-sector workers and employers to an Occupational Retraining Fund, and also from the general budget.

The Programme is considered an example of best practices for several reasons:

- The *first* is that it creates linkages between the job supply and the demand for jobs, as all the training it provides is adapted to reflect employment trends. This is facilitated by the fact that the Programme is funded in part by workers' and employers' associations and that it represents a cross-sectoral initiative by different State institutions. In addition, PROJOVEN obtains providers for its training courses by extending public invitations to bid, with the stipulation that the providers should adapt the course content to the demands and requirements of businesses that hire workers.

- *Second,* the Programme targets groups that not only are vulnerable themselves, but also tend to reproduce vulnerability. The Programme focuses on young men and women who have not finished secondary school and do not have formal jobs, most of whom have dropped out of the educational system and lack both work experience and the skills they need to obtain work. Within this group, the Programme gives preference to those who are already heads of household (fathers and/or mothers).
- Third, the Programme offers a variety of training options to meet the needs of subgroups with different levels of difficulty. It combines three basic modules: specific or technical training (200 hours), a vocational orientation workshop (50 hours) and job placement supported by information, business contacts and follow-up (up to 3 months), along with two complementary training programmes (150 hours) and a training internship (3 months). For young people with additional needs, these courses are supplemented with basic skills training in reading and writing and in interpersonal relations, to strengthen the general abilities required in the world of work. The Programme also takes advantage of the benefits available under Uruguay's Youth Employment Act, which encourages firms to hire young people in order to promote on-the-job training and fosters linkages between vocational training institutions and businesses.

Follow-up surveys of beneficiaries who have completed the Programme show a 36 per cent reduction in the number of young people without work, a near-100 per cent increase in the number who are working and a gross workforce participation rate of over 50 per cent for all beneficiaries. Programme participants also tend to obtain higher-quality jobs in terms of both remuneration and fringe benefits.

An interesting initiative by a local-government agency is the Primer Oficio ("First Job") Programme developed by the Municipal Youth Secretariat of the municipal government of Curitiba, Brazil. This Programme, which was started in 1989, has the aim of providing unemployed adolescents with opportunities to join the labour force and earn an income. This is accomplished through a job placement programme in partnership with various firms located in the city. Circa 1998, some 115 firms in Curitiba participated in the Programme, which was financed entirely with local-government funds.

One positive aspect of this initiative is the high rate of participation by businesses located in the city. Also noteworthy is the fact that Latin America does not traditionally have city services that match unemployed young people with businesses' demand for workers. Another interesting point is that, far from representing an alternative to formal education, the Programme requires the young people selected to stay in school, and monitors their school performance. The beneficiaries take an introductory course to enable them to fill available vacancies in the firms in the city that support the Programme, and after they are hired the specialists of the Municipal Youth Secretariat follow up on them to assess their school performance, adaptation within the firm and family situation. Thus, this initiative is not merely a municipal youth employment agency, but a comprehensive programme that takes the beneficiaries' educational, work and personal lives into account.

Non-governmental organisations offer many youth participation programmes, but far fewer of them operate in the specific area of employment, as national and local governments are usually the ones that have the necessary resources, influence and institutionalized links with the business world. One non-governmental programme is the *AXÉ Project/Programme* run by the Association of Parish Communities of Salvador de Bahia, Brazil. This non-governmental organisation, founded in 1991, addresses the needs of street children and adolescents at risk. The Project/

Programme's objective is to provide street children with an educational process in which work is regarded as an essential tool for building good citizenship. The aim is to create opportunities for employment and production as a means of generating income and facilitating the beneficiaries' social, family, educational and productive reintegration. The initiative is funded by the federal Government (20%), the local government (10%), international cooperation (35%) and private contributions (3%), in addition to a self-financing component (32%).

The programme has several distinctive features. First, the kind of training provided takes young people's motivations and generational sensibility into account. Priority has been given to the fashion industry as a teaching instrument and as a foundation for productive development, reaffirmation of cultural identity and reinforcement of self-esteem. Second, the programme targets the population at highest risk – i.e., street children in a city with a high level of extreme poverty. Third, the teaching strategies used seek to break down the dichotomy between vocational training and citizenship-building and between social projects and economic activity by combining liberal arts education with complementary technical and occupational training. Lastly, the initiative takes a pragmatic approach that strongly encourages the autonomous business management of training and production workshops and focuses on establishing links with private firms.

The Situation of Education and Learning in and out of School

Latin America and the Caribbean traditionally has a good reputation for its high primary school enrolments rates – at this point almost universal (97%) – and opportunities for school-age children. Retention and completion rates have also improved, although repetition remains high, socially devastating and costly: an estimated US$ 12,000 million are wasted every year in primary and secondary school repetition (UNESCO-OREALC, 2007). Other important developments in recent years have been:

- the expansion of compulsory education beyond primary and even lower secondary education in many countries;
- increased attention to early childhood and pre-school education, often including one or two years of pre-school within basic/compulsory education; revised curricula;
- renewed teacher training efforts;
- networking in many areas and fields;
- increased investment in school infrastructure and equipment including ICTs; and
- student achievement assessment and evaluation systems in place at regional level and at national level in many countries.

The biggest quantitative progress over the past decade has been on secondary and tertiary education: the proportion of youth aged 20-24 years who completed upper secondary education grew from 27 per cent to 50 per cent, and the proportion of youth aged 25-29 years who completed at least five years of tertiary education grew from 4.8 per cent to 7.4 per cent. Such increases benefited mostly middle and upper classes (CEPAL, 2007). Completion of studies is always lower among the poor, showing that equal educational opportunity for all is not a reality.

Quality and equity remain major unresolved issues, related – in this order of importance – to:

(a) socio-economic condition,

(b) zone of residence (urban-rural),

(c) ethnic identity, and

(d) gender, as confirmed by numerous studies and evaluations in the region.

There are no indications of improved student learning over the past decade in any country, despite the many education reforms and the increased investment in evaluation efforts, as revealed by the two regional studies conducted by the Latin American Laboratory for the Assessment of the Quality of Education.

The Latin America and Caribbean: Youth Leadership Summit

Countries in Latin America and the Caribbean, like those in other regions, are taking steps to fulfill the promises 190 governments made at the United Nations Millennium Summit in September 2000 to cut extreme poverty by half, achieve universal primary education, empower women, reduce maternal and infant mortality rates, reverse the spread of HIV/AIDS, and ensure environmental sustainability by 2015. In this endeavour, youth - who comprise a sizeable and growing proportion representing more than one-fifth of the total population - have a vital role to play, given their dynamism, imagination, idealism and role as the conscience of society. Achieving the Millennium Development Goals (MDGs) will only be possible through a mobilization of all sectors of society, including groups affected by exclusion and inequality. Though they represent the 21st century's first generation of leaders and are often extremely effective in grassroots outreach, the voices, possible contributions and needs of young people are often ignored. That is why the United Nations Development Programme (UNDP), the United Nations New York Office of Sport for Development and Peace - a new unit which reaches out to the media, the private sector, sports personalities, as well as artistic and cultural leaders as a tool for improving the quality of people's lives - and their partners have decided to engage young people in the drive to reach the Goals. Working with the Global Peace Initiative of Women, they are cultivating and supporting a new movement by youth and youth-related organisations that contributes to achieving the MDGs. The Latin America and Caribbean Youth Leadership Summit aims to help the youth leaders in the region face these challenges and will enable young men and women to develop and implement programmes and to connect youth movements to achieve the MDGs and provide a global platform for their voices.

Over the last two decades, Latin America and the Caribbean - home to one of the largest populations of young people in the world - has achieved significant progress toward the establishment of democratic regimes in the region. This is largely due to the mobilization of civil society, local governments, organisations and young people, who are leading the way toward a more participatory and inclusive society. However, the stability of many of these democracies remains fragile due to the increasing social problems that plague the region, including the rising poverty levels, the increased prevalence of HIV/AIDS, especially among people in the 25 - 44 age group, along with unemployment, drug trafficking and the eruption of internal violence. The region also faces a number of emergent challenges such as environmental degradation and pollution, as well as persistent problems including gender, racial and socioeconomic inequality, which, if not addressed, could become unmanageable, reversing the gains made in economic and human development in the last decade. The next generation of leaders will need all the guidance they can get to build a hopeful future. The Latin America and Caribbean Youth Leadership Summit seeks to identify, mobilize and support young leaders, giving them access to training, knowledge, networks and skills to meet the challenges facing their countries and communities, creating an environment for debate and the development of proposals. Responding to the most critical problems confronting the world, the United Nations General Assembly has adopted the Millennium Development Goals, to be achieved by 2015. They are:

- eradicate extreme poverty and hunger;
- achieve universal primary education;
- promote gender equality and empower women;
- reduce child mortality;
- improve maternal health;
- combat HIV/AIDS, malaria, and other diseases;
- ensure environmental sustainability; and
- develop a global partnership for development.

One way in which the United Nations is encouraging and supporting countries in their quest to fulfill these promises and achieve a more peaceful, prosperous and sustainable world community is through young people. The Summit forms an important part of Latin America Caribbean 2015, an initiative of the UN New York Office of Sport for Development and Peace to boost ongoing efforts and trigger bold new steps to support achieving the Millennium Development Goals in the region. A critical challenge is HIV/AIDS, where early policy response can save millions of lives. This is an area where young people have to take the lead. The Summit looks at how the MDGs are faring in Latin American and Caribbean countries and what projects youth leaders and youth movements can initiate and/or contribute to increase the momentum.

REFERENCES

Alexis, A. (Year of Publication not Mentioned). *"Mainstreaming Youth in the Development Process"*. Public Lecture to Mark Youth Month 2000, University of Technology Jamaica. Mimeo. Guyana: Commonwealth Youth Programme.

Barker, G. (1995). *"Situational Analysis of Drug Abuse among Youth at-Risk in the Caribbean: A Needs Assessment of Out-of-School Youth in St. Vincent and the Grenadines, Trinidad and Tobago, St. Maarten and Jamaica"*. Mimeo. UNDCP.

Caribbean Country Management Unit, Poverty Reduction and Economic Management Unit, Latin America and the Caribbean Region (2003). *"Caribbean Youth Development: Issues and Policy Directions"*. World Bank.

Caribbean Community (CARICOM) (2002). *"Women and Men in CARICOM Member States: 1980, 1990 and 2000 Rounds of Population Censuses"*. Caribbean Community (CARICOM) Secretariat, Georgetown, Guyana.

Danns, G.K., Henry B.I., and LaFleur, P. (1997). *"Tomorrow's Adults. A Situational Analysis of Youth in the Commonwealth Caribbean"*. London, UK: Commonwealth Secretariat.

Fawcett, Caroline (Year of Publication not Mentioned). *"Latin American Youth in Transition: A Policy Paper on Youth Unemployment in Latin America and the Caribbean"*. Sustainable Development Department, Social Development Division, Labour Markets Policy Briefs Series, Inter- American Development Bank.

O'Higgins, Niall (2002). *"Government Policy and Youth Employment"*. Produced for the Youth Employment Summit (YES2002).

Helena, Helve M. (Year of Publication not Mentioned). "The Situation of Girls and Young Women." Helsinki University.

Hoikkala, Tommi and Mustonen, Juha (Year of Publication not Mentioned). *"Overview: Priorities for Global Youth Policy"*. Finnish Youth Research Network, Helsinki.

Hopenhayn, Martin (Year of Publication not Mentioned). *"Youth and Employment in Latin America and the Caribbean: Problems, Prospects and Options."* Economic Commission for Latin America and the Caribbean (ECLAC) for the Youth Employment Summit Alexandria, Egypt, September 7-11, 2002.

International Labour Organisation (ILO) Caribbean Office and Multidisciplinary Advisory Team (1997). *"The Challenge of Youth Unemployment in the Caribbean: the Role of Youth Employment Training Programmes"*. ILO.

International Labour Organisation (ILO) (2002). *"Generating Decent Work for Young People: An Issues Paper Prepared for the Secretary-General's Youth Employment Network"*. Youth Employment Network. ILO.

International Labour Organisation (ILO) (2001). *"Meeting the Youth Employment Challenge: A Guide for Employers"*. Geneva.

International Labour Organisation (ILO) (2001). *"Reducing the Decent Work Deficit: A Global Challenge"*, ILO, Geneva.

Morales, C. (2001). *"Youth and Social Exclusion in Chile"*, in E. Gacitúa Soto and S. Davis (Eds.), *Social Exclusion and Poverty Reduction in Latin America and the Caribbean*. San Jose Costa Rica: FLACSO/The World Bank.

Pantin, Dennis A. (Year of Publication not Mentioned).Volume 1 of a Working Draft of a Conference Paper Titled *"Revisiting the Challenge of Youth Employment in the Caribbean"*. Commissioned by the International Labour Organisation, ILO Caribbean Office, Trinidad and Tobago.

Townsend, P. (2000). *"Ending World Poverty in the 21st Century"*, in *Tackling Inequalities: Where Are We Now and What Can Be Done*, C. Pantazis and D. Gordon, eds. Bristol, The Policy Press.

United Nations (2003). *"Follow-up to the World Summit for Social Development and the Twenty-fourth Special Session of the General Assembly: Review of Relevant United Nations Plans and Programmes of Action Pertaining to the Situation of Social Groups.*

World Youth Report 2003. Report of the Secretary-General". United Nations.

United Nations (2000). *"United Nations Millennium Declaration"*. United Nations.

United Nations (Year of Publication not Mentioned). *"Report on the International Conference on Financing for Development"*. Monterrey, Mexico, 18-22 March, 2002. United Nations, New York.

United Nations (1995). *"Report of the World Summit for Social Development"* (Copenhagen, 6-12 March 1995). United Nations.

United Nations (2001). *"Road Map Towards the Implementation of the United Nations Millennium Declaration. Report of the Secretary-General"*. United Nations.

United Nations (Year of Publication not Mentioned). *"We the Peoples: The Role of the United Nations in the Twenty-first Century"*, Report of the Secretary-General (A/54/2000). United Nations, New York.

World Bank (2000). *"HIV/AIDS in the Caribbean: Issues and Options"*. Washington, DC: The World Bank.

http://www.unesco.org/fileadmin/MULTIMEDIA/INSTITUTES/UIL/confintea/pdf/GRALE/confinteavi_grale_lac_synthesis_en.pdf, Accessed on July 8, 2012.

7

Youth Education and Employment

– J.Anuradha

Youth has emerged as a distinct and powerful socio-demographic group in India. Youth is the most important asset and strength of the nation and plays an important role in the development of the nation. Therefore, it is imperative to develop the youth with a view to make them educationally sound, socially useful and financially self-dependant. If anything happens to youth, the whole society gets affected. They form about one third of India's population. Unfortunately, the state has failed to develop and channelize the power and potential, energy and enthusiasm of the youth into socially productive ways. Consequently, the precious human resource of the nation is being wasted away.

Youth has emerged recently as a distinct social category, not because they form the majority of a nation's population but due to reasons of their specific characteristics, needs, psycho-social traits and pattern of behaviour. Youth are the human property of nation, who represent strength, vitality and vigour and are the hope for the future of a nation. "Youth are the carriers of culture, custodians of national honour and trustees of the freedom of the country." The youth of today are the citizens of tomorrow. They are the treasures of human resources of the nation having a lot of talents dormant in them, and if tapped in the right direction, would bear great fruits. "They are the store houses o f energy and knowledge" says Nair, Vinita and if given a right direction, can work wonders. Indian youth, in spite of all their energy, enthusiasm and courage, have continuously been loosing a balanced perspective and orientation towards social reality and for this, both the characteristic feature of this period of personality development and striking imbalance in the modern social order are to be held accountable.

The problem of unemployment among the educated youth is one of the gravest that the nation is facing today. The nation is being deprived of the services of the millions of educated and professionally trained youth force, on the one hand and wasting the human resources of the nation, on the other. This has invited the anger of our youth and they are increasingly indulging into the illegal, anti-social and other violent and criminal activities day-by-day and tend to destroy public property very often. This is the expression of their distrust to the system. The attempt to get preferential treatment in the matters of recruitment, further generate some socio-economic problems like corruption, nepotism, casteism, regionalism and linguistic confrontations.

Therefore, determined efforts are needed and appropriate policies are to be made so that our young men and women can become job creators and not remain job seekers. According to the sociological point of view, youth should develop and expand the elementary social skills and capabilities, acquired in childhood to the extent that the complex degrees of competence necessary to achieve adult status. Youth is a phase of life in its own right with its own quality of experience and at the same time they are the product of society and culture.

The manifold investigations into the crisis in training, unemployment, drug-taking, political extremism and other problems during youth have indeed concentrated predominantly on a definite phenomenon of behaviour among young people, to which immediate attention is being drawn in public discussion. There is a lack of comprehensive theoretical models which include various problem areas and institutions, which analyse their way of functioning and thereby are in a position to classify and then to qualify the many individual results. If research into youth is to make an effective contribution to clearing up the conditions affecting the main outline and regular features of the development personality in youth, can contribute to the solution of the problems confronting youth people.

Young persons in the process of building up their personality are confronted by contradictions and inconsistencies in what society expects of them in their environment. In these circumstances they have to rely on the organising force of the way society which defines their movement from one status to another. The theme of youth has attracted a galaxy of scholars, academicians and teachers of various disciplines of social sciences like Psychology, Sociology, Criminology, Political Science, Anthropology, Economics and Law. A good deal of research has been done on rural problems and aspects of life related with youth. Mainly three types of literature can be found on the youth and related subjects:

- One is Journalistic literature scattered in various Periodicals, Newspapers, Editorials and Survey Reports;
- Second type of literature is academic literature that is based on the Observations, Insights and Research of the scholars; and
- Third type of literature is available in Government Reports, Documents and Offices which is termed as Statistical Literature.

Department of Youth Affairs and Sports has also in its possession, the statistical information relating to youth. Apart from that some International Agencies and Organisations also prepare statistical Bulletins and circulate through the member countries. During 'International Year of Youth', the Statistical Office of United Nations Secretariat had prepared a booklet of Statistical Indicators on youth in cooperation with the Centre for Social Development and Humanities Affairs of the Department of International Economics and Social Affairs, United Nations Secretariat and the Statistical Office of ILO, FAO, UNESCO and WHO. Forty statistical indicators have been outlined from International Data Sources in the fields with immediate concern of youth related to population composition and change, education training and literacy, economic activity, family formation and fertility life expectancy and morality.

Vishwa Yuvak Kendra, New Delhi is doing an enormous task to undertake youth studies, to collect statistical information and to promote publication of the literature. It prepared a list of the available literature on youth and published in India and abroad under the title' Youth in Print.' India was basically and pre-dominantly an agrarian country. The young generation got mainly enchanted of the mirky lights of electronic gadgets. The education developed a kind of complex and bias against manual labour, thus rendering education youth an idle lot of luddites. The dignity of labour got lost at the time, one entered into campuses from fields. There is a general saying that when the son left home for studies at the first time, trunk was on his head but at the second time it was on the head of his father.

India has emerged as the biggest garbage pot of human resources and affords high cost of its idiotity. Education has proved to be a bane not only for the educated but for the nation and the society at large. The queues of educated people looking for jobs have grown longer every day. It is usually argued that most of the youth remain unemployed because they are unemployable. The vast army of youth passing out graduate courses from faculties of Arts, Science, Commerce, Law and Education, Medical Sciences and Engineering every year has to wait years before they get any job, even inferior to their qualifications and thus allowing dust upon their learnt skill.

Engineers selling pop-corns, doctors driving rickshaw, graduates resorting to shoes polish and other demonstrating as scavenger's job are common methods of protest of unemployed youth against the government policies regarding employment. A large number of highly skilled man power drain abroad in search of work. Most of the youth population have emerged to be traditionally employed and women are married who have to bear household responsibilities. Those without formal education have either to resort to domestic occupations or as menial workers. Therefore pressure of employment seems to be upon those educated up to graduate level or above. Prospects of career can exist and dues exists for graduates from any faculty depending on how well they had done and the socio-economic stratum from which they come. The possibilities of a career are, therefore, confined to a very limited proportion of youth.

In India, we have no authentic and fool proof system to know the gravity of the problem of unemployment. Varied kinds of apprehended, data is available but is absolutely unreliable due to many inbuilt structural factors and technical fallacies. Even the qualitative studies, impact studies and other kinds of research have been wanted since long but insufficient and scanty. I.L.O. have tried to assess the problem of unemployment in developing countries and particularly in Indian context but their focus have been on economic repercussions rather than socio-psychological consequences of unemployment. Reality is that it brings personality disaster to the individual and creates many problems related to his adjustment, intra-personal and inter-persona and even societal. It brings family into crisis and some times causes disintegration into it. Instead of bearing the burdens of the family liabilities an educated unemployed remain a burden upon the society and particularly on the family.

- Many theories have been laid down as to who is responsible for unemployment. There are basically three schools of thought which try to explain aetiology of unemployment.
- One notes that unemployment is a penalty for deviating from laissesfaire.
- Second views unemployment as a result of trade cycle.
- Third describes unemployment in terms of lack of effective demand.

Sociologists also could not move beyond accusing the fruitless education system. There are many more causes like corruption, casteism, regionalism, nepotism, political nexus, bureaucratic biases and many more. Learning disability and unemployability of the candidate are also important factors. Merit has got the back seat and the maneavouring rests on the front. Leakages of the question papers of different entrance exams is a common failure. The personality tests and interviews have lost their credibility. Universities are filled with third grade teachers who are supposed to impart education and training. It creates frustration among those who are deprived but deserve. It further leads to alienation of youth from the society who appear with a non-conformist image.

'Bekari Hatao' (Banish Unempoyment) has been our cherished goal since Fourth Five Year Plan. Many Employment Generation Programmes and Twenty Point Programmes appeared since then but the problem has become worst. Slogans of rights to work proved to be just a lip service for youth in order to create a distinct vote bank. Employment Guarantee and Employment Generation Schemes have proved to be a myth for the poor and benefits are being cropped by affluents. It seems responsible to address the role of social work profession in promoting more responsive social policies and services on the one hand and to provide direct services and relief to unemployed on the other.

Unemployed youth have tangible needs which must be met. Many unemployed people need to learn how to tap necessary resources to maintain food and shelter for their families to survive the social and emotional crises which result from unemployment. People need to help to maintain their physical and emotional health during unemployment. Unemployment like any life crises can provide individuals, families and communities with an opportunity for growth. Old patterns may be reviewed and better patterns for living may be developed. The whole community need to assure the unemployed by strengthening their moral support for always he views himself as a failure in life. Unemployment for most people is experienced as a loss of self and a loss of some aspects of personal functioning. He is confronted with the loss of many things like food, shelter, identity, security, competency, independence and self-esteem. Even the loss of social networks on which the person depends for the expression of feelings and gratification of emotional needs are observed.

Colin Murray, Parkes (1972) lists seven features, of bereavement, of unemployed youth.

- Realisation of loss
- Alarm reaction
- Urge to search for and find lost object
- Anger and guilt
- Feeling and internal loss of self or mutilation
- Identification with symbols of a job and
- Pathological variants of a grief

Economists tend to regard employment as only a means to pay cheque. However, one's job is major component in one's identity. The job provides structure around which people build their lives. The job provides social outlets. Atchley (1977) that the greatest tragedy for a woman is widowhood and for a man is unemployment or joblessness. Number of persons take up casual jobs and part time employment which pushes them below poverty line. Thus, poverty has a relation with unemployment. Unemployment is the worst evil that can befall a country. The frustrated aspirations are heading the dilemmas of contemporary youth and that the overall quality of youth is decreasing perhaps due to the failure of our education system. It is evident that most of the youth do not look for any specific job but just a job of any nature.

Plato said, 'The best way of training the young is to train your self at the same time. Do not admonish them but always carry out your own practice.' Indian youth tend to nurture materialistic aspirations. Hardly any one wants to be a Nehru, Buddha, Gandhi etc, rather most of them just want a happy secure and prosperous life.

Social work is a problem-solving profession and assists individuals, groups and communities in distress. Unemployed youth form a part of the clientele of social work profession. Social work, group work, community organisation and social action are the methods of social work which can be used to deal the problems of the unemployed youth. The long term perspective includes the change in the education system and in the socio-economic structure in order to ensure a job for the unemployed. The education system and man power needs of the nation must be co-ordinated in order to save the waste of human resources. Higher education system must be highly selective. The process of socialization needs to be modified so that youth may not be subjected to job phobia. This will save youth from falling into psychological complexes and will enable to build their career on the basis of their own initiative and self-determination.

The Department of Youth Affairs and Human Resource Development is harnessing many nation building activities. The involvement of non-student youth in nation building is promoted through the Nehru Yuvak Kendra. The Department of Youth Affairs and Sports continued its efforts through national integration camps, festivals for university students, adventure programmes and exhibitions for youth. Vocational training is also provided to young men and women to prepare them for taking up self-employment.

REFERENCES

Acharya, L.K. (1990), 'Evolution of Ideas on Unemployment', Financial Express, New Delhi.

Bhattacharya,B.B. (1988),'Reorient Planning Strategy Yojana', Vol. 33.

Chandra, Bipin (1984), 'Communalism in India', Vikas Publication, New Delhi.

John Hayes K Nutman(1981), 'Understanding the Unemployed', London, New York.

Nair, Vineeta (1987), 'Youth on the Brink', Pioneer Publications, Lucknow.

Saraswati, S (1988), 'Youth in India', Department of Youth Affairs and Sports, Ministry of Human Resource Development.

8

Education and Social Empowerment of Youth

– Y. Bhaskaracharyulu
– K. Ananda Rao

> "Young people in all countries are both a major human resource for development and key agents for social change, economic development and technological innovation. Their imagination, ideals, considerable energies and vision are essential for the continuing development of the societies in which they live. The problems that young people face as well as their vision and aspirations are essential components of the challenges and prospects of today's societies and future generations."
>
> (*United Nations, 1995*)

Introduction

Unemployment and underemployment among youth is a problem everywhere. This is a true as part of the larger struggle to create employment opportunities for all citizens. The problem of unemployment has worsened in recent years because of the global recession which has affected developing countries the most seriously. The disturbing fact is that economic growth is not always accompanied by growth in employment. The difficulty of finding suitable employment in insufficient training and is worsened by periods of world economic slow-down and by overall changing economic trends.

The developing world is home to nearby 90 per cent of the economically active youth, with Asia alone accounting for some 60 per cent. India, with ahlf its populations under 25 years of age, has huge stakes in shaping the prospects of an entire new generation. The importance of guaranteed minimum income and social welfare protection for this segment of the em is created predominantly in the informal sector, which is under-regulated. The absence of compulsory education beyond 14 years in countries such as India, which induces premature and forced entry into the labour market and many short comings linked to education, skills and employment. Given that a strong base in skills is pivotal to the emerging knowledge – based economics of this century, it is only logical that skills development should receive priority. In this context, this paper mainly addresses the present employment trends and the challenges before the youth in the present scenario.

Youth constitute an important asset of the society. The investment in their development is investment of our future. The importance of youth in human life and youth population in a nation is considerably significant. Today's youth is tomorrow's leader and pacesetter. Education is a major challenge for empowerment of youth. The global situation of young people today is characterized by striking paradoxes, i.e. extreme disparities in terms of economic, technological, social and cultural resources which vary enormously across regions, countries, localities and population groups. Almost 85 per cent of young people live in developing countries, with approximately 60 per cent in Asia alone. Despite mass urbanisation, the majority live in rural areas. Young men outnumber young women (525 million versus 500 million), while 57 million young men and 96 million young women are illiterate. In developing countries, rapid changes are taking place in the social conditions of young people as a result of changing socio-economic and policy structures and wider global change mean that they face a more precarious future than any preceding generation. Today's young generation experiences widening social gaps and faces manifold challenges. Education is the only instrument makes awareness about the problems and how to overcome all the barriers in human life and get empowered through self-sustaining perspectives. The present paper addresses about the main principles and strategies for youth empowerment through education to achieve youth aspiration and develop their capabilities. The paper also depicts the current challenges and opportunities are diagnosed to design appropriate educational plans that overcome shortfalls and maximize benefits.

Definition of 'Youth'

Most of the national youth policies attempt to define 'young people' in order to determine the main beneficiaries of policy interventions. Defining 'youth', however, is not a simple task since there is no international consensus on what the term implies or a clear-cut indicator such as age intervals to define it. A quick look at the youth policies of more than one country will show how broadly the term can be defined. Who is designated a 'youth' in your county will depend on a variety of political and cultural factors. Flexibility of interpretation is essential in overcoming the difficulties of age definition. It is equally significant to acknowledge that young people may not be seen as a single demographic unit, but must be considered as a broad category encompassing many specific subgroups, which might require specifically targeted policies. The UN defines 'youth' as people aged between 15 and 24 and young people as people aged 10-19, and for the sake of consistency and to facilitate comparisons across national borders, we encourage the use of this definition.

Globalization and Prospective Challenges

Today's young generation experiences widening social gaps and faces manifold challenges: it is the young who - perhaps more so than any other social group - encounter the uncertainties and risks generated by the process of economic and cultural globalisation. Even though, in some parts of the world, young people are better educated than ever before, they are faced with increasing insecurity in the labour market. Those who have the opportunity to go to school are forced to study longer and longer as job opportunities become scarcer, less well-paid and less secure, delaying the age at which they become financially independent from their parents. Those who do not have the opportunity to pursue their education or who choose to leave the school system at an early age face marginalization from the broader community from which they may never recover, either as a result of long-term unemployment, or low-paid, insecure and even dangerous jobs. Sixty-six million young people throughout the world are unemployed, some 40 per cent of global unemployment. Hundreds of millions more work fewer hours than they would like, while still others work long hours with little gain and no social protection. In terms of health issues, the recognition of youth as a unique group in society due to the many aspects of vulnerability it contains reveals some shocking truths. One-third of the 20 million people throughout the world who have already died as a result of HIV/AIDS-related illnesses were young people and another 6,000 are infected every day. Young people continue to lose their lives to acute respiratory infections and vaccination-preventable diseases and malnutrition. Violence and suicide are growing problems in some communities, as is drug dependency among the young.

Youth all over the world thus increasingly emerges as a specific social category which is laden with risk and uncertainty. The pronounced difficulties young people experience in terms of their socio-economic, political and cultural inclusion in an ever more volatile world are the subject of wide-spread concern at both the national and international level. Since the ways in which these challenges are addressed by policies will not only shape the present but profoundly determine the future of any country, the need for an adequate policy relating to young people arises as one of the highest priorities of society.

Education for Social Empowerment of Youth: Strategies and Principles

As society kept on changing, it was realized that to adapt to change, the change need not necessarily come from formal schooling but also it could come from the wider society and other sectors within the society. The single most important factor for young people is to lead productive and responsible lives. National youth policies relating to educational issues should foster equal access for all to the formal education system, especially in order to combat illiteracy, which continues to be an enormous problem for many young people in the world. Not to be limited to the skills on which the labour market is focused. Education contributes, from an early age, to the socialisation, integration and empowerment of individuals. According to Hoppers (2005) and Rogers (2004) the flexibility with which the programmes is developed and managed will largely depend on the nature of the group. The education providers should therefore understand group dynamics and organisational theory. Such knowledge should also guide the education providers to increase enrolment of the out of school youth in nonformal education programmes. Within the modern thinking about non-formal education internationally, therefore, there is need to give an alternative form of education to the out of school youth who are faced with many challenges (Kenyon, 1998).

Place renewed emphasis on life-long learning schemes to provide culturally, socially and economically appropriate education. Life-long learning schemes can provide various benefits, especially for people in countries lacking access to universal education (Fordham, 1993). Education and learning should be based on the principle of "The search for

Knowledge" by making education and learning a collective process including students and teachers as well. Education reform aiming to youth empowerment entails the formulation of integrated reform approach/perspective through projects implemented by the community in line with comprehensive vision linking the political reform to economic and education reform.

Empowerment of Youth through Policies

It is important that a national youth policy be formulated as independent legislation, it is essential to subsequently integrate it into the overall national development plan. Youth policies need to be related to and co-ordinated with sectoral policies and relate to the overarching objectives for national development only as such will the needs of youth be considered an integral part in national planning and policy-making. Policy formulation could become a rather inefficient and futile exercise, if no attention is paid to cutting across sectoral lines, i.e. to the mainstreaming of youth issues and youth policy in your country. Consequently, there is a great demand for the sharing of experience in formulation, implementation and best practice as concerns strategies for youth participation and involvement. There is a high potential for cooperation in this field, particularly through networking of both governmental and non-governmental youth organisations on a regional and international scale (UNESCO, 2004).

Education cannot Act as Factor of Ascending Social Mobility

In transition countries, 9 million youth or a third of the population aged 15-18 years old is out of school. Most countries allow students to leave school as early as 15 years old with the completion of basic education, and some in Southeastern Europe require an additional year of education. In Central Asia, evidence suggests there is increasing number of children who do not even complete primary education. Research in the West has found strong correlations between leaving school at an early age and unhealthy behaviours, and there is also a risk of long-term social exclusion of these youth (Quintana, 2002:7). Youth employment is characterized by higher levels of exclusion than the general population. Youth unemployment rate for 18 of the 27 transition countries stood at 30 per cent, 15 percentage points higher than the overall unemployment rate. Youths are extensively affected by unemployment, accounting for half of the total unemployed population (Quintana, 2002:7). Moreover, this trend of unemployment among the young is increasingly rising. Most Latin American youths either do not have enough "educational capital" to have access to comfortable job positions nor the necessary "social capital" especially important for the first-time job searchers. The Youth PATH (Youth Poverty Alleviation through Tourism and Heritage) project was launched in January 2003 by the UNESCO Office in Kingston; Jamaica. This project seeks to implement new community-based initiatives such as community tourism to empower young people to achieve economic freedom and self-esteem. The project goals relate to the training of marginalized youth in the development and documentation of heritage sites, the development of marketing tools and entrepreneurial skills and the use of electronic networking and relevant business strategies, including micro-credit. The project aims to provide not only economic viability but also life skills to young people in rural areas in the Caribbean. So far, each project site has attracted a large number of marginalized youth in the community and partnerships have been formed with the private sector in order to ensure sustainability of these projects.

Significantly increase in social cohesion, through the integration of youth at risk from different socio-cultural backgrounds. In a conflict-affected country with youth unemployment estimated at nearly 70 per cent, community based approaches to youth development (through activities disseminated in youth centers throughout the country, including rural areas) and institutional capacity building are the two main strategies being employed for youth empowerment and conflict prevention. Life skills aim at promoting responsible citizenship and life-long learning. Livelihood skills, increasingly recognized as an important requirement for better preparation of young people in securing employment, include job-searching skills, interviewing skills, leadership skills, and entrepreneurial skills as well as specific marketable skills appropriate to the local economy. Linkages to private sector groups are being developed to provide apprenticeship and placement opportunities (Commonwealth Youth Programme, Asia Centre 1996).

Suggestions for Social Empowerment of Youth through Education

- Creating a comprehensive vision for youth education
- Ensuring adequate funding
- Developing decentralized education administration
- Ensuring the participation of civil society
- Increasing the culture of understanding in the primary stage and expand the effort for illiteracy eradication.
- Guaranteeing secondary education for all
- Providing the basics for social justice in the higher/university education.
- Developing the education structure based on the principle of diversity within unified approach
- Linking education to youth life and to the socio economic conditions.
- Developing educational curricula
- Setting democratic social organisations in teaching–learning relationships.
- Seeking alternative vision for girl's education
- Providing continuous education and ensure complementarities for formal and informal education
- Enhancing cooperation in the field of youth education.

Conclusion

Every country thus needs effective strategies able to help young people to make the right choices, protect them from exploitation and neglect and ensure their participation in all spheres of society. National youth policy strategies that are effective and beneficial for youth and empowering young people to actively influence and shape the political agenda. There is in the Commonwealth a wide recognition that young men and women constitute a community of interest whose needs and aspirations require specific attention. Today young men and women form a significant proportion of most national populations; need a supportive, participatory and informative environment to move successfully from the dependence of childhood to the autonomy and responsibility of adulthood. They have a unique contribution to make to national development due to their energy, enthusiasm, resilience and ability to inject a fresh focus. They have had less life experience and often significantly less exposure to information, resources and power over their lives than older people, making them more vulnerable to neglect, abuse and exploitation; and often represent the most 'at risk' group in terms of major socio-economic challenges including unemployment, low income, physical and sexual abuse, substance abuse and a wide range of health issues including HIV/AIDS – young women being most disadvantaged in these areas. A progressive national youth policy obliges traditional decision-makers to work not only for young people, but with them and let their experiences inform the development of appropriate interventions and services. It is the essential role of governments to ensure that the concerns of young people are taken into account in all areas of government policy and decision-making, and not just those deemed to be 'youth issues', and that young people's views, priorities and desires are encouraged, listened to and acted upon.

REFERENCES

Commonwealth Youth Programme, Asia Centre (1996), Consultative Meeting of Senior Officials on Youth Policies and Programmes: Report, Chandigarh.

Fordham, P.E. (1993). Informal, Non-formal and Formal Education Programmes in YMCA George Williams College ICE301 lifelong learning unit 2. London: YMCA Gorege Williams College.

Hoppers, W.K. (2005), Summary Report on the Electronic Discussion Forum on "Challenging Non-formal Education in Africa; Where do we go from here; what Role for an ADEA Working Group?

Kenyon, P. (1998), Formulation, Implementation and Evaluation of National Youth Policies: An International Overview (I.D.E.A.S. (Initiatives for the Development of Enterprising Action and Strategies), York, Western Australia, June).

Quintana, R. (2002), Desk Review: Los programas de juventud en America Latina y el Caribe: Contexto y Prinicipales características, IDB Washington DC.

Rogers, A. (2004), Looking Again at Non-formal and Informal Education Towards a New Paradigm; the Encyclopedia of Informal Education. Accessed at http//www.infed.org/biblio/non-formal-paradigm.htm.last update.

United Nations (1995), World Programme of Action for Youth to the Year 2000 and Beyond (General Assembly Resolution 50/81 of 14 December 1995).

UNESCO (2004), *Empowering Youth through National Policies*, UNESCO: France. Accessed at: http://www.unesco.org/youth.

Website: http://www.unesco.org/youth

Website: http://www.unesco.org/youth

SECTION – II

YOUTH AND HEALTH AWARENESS

9

A Study on Youth and Health Awareness (HIV/AIDS) in Tamil Nadu

– G.Vijayakumari
– K.Nachimuthu

Introduction

Youth empowerment is an attitudinal, structural, and cultural process whereby young people gain the ability, authority and agency to make decisions and implement change in their own lives and the lives of other people, including youth and adults. Youth empowerment is often addressed as a gateway to intergenerational equity, civic engagement and democracy building. Many local, state, provincial, regional, national, and international government agencies and non profit community-based organisations provide programmes centered on youth empowerment. Activities involved therein may focus on youth-led media, youth rights, youth councils, youth activism, youth involvement in community decision-making, and other methods. Everyone seems to be talking about empowerment these days, female empowerment, worker's empowerment, and youth empowerment are just some of the phrases that are flying around.

National Programme for Youth Adolescent Development (NPYAD) has been formulated by merger of four 100 per cent central sector grants-in-aid schemes of the Ministry of Youth Affairs & Sports during 10th Plan namely, Promotion of Youth Activities & Training, Promotion of National Integration, Promotion of Adventure and Development and Empowerment of Adolescents, with a view to reduce multiplicity of schemes with similar objectives, ensuring uniformity in funding pattern and implementation mechanism, avoiding delays in availability of funds to the field level and institutionalizing participation of State Governments in project formulation and its implementation.

As of 2005, an estimated 40.3 million people around the world were living with AIDS/HIV. About 3.1 million people have died form AIDS related disease in the year 2004. The surveys showed that, HIV infection rates among pregnant women were rising, tripling to 1.25 per cent between 1995 and 1997. the State Government acted decisively. It set up an AIDS society, with worked closely to NGO's to active AIDS prevention campaign. India is currently had to over 5.1 million AIDS patients. The number of People living with HIV in 2007, in the world was 36.1 Million and the adults are 33.6 million, children under 15 years are 2.5 million. In Total 2.4 million and children less than 15 years are 3,80,000 are under Aids deaths in 2007 in the world. (World Health Organisation, Library Publishing Data, 31, Dec 2007)

Objectives of the Study

The objective of the Youth and health awareness (HIV/AIDS) behaviour survey is to obtain trends and measure on risk sexual behaviour among related groups.

Sample for the Study

The survey conducted in Namakkal District of Tamilnadu in India, which covers four main taluks namely, Rasipuram, Velur, Namakkal and Tiruchencode. In total 1250 respondents were interviewed in terms of Knowledge, Sexual behaviour, Condom usage, Risk perception and Preventive messages.

The sample consists of Housewives, (HW), Commercial Sex Workers (SW), Truck drivers –Male (DM), Factory Employers -male & female (FMW), College Girls and Boys (CMW) and Youth (uneducated) of 15-25 years (YMW). The data collection was completed within one month. The Sample for the Youth and health awareness (HIV/ AIDS) behaviour survey study was described in Table 9.1.

Table 9.1: Sample for the Study

Code	Category	Namakkal	Rasipuram	T.Code	Velur	Total
HW	House Wives	40	35	35	30	140
SW	Commercial Sex Workers	27	07	18	08	060
DM	Truck Drivers (Male)	110	24	102	20	256
FMW	Factory Male & Female Employees	50	24	45	20	139
CMW	College Boys & Girls	125	64	106	57	352
YMW	Youth Boys and Girls uneducated	125	37	106	35	303
Net	Total	477	191	412	170	1250
Ave	Per cent	38%	15%	33%	14%	100

From the above Table 9.1 illustrates the sample for the study consists of Namakkal (urban) respondents were 38 per cent (477), Tiruchencode (urban) respondents were 33 per cent (412), Rasipuram (rural) respondents were 15 per cent (191) and Velur (Rural) village respondents were 14 per cent (170). In the above said sample, the investigator collected more number of youths in educated and uneducated level. The lowest respondents were commercial sex workers (60); because the investigator reached those workers only by the help of police people. Tiruchencode and Namakkal areas were lorry and truck constructed areas. So that reaching to the truck drivers (n=256) respondents were very easy.

During the data collection, data entry and analysis, we adhered to strict quality control measures to ensure the quality of the data and the findings. The questionnaire was standardized by the experts as well as interviewers and the reliability was 0.73 and content validity was established. In the age concern, SW (Commercial Sex Workers) had the mean age of 27.5 years and the DM (Truck drivers) been 30 years. The mean age of FMW (Factory Male &Female Employees) was 18 to 30 years only. The college students were 18.5 mean age years and the uneducated youth were 18 years respectively. From the part of marital status, 75 per cent of the sex workers are married but only 25 per cent are living with their own child and their life partner. Rest of them were widowed/divorced. Form the part of Truck drivers 45 per cent are unmarried.

Findings of the Study

'Youth' would cover persons belonging to the age group of 13 to 35 years and 'adolescent' would cover persons in the age group of 10-19 years under the scheme. The targeted beneficiaries of the programmes include members of the youth clubs affiliated to the Nehru Yuva Kendra Sangathan, National Service Scheme, and State Government Youth Organisations, Bharat Scouts & Guides or student youth in Schools, Colleges and Universities. Adolescents and Youth from other established youth organisations or NGOs may be considered provided they are the registered members of such organisations. Preference may be given to the youth with special abilities and youth belonging to scheduled caste, scheduled tribes, minorities and weaker sections.

If any government project concentrates the comprehensive youth workforce development programmes conducted, the following activities are included. That five developmental areas are as follows:

1. **Learning** includes developing both basic and applied academic competencies and skills. Research indicates that youth learn best when they are involved in authentic learning environments with opportunities to explore and with real world application.

2. **Thriving** relates to physical and mental health and overall well-being. Effective youth development activities prepare, support, and assist youth in making healthy choices in all phases of their lives.
3. **Connecting** relates to the development of positive social attitudes, skills, and behaviours so that youth feel a part of programmes and their community. Mentoring is an example of the type of activity that can contribute to the feeling of connectedness.
4. **Working** relates to occupational and career skills, attitudes, and behaviours that are needed for success in the workplace. Employment and work-based activities help youth to validate their self-worth, as well as to explore their abilities and interests.
5. **Leading** activities and opportunities help youth develop positive civic attitudes, skills, and behaviours. Youth need to contribute to their community, school, and family in order to develop to their full potential.

The major findings of the above said study were, knowledge of prevention of AIDS has reached 90.5 per cent in many of the samples. 15 per cent of the Truck drivers have involved in non-regular sex in different state females and they have approached with Mr. X parties also (both Male & Female external characters in a single). For female factory workers, in their knowledge level part, the condom usage was very low as compared to the men. Condoms are also easily available in most places where the trucker halts. Knowledge about homosexual behaviour is high among both male and female students at school and college level. Youth reported that, the alcoholism is another factor; which motivate them to seek sex.

From the statistical data, the knowledge level of the prevention of the HIV/AIDS, without misconceptions has increased. In Namakkal district, the voluntary condition procurement of the Social workers has increased steadily (75%). 90 per cent of girls and boys in colleges have got individual education on HIV/ AIDS prevention. How ever, lesser proportion (40%) of educated youth of male and female are educated. In concern with Condom usages, 85 to 90 per cent was increased in Truck Drivers, 80 to 85 per cent for regular clients and Cent per cent in married Teacher training adults. (College girls & Boys). From the level of behaviour modifications, the uneducated youth in rural areas have involved in non-regular sex regularly (60%). And also the sexual relationship with a paid partner has increased among the DM group (70%), but the condom usages with non-regular partner has increased between DM and SW groups. 7 per cent of the DM group and 10 per cent of YMW group had sexual relationship with same sexual partner.

Conclusion

Many people are trapped in some kind of a bad habit that they wish they never had. Bad habits are formed more easily than good habits, and are usually the hardest to get rid of. Smoking, drinking, gambling, overeating, and eating fast food are all examples of bad habits. Many people, who know of their bad habits, want to change, but no matter how hard they try, they usually find themselves not being able to. To change, we have to have an intention and high motivation. It is easy to develop bad habits, especially when a person is young. This is because when a person is young, it is hard for him/her to distinguish the difference between right and wrong because of their inexperience. Bad habit is a process that starts from our mind-our thoughts. Habit is formed by a step-by-step process which involves thought, action, and repetition. Thought is the backbone of creating bad habits. Our mind plays a very important role in creating habits. Being humans, we do not realize the consequence(s) of turning our thoughts into reality.

Many teens feel that they need to drink, smoke and take drugs to be considered cool. In today's society, the peer pressure to drink, smoke or use drugs to fit in is all around our youth. Often, teens are anxious to find an alternative way to have fun and to escape from the 'boringness' of movies and television. For this reason, they jump at the chance to gather in a large group to socialize. This event is otherwise known as a party. They are willing to pay for a cup of beer, even if they know that drinking under the age of twenty-one is illegal. When there is nothing else to do or nowhere else to go, teenagers will find something to take away their boredom, even though their actions could jeopardize their future and even their lives. Drinking alcohol comes with many responsibilities. Smoking is another large issue within the college community. Many teenagers who smoke have been smoking for a few years and started smoking at an early age. Drug usage is the third huge area of abuse among students in college. The majority of these teens have tried the most common gateway drug, marijuana. Many of these teenagers said they have also tried mushrooms, ecstasy, and speed. They all agreed that heroin is the most dangerous drug and they would never think about trying it.

Due to Government organisation's advertisements, the usages of condoms also increased and the adults in the schools and colleges they have no sigh to discuss the sex education and its importance. Many parents know only the folk terms for sexual organs and sexual processes, not for the exact disease and its preventions. Sex education can be imparted in a better way if teachers, parents, youth teachers and social workers work hard, had in hand of shifting the responsibility. Thus to begin with, it is necessary to motivate a small group of students in each institution. So that the students group, in turn can act as communicators or educators for the new groups. Medical students at the end of their pre-clinical training are ideal peer group communicators. By this time they are informed about the nature of the HIV virus and the mode of transmission. The prevention activity includes designing posters and pamphlets and distribution and display in clinics, and other public places.

The college and school activities include oratorical competition, drawing competition, debate, drama and awareness-street plays about the sex education. The media activity includes radio talks and the use of programming arts such as story telling, drama shows and role-play. The community and different groups can be reached by using existing organisations such as women's groups, youth organisations, community and religious leaders and educational institutions.

REFERENCES

Information and Knowledge for optimal Health (INFO) Report (2005). Population Reports about AIDS and its Controls in 2005, USAID, Baltimore, USA.

Nachimuthu, K & Vijayakumari, G. (2008). Prevention of HIV/AIDS Among Youth, Endeavour: Journal of Youth Development, RGNIYD pub, Chennai, Vol. II, No.1., Jan-Jun 2008, pp. 55-58.

Prakash, S. (1994). On the Horizon of Adulthood, UNICEF Publications, New Delhi.

TNSACS, (2005). Health & Family Welfare Department, Report about Tamil Nadu State Aids Control Society (TNSACS) Activities, 2005.

United Nations Dept. of Economic and Social Affairs. (2005). Population division- 2005, HIV/AIDS, New York, UK.

Vijayakumari, G (2011). Role of Educational Games Improves Meaningful Learning, Journal of Educational Technology, Vol. 08, No. 02, July-September 2011, pp. 08-11.

10

Youth and Drug Abuse in India

– Mande Suresh

ABSTRACT

"The youth of a Nation are the trustees of posterity" - Benjamin Disraeli (1804-1881)

British Politician & Author

The present study is an attempt to examine the Youth and Drug Abuse in India, reviewing a microcosm of drug situation among youth in Andhra Pradesh, particularly Visakhapatnam City. It focuses on the perceptions of the substance abusers, the causes for their addiction to drugs, smoking and alcohol; the role of their families, friends and social environment and the law enforcing agencies in curbing/ spreading this menace. The study has taken 200 youth by following snowball sampling method. The youth of the affluent and the middle-classes are in abundance in the City. As they have access to material comforts, most of them try to lead lavish and stylish life that subsequently offers them a wide variety of things to experiment with. In this process they taste the thrill of cigarettes, alcohol and drugs- just for a change but unfortunately, they are caught in the vicious circle of addiction to harmful substances and drug abuse.

Introduction

Drug Addicts in India, A Fearful Statistics

In a nation with a big population of more than 1 billion individuals, what lies ahead if one-third of the youth population would become drug addicts? It might not be frightened to learn that an estimated 7.5 crores Indians are drug addicts and the amount is working over significantly, drugs are now opening to semi-urban and backward areas, according to formal numbers. Reported to the major officials of Ministry of Friendly Justice and Empowerment, drug and alcohol abuse is becoming an area of interest in the Indian community. Reported to the National Survey on Extent, Pattern and Trends of Drug misuse in India conducted by the Focus in collaboration with UN Office on Drugs and Criminal Offence, the actual preponderance values inside the age group of 12-18 age was Alcoholic Drink (preceding 21), Cannabis (3), Opiates (0.7) and other illicit drugs (3.6%). This is an alarming statistics in India (UNODCO, 2009)

According to the survey, a high concentration of drug addiction goes in certain friendly sections and high-risk groups, much as, commercialized sex workers, transportation workers and street kids. Among full the provinces, usage is higher in North Eastern states/border areas & opium development areas of the nation. The drug insult prevalence is uneven in the state. A last point of alcohol abuse was according from the North Eastern states, high cannabis function from North East and Eastern regions and high opiate use in North East, North and Western geographical areas around the world. The National Survey in year 2010 indicated the prevalence of drug misuse among 371 women out of the try out size of 4,648 persons which is 8 per cent. It is figured that on that point are most 6.25 crores alcoholics, .90 million

Cannabis and 0.25 gazillion opiates and nearly 1 million illicit drug exploiters in India. What does the administration state regarding kids and students? Ministry references said on that point is no authentic information to indicate that on that point is a development menace of drug addiction in the country particularly among kids and students as zero timeline information for are available. Nevertheless, they said that students at the secondary and higher associate levels are insecure to slipping into drugs and substance abusing behaviours due to family circumstances, peer pressures in society, distress elements and social stigma that match the mold of the younger generations in India.

Etimology of Youth

There are more than a billion youth in this world and developing countries account for 850 millions of them. About fifty per cent of the population in the developing countries lives in urban areas. The United Nations Organisation (UNO, 2005) defines youth as a group that falls in the 15-24 years category whereas for Commonwealth Youth Programmes it is between 16 and 24 years. According to the Government of India, youth is the sum of individuals falling in 15-35 years age group. However, despite its limitations the definition of age is useful in forming statistical details and offers the practical convenience of a definitive social group with it own specific needs and problems.

Youth are of different categories such as male and female; rural and urban; literate and illiterate; employed and unemployed; skilled and unskilled etc. Youth is a period of life which is heightened in its emotional aspects. Sexual drive is the highest at this stage of life, which the youth need to be able to control and sublimate through socially approvable behaviour. This is a period where right interaction with the opposite-sex is learned. It has been identified that reproductive health problems are steeply rising among teenage marriage and pregnancy, teenage pregnancy outside marriage, sexually transmitted infections two-thirds of STI problems are estimated to be affecting the youth. AIDS is reported to be a critical problem among the youth in major metropolitan cities and drug addicts; high rates of anemia in female adolescents after menarche. Accidents are also on the rise; about 15,000 to 20,000 accident deaths and an equal number of permanent handicaps in youth take place every year; 15,00 to 20,000 suicidal deaths and 1.5 million to 2 million suicide attempts are recorded every year. Further, smoking, alcohol and drug abuse add fuel to the fire of youth problems (WHO, 1986)

Youth in Highly Urbanized Cities

The last decade of the twentieth century brought with it some fundamental changes in political, economic and socio-cultural spheres. Young people were both agents and victims of those changes. They were in a dilemma whether to be integrated into an existing order or to serve as a force for transforming that order. The onset of market economy had witnessed a phenomenal growth in trade and industrial activity which in turn necessitated recruitment of larger workforce. Thus, drug proliferation started the process of urbanization in India. In fact, urbanization is a process of switch from spread out pattern of human epicenters. As a result, urban areas are flooded with migrant people, swelling them in number. With the establishment of new factories, industries and other employment creating avenues, the standard of living rises along with the cost of living.

A significant chunk 84 per cent of the youth in the City was addicted to drugs and had also consumed prescription drugs. The study revealed that youth respondents have had taken a sample consume hemp, opium and prescription drugs. It is noteworthy that instances of cocaine, heroin and brown sugar are not reported by the sample of the study indicating that the availability of these substances is not within their reach and is confined to the rich and elite classes of the city.

Table 10.1: Population of Youth in India Population in Age-Group By Residence and Sex

Age-group	Total			Rural			Urban		
	Persons	Males	Females	Persons	Males	Females	Persons	Males	Females
10-14	124846858	65632877	59213981	92382322	48602745	43779577	32464536	17030132	15434404
15-19	100215890	53939991	46275899	70061823	37748418	32313405	30154067	16191573	13962494
20-24	89764132	46321150	43442982	61398904	31127482	30271422	28365228	15193668	13171560
25-29	83422393	41557546	41864847	57685140	28377173	29307967	25737253	13180370	12556880
30-34	74274044	37361916	36912128	51828879	28688779	26140100	22445165	11673137	10772028

Source: Census of India 2010.

The total population of youth in India (15-34 years age group) is 34,75,76,469 out of which the rural youth are around 24,09,74,746 and the urban youth are 10,67,01,713. The percentages of rural youth and urban youth to the total population of the country are 69.33 per cent and 30.67 per cent, respectively.

Profile of Drugs Usage in India

World Drug Report 2006 of United Nations has given a figure of 16 million opiate addicts world-wide. This figure is not inclusive of other addictives or alcoholics. Opiate is the prime drug of abuse. According to a 2004 United Nations Office on Drug and Crime (UNODC) and Govt. of India report, India alone has nearly 9 million cannabis users, followed by 2 million opiate users and 0.3 million sedative hypnotic users. Besides, 62 million alcoholics as much size of the population of France were reported in India.

India has moved from the traditional stable society, mostly agrarian, to a highly developed, industrial and space society. The traditional joint cohesive family has changed to a micro and non-cohesive one. There has been a change from rural to urban living. In such a society, where the youth come from various strata of society, language and life styles, the youth experience difficulty in adaptation to the changing roles and value systems. This results in alienation, withdrawal, interpersonal relationship difficulties, depression and even suicidal tendencies. The problem gets intensified when the parents come from different religions and cultures and expect their children to be mature and develop their own value systems and roles without guiding them appropriately. (Johnston, L.D., O'Malley, P.M., Bachman, J.G., 2002).

Substance abuse is an important issue related to youth health worldwide. In NFHS-3, data were collected on tobacco consumption and alcohol consumption by men and women. Annually, about 5 million people die worldwide due to tobacco-related diseases which are more than deaths caused by any other single agent (Global Tobacco Surveillance, 2007). According to (Mishra et al., 2005), if the current consumption of tobacco trends persists, tobacco related deaths will be around 10 million per year by 2030. While cigarettes are the dominant form of tobacco use in much of the world, oral use of smokeless tobacco like chewing or applying to the teeth and gums and smoking of bidis are the dominant forms of tobacco consumption in India.

World Drug Report 2006 of United Nations has given a figure of 16 million opiate addicts world-wide. This figure is not inclusive of other addictives or alcoholics. Opiate is the prime drug of abuse. According to the United Nations Office on Drug and Crime (UNODC, 2004) and the Govt. of India Report, India alone has nearly 9 million cannabis users, followed by 2 million opiate users and 0.3 million sedative hypnotic users. Besides, 62 million alcoholics as much size of the population of France were reported in India.

The present drug control strategy of India can be traced back to the Single Convention on Narcotics Drugs of 1961. This was enforced in December 1964 and amended in 1972. The developing countries became puppets in the hands of U.S., via the UN. Increasingly we witnessed the incursion of international drug legislation into the national scene as aid became conditional on countries accepting the U.S. inspired drug laws. This threat was posed (among others) to Nepal when it refused to implement national drug laws modeled on international requirements. Western tourists tipped up the scales for cannabis especially those countries like Canada, USA and UK where cannabis is deemed legal use. Their demand modified the traditional association with drugs that existed in India, roping in several Indian youngsters. It became a sought after substance in certain elite echelon of society. In 1981 the member states formulated the International Drug Control Strategy that was supposed to cover all aspects of the drug issues: use, abuse, trafficking, treatment, rehabilitation and crop substitution. In 1984, though the member states pledged to include economic, social and culturally relevant alternative programmes, they had no strategy on how to deal with problems arising from the criminalization of centuries-old cultural habits in India. The demand modified the traditional option of drugs that existed in India. It became a sought after substance in certain strata of society.

Indian Law on Drugs

Nevertheless, the Indian government enacted the Narcotic Drugs and Psychotropic Substances Act, (NDPS Act), which did not take into account the Indian situation and its plural cultures. The NDPS Act was designed to conform to the Single Convention of 1961, which the Indian government had signed in 1964. India subscribed to the international goal of eradicating all cultural uses of cannabis within a 25-year period. Since the decision was taken without any planning, little or no attention was given to the methods used to achieve the stated goals and implications. There was no real public debate on the new legislation, and it was adopted without much research. The government's mismanagement has led to the leakage of opium produced from licit to illicit channels. After the enactment of the NDPS Act in 1985, there has been an attempt to reduce the area of cultivation. Some high yield varieties of poppy had been introduced, producing over 42 kg. of opium per hectare, whereas the official computation of productivity remained for long at 28 kg per hectare. Further, there was a decrease in the floor purchase price of opium from Rs. 280 to Rs. 270 per kilo, inducing the farmers to divert sales to drug traffickers instead. The commission payable to the lambardars (agents who buy opium from the farmers and sell to the government) was reduced from 3.5 per cent to 0.75 per cent. This paved way to corruption, smuggling and trafficking.

With a purview of preventing arms-cum-drugs trafficking, the Indian government is building fences along the Jammu and Kashmir border. It was hardly known that as long as the conflicts persist, this area continues to be affected by drug trafficking. Political disturbances do not occur in a vacuum. When a region craves for independence, vested interests or negligence from the centre sometimes leads to deprivation. This was clearly the case in the North East – region whose underdevelopment is exacerbated by violent conflict, closing down of educational institutions and so on. In this situation of heightened insecurity, even school children have turned to drugs. All these conflicts have facilitated the smuggling of heroin from multiple sources, thereby multiplying potential sources of supply within India. Although a hard-to-quantify proportion of the heroin smuggled into India is re-exported abroad, it seems reasonable to assume that some of it becomes available for Indian consumers. As more heroins become available, more incentives are generated to become involved in selling it in the domestic consumer market. Therefore, a 'pressure of supply' is generated on the domestic consumer market, first in the areas of conflict and then in the country at large. The pressure of supply is coupled with a strong pressure of demand resulting from the poor and stressful living conditions of the population of the areas of conflict, especially the young.

A system of supply and demand that characterizes the Indian drug market is that the users and traders are often the same. To fund the drug consumption many users commit petty crimes, such as theft. Many have resorted to selling drugs in order to bankroll their own habit. The outcome is to multiply sources of supply at the retail level, thereby increasing the chances that more people will become addicted, and resort to crime and peddling to fund their habit. The drug scene in Mumbai provides a good illustration of the situation prevailing in most Indian cities. In the late sixties, heroin use in Mumbai was restricted to the circles of the rich since it was expensive to buy. Drug users in India make up a substantial proportion of the petty thieves 'working' in the city, but they are seldom arrested nowadays. While poor users do face problems when they become marginalized, the process of marginalization can be extremely painful to persons from the richer strata of society, who find it extremely difficult to adjust to the realities of street life in India. In addition, some users have died in custody. Others have developed a strategy to avoid arrest altogether: they slash themselves with a razor blade, usually on the chest or hands. They use a new blade each time for this purpose since they say 'it is safer'. Police officers are put off by such seemingly 'crazy' behaviour and would rather avoid having to deal with it.

Marginalized users are the main victims of drug use. When their daily heroin intake becomes impossible to afford, users get involved in rag picking, begging or manual labor. Another widespread means of earning a living is by stealing. Petty drug peddling has become an all-important source of income for some users. Some become regular assistants to peddlers, often receiving drugs, food and a place to sleep in return. They may eventually discontinue the habit as a result of friction between the police and the petty peddlers under whom they work. It is the purchaser or the intermediary who arranges for the sale of stolen goods. They can make better deals since they are aware of the desperate need of users for the drug. One user explained that it was difficult for them to pretend to be ordinary vendors because they sell their goods only when they are in urgent need of money for drugs, and seldom wait for a good bargain. Besides, they are afraid of being noticed by the police as they carry telltale signs of their habit: black marks on their fingers which were resulting from burns from the match sticks used to heat up the heroin.

Another strategy that users have developed in order to avoid the police is to apply human excreta or filth from the gutters onto their bodies. While many policy-makers advocate tougher law enforcement, few have bothered to understand the extent to which lives are wrecked through the criminalization of drug use. Previously, the users avoided creating trouble to society. When new legal sanctions came up, antisocial activities became rampant, depending on the extent of their craving. The move towards a drug free existence is a long term process depending upon the user and cannot be attained merely through enforcement.

Crime and Drugs Scenario in India

Organised crime in India was not born out of the drug trade but out of the national tariff barriers, foreign exchange and import restrictions that existed before the introduction of the new economic policies of liberalization. Thus, Indian import policy left loopholes for illegal trade. In the case of gold, India did not have commercial links with its largest supplier – South Africa. It was then channeled through third countries on its way here. Illegal channels got strengthened with the Gold Control Act. This created its own infrastructure and related services, such as transporters, landing specialists, couriers and money holders, which in turn facilitated the development of other forms of smuggling. With the demand for other foreign consumer goods, with the 'imported quality' prestige that the Indian middle class attached to Taiwan, Japan and Singapore-made, the underworld geared itself to cater to these needs. However, with the rise of liberalization of trade and the lowering of barriers previous profit margins plummeted and the players disappeared, but the infrastructure remained intact. So when brown sugar emerged in a early eighties, the freeway was already available. By criminalizing culturally sanctioned drug use and supply, the new legislation has left users free to establish their own individual norms regarding use, and paved the way for an exclusively for-profit motive on the part of the suppliers. Under a prohibition regime, profits become substantial because drug delivery happens despite the law. The special abilities required to do this on a continuous basis usually belong to organised crime.

In three states of North East India, No 4 heroin, smuggled from Burma where it is manufactured on a large scale, is taken through intravenous injection. This region of India has the highest incidence of HIV infection among drug users, mostly youngsters. Their life reels under strict military control, imposition of a curfew after 6 pm. The situation is so bad that some start using heroin at age nine. Brown sugar had not appeared till 1978; earlier studies do not even include brown sugar in the interview schedule. In the early eighties brown sugar emerged in Kashmir, Bhubaneswar, Madras, Coimbatore, Pune, Hyderabad, Goa and Bombay. Border villages lying on trafficking routes were also affected like patients coming to Chennai for treatment from the fishing communities of coastal Tamilnadu located on major international heroin trafficking routes.

The current drug scene is characterised by the continuing presence of traditional substances which can be used for either cultural or secular purposes, and the spread of new products, all of which are used in a secular way. The use of opiates is evident in parts of the country such as the highly urbanized cities, tourists' spots, some border areas and areas located near poppy crops or manufactures of opiates. In India, the commonly used derivatives of opium for non-medical purposes are morphine, brown sugar, pure heroin and codeine. Besides heroin, abuse of pharmaceutical drugs has become common in certain parts of the country.

The lack of proper procedures in the treatment of drug abuse has created a situation where addicts buy prescription drugs over the counter for self-medication and self-detoxification without proper guidance. This leads to a different kind of addiction. The abuse of pharmaceutical drugs among women is more common than the use of substances such as heroin and cannabis products chiefly because pharmaceutical drugs are purchased from legitimate sources and can be consumed under the guise of treatment for an illness. Pharmaceutical companies can market a product for a short span of time (two to three years), and subsequently withdraw it when the adverse effects generate criticism. However, in the process they retain the ability to market a 'drug' and yet be clean in the eye of the law. At present in the rural parts of India, cultural norms are still the order of the day; the question is how long this constructive form can last out against the attack of commercial trafficking networks. It is feared that the criminalization in the cities and the North East will be replicated in these parts and with many drug users become more vulnerable to HIV/AIDS, chances are this reality remains hidden in a multi-faceted culture of India.

Present Scenario of Drug Use Among Youth

Drug abuse is a complex phenomenon in India. In most recent studies, it is known that Visakhapatnam, Andhra

Pradesh, is envisioned as a growing industrialized mega city in the coming decade, various social, cultural, biological, geographical changes lead to the proliferation and prevalence of drugs. India ranks second to Afghanistan in production of illicit opium and probably the only country producing gum as found by the Indian Central Bureau of Narcotics. Opium poppy is grown in the central Indian state of Madhya Pradesh (Mansaur), Rajasthan (Kota, Jodhpur, etc.) and Uttar Pradesh (Gazipur). By the turn of the century the Indian government licensed nearly 160,000 farmers to cultivate opium on 35,000 hectares. In the year 2010 over 1,300 metric tons of opium was harvested, the largest amount in many decades.

While, Afghanistan produces almost 90 per cent of world opium followed by Myanmar. Many of the Indian states i.e. Jammu and Kashmir, Uttar Pradesh, Manipur, Mizoram, Nagaland and Arunachal Pradesh have been found to indulging in illegal growing of opium poppies (Narcotics Control Strategy Report 2000). Since the early 1980s use of opium derivatives like heroin has been wide spread in the major metropolitan cities of India like New Delhi, Kolkata, Chennai and Mumbai, etc. and most of what is available is impure and crude. A purer variety known as 'white sugar' or 'number four' is available in the states of Manipur, Nagaland and Mizoram, which are closest to the source of heroin. A part of the heroin available in India is trafficked from the Golden Triangle, in particular from Myanmar.

Claim of Youth using IDUs

Drugs and substance abuse is an important issue related to youth health worldwide. In NFHS-3, data were collected on tobacco consumption and alcohol consumption by men and women. Annually, about 5 million people die worldwide due to tobacco-related diseases which are more than deaths caused by any other single agent (Global Tobacco Surveillance, 2007). According to (Mishra et al., 2005), if the current consumption of tobacco trends persists, tobacco related deaths will be around 10 million per year by 2030.

Drug use, misuse or abuse is also primarily due to the nature of the drug abused, the personality of the individual and the addict's immediate environment. The processes of industrialization, urbanization and migration have led to loosening of the traditional methods of social control rendering an individual vulnerable to the stresses and strains of modern life. Though India does not appear to have a widespread culture of professional injectors, or 'street doctors', as in some other Asian countries, there do appear to be 'shooting galleries' where IDUs come to a site and inject. As a general rule injecting equipment is discarded inappropriately. Often they are thrown onto garbage heaps in the neighborhood, and even though they are a risk to the local communities, they are frequently collected by people, washed and sold to others at a cheaper price.

Among India's IDU community sharing of injecting equipment is widespread and in many circumstances it is considered normal. A recent Rapid Survey in India showed that most addicts had at some stage shared their needle and syringe (within a period of six months). It has been found that the rates of sharing in metropolis of Delhi, Chennai, Mumbai and Kolkata ranges from 50 per cent to 78 per cent, while Imphal tops with 86 per cent (Manning, G., 2001). Though many druggies clean their injecting equipments, the majority did so inappropriately for protection against blood borne viruses such as HIV/AIDS and hepatitis C. The IDUs also indirectly shared common spoons, solutions, cotton swabs and at the same time dipping of a needle into an ampoule of a pharmaceutical drug was also noted.

Drug abuse has led to a detrimental impact on the society. It has led to increase in the crime rate. Addicts resort to crime to pay for their drugs. According to this research, drugs remove inhibition and impair judgment egging one on to commit offences based on self-consciousness, feelings and repercussions that the drug users are inclined to take. Incidences of teasing, group clashes, assault and impulsive murders increase with drug use and abuse. Apart from affecting the financial stability, addiction increases conflicts and causes untold emotional pain for every member of the family. In this study, it is revealed that with most drug users being in the productive age group of 15-35 years, the loss in terms of human potential is incalculable and damaging. The damage to the physical, psychological, moral and intellectual growth of the youth is very high especially among non-youth category. Among the youth category, the rising trends becomes a fashion in society especially those who belong to the elite members of community.

Adolescent drug abuse is one of the major areas of concern in adolescent and young people's behaviour. It is underscored that India has braced itself to face the menace of drug trafficking both at the national and international levels. The kind of menace has already beset urban cities like Visakhapatnam, although, limited information has been provided to give a clear and in depth understanding of the drug use and abuse situation in the City. Several measures involving innovative changes in enforcement, legal and judicial systems have been brought into effect such as arrest of culprits and conduct of raids in pubs and bars where drugs are commonly proliferating.

The introduction of death penalty for drug-related offences has been a major deterrent. In India, the law is constraint only under the rules and provisions of offense and crime but not considered heinous crime. Perpetrators who violated the law are only arrested but not dealt sternly, so there is a great tendency that the crime will be repeated itself because more damages it will divulge to the growing younger populace in the city. The epidemic of substance abuse in young generation has assumed alarming dimensions in Visakhapatnam. Changing cultural values, increasing economic stress, constant migration of families and dwindling supportive bonds are leading to initiation into substance use.

Substance abuse like the use of cannabis, heroin, and Indian-produced pharmaceutical drugs are the most frequently abused and used in India. Owing to various stress factors and increased influence of the internet exposure, media, the young people especially the student and non-student youth, generally get distracted as they have tendency to mimic the production of so-called and easy access to "designer drugs" is soaring out of control throughout the entire society. Major trends in drug abuse and trafficking in India and around the world as reported by the United Nations International Narcotics Control Board (INCB) has further show an increasing strategy to combat drugs related problems. Their potential can be proved in academics, social circles and other useful crafts of life. The lack of self-discipline, parental control, pampering, and peer pressure and their own vulnerability to get hooked to new and fascinating things – all these play havoc with the lives of the present generation of youth.

Findings of the Study

The present study provides an insight on various parameters of drug abuse in Visakhapatnam as evident from the foregoing analysis of the primary data. It was revealed from the recent data that the youth age 15 and above have experienced the blatant effect of individual characteristics and, if so, whether the effect was similar to dependency and abuse or victimization of the young users and offenders.

There were two clear findings emerged. First, the characteristics of the youth in which the people live do play some part in influencing their delinquent and drug using behaviour, although fewer of these factors were significant as compared with individual characteristics and the explanatory power of the impulsivity measure was stronger than that of any of the significant youth characteristics. It is likely that the inclusion of further individual level explanatory variables would weaken the impact of drug abuse in the city even further, which is broadly in line with the findings of other cross-sectional analyses.

The finding is supported to an extent by the report of Drug Control Agency that confirmed the menace in Visakhapatnam these days. It is pertained evidence that weak law enforcing agencies affect in explaining trajectories of drug offenders, particularly for those who start offending later in adolescence. The second main finding from this analysis is that there are distinct differences in the characteristics of the city that impact on delinquency, cannabis and hard drug use, which suggests that quite different explanatory frameworks are required. The evidence presented here suggests that delinquency among the youth thrives within areas experiencing structural adversity and economic deprivation. This is consistent with other recent evidence from the research study that shows those living in highly urbanized city were less likely to desist from offending than those living in more affluent environment. Such evidence highlights the contextual importance of the places that youth who grow up and are broadly.

The relatively significant ratio of youth in Visakhapatnam City cohort members who reported taking hard drugs may have had some bearing on the model results for these dependent variables in the study. The scientific explanation for hard drug use among the youth showed some consistency with both the delinquency in smoking, alcohol and cannabis in terms of the individual factors that emerged as significant. Like both delinquency in drug use and other substance increased hard drug use at age 15 and above was associated with having experienced family stress, social pressures, separation and loss with having a more impulsive personality traits among the youth. In contrast, there was a relative increase in the influence of self-consciousness, feelings and repercussions among the youth who have experienced great turmoil in their early formative years.

Drug Trends in Visakhapatnam City

The growing trends in society also have severe influence of impulsivity in explaining hard drug use. Impulsivity was still a stronger explanatory factor than the one emerging social and economic factors. Like the drug use and abuse, cannabis is becoming a common outlet and gender was not significant in explaining increased hard drug use. While most likely that delinquency among the youth has thrived significantly, drug use has increased by factor of familial socio-economic status. In contrast to both of the previous data, neither of the census measures proved to be significant in explaining more frequent involvement in drug use of the youth at an early age of 15 and expanded through the years.

The only area level variable to emerge as significant within the drug use was living in the highly urbanized city with a high incidence of crime and drug proliferation such over the counter prescription drugs. It is not exactly clear how living in an area with a higher rate of crime such as Visakhapatnam can cause severe social damage, stealing and violence might precipitate a greater level of drug use, especially among the youth since this variable had tremendous bearing on frequency of youth offenses and delinquency. There was an indication that concentrated deprivation, social dis-integration re-organisation, poor collective efficacy or social disorder had an impact on increased levels of drug use within the study area. In addition, when the measure of smoking, alcohol and cannabis acceptability was included in the research, it proved to have major impact on drug use which discounts general drug tolerance as an explanation.

The influence of substance use and drug abuse was disturbing among the youth in Visakhapatnam City. In a general perspective, it was a known fact that the vast majority of drug users were also smokers, alcohol consumers and cannabis users. When frequency of cannabis use itself was taken into account, it proved to be highly significant in explaining more frequent drug use, which shows a strong link between these three dimensions on self-consciousness, feeling and repercussions. Even though controlling for frequent smoking and cannabis use, the offenses and crime measure remained within the context of the study. It seems likely, therefore, that drug users are a very distinct subpopulation – quite different from the majority of general youth – and that a range of other individual youth factors might be more important in terms of explaining their deterrent behaviour. It is also possible that the offenses and crime committed by those drug users and abusers varied on acted upon influence as a proxy for other more pertinent city-wide analysis and scope of study. These influencing factors were included in this analysis, such as drug availability and vulnerability among the youth.

In contrast, more frequent cannabis use was found to be associated with economic prosperity – both at the individual and the self-consciousness level. The association between drug use and economic prosperity has recently been noted. In this study, it is argued that those living in 'highly urbanized areas such as Visakhapatnam, (which included affluent, prosperous professional and better off executive areas) had the highest levels of drug use (of which the most common type was cannabis use). This strongly suggests that there are cultural factors at work in terms of explaining drug use, which may be in part environmentally determined (e.g. through the availability of drugs or the collective approval of such behaviour, although the study did not find this to be the case from previous data analysis) and that the developmental processes involved in drug use are quite distinct from those of youth delinquency. Moreover, increased smoking, alcohol intake level and cannabis use is associated with areas characterised by a younger age group, more transient population which is somewhat supportive of the study recount. The finding showed that drug use was more frequent within areas of high recorded city based crime is quite difficult to interpret, since it is highly unlikely that this in itself is a causal factor among drug users and abusers. It is probable that the police crime records were lacking in terms of absolute measure was acting as a proxy for some other pertinent characteristic, such as drug availability and vulnerability.

The fact that different explanatory frameworks are required to suggest that different government policy responses are also needed to address these drug related problems among the youth. The differences in the social, economic and cultural perspectives examined in this study only imply that community-based strategies which take a uniform approach to tackling offense, crime and drug use are unlikely to be entirely successful and that more specifically targeted approaches are necessary. The findings are supportive of crime control policies aimed at tackling underlying aspects of structural deprivation. However, such initiatives are unlikely to have much impact on reducing drug use, which is associated with greater social affluence and economic prosperity.

There is great emphasis to be placed on targeting health education, media campaigns particularly within the communities that have a high population of young people and transitional populations. Although, it appears that strategies for reducing drug use may be best targeted within the highly urbanized cities, it is likely considered that much more needs to be understood about drug use and abuse within a population as young as 15 to 35 years old before policy implications can be considered.

While the primary focus of this research has been on the impact of drug use and substance abuse among the youth of India, the level factors did prove to be strong explanatory in three dimensions on the behavioural problems of the youth and revealed both similarities and differences. It seemed to appear that risk factors underlie problematic behaviour among the youth in particular. There is evidence that they may impact differentially on delinquency and drug use, with impulsivity being more important in explaining delinquency and family disruption being more pertinent to the development of drug problems. These findings supported the need for initiatives to provide parents with the skills to deal effectively with difficult children and to advise and support families, social institutions and law enforcement agencies particularly in the context of Visakhapatnam.

Conclusion

Account of addicts in India has always been a difficult task and this still remains the case. It was estimated in late

1980 and early 1990s that India had five million opium users and one million heroin addicts respectively. Most of the drug users in India are male but in many drug treatment centers female drug users may constitute up to 10 per cent depending on the city and geographic region; and it is proliferating (UNAIDS and UNDCP 2010). A New Delhi study of female drug users although of small sample size shows that 30 per cent were commercial sex workers (CSW). Only 15 per cent admitted to being IDUs, though, it was not clear if these people were also Commercial Sex Workers (NEIDAC, 2000).

Rapid survey data on drug use show that the onset of drug use in various major cities starts as early as 15 to 21 years of age. Experts agree that the ages of starting injecting are similar in most of the states. Sizeable number of drug users is from a lower socio economic status with substantial numbers having almost no education and they work in insecure positions or are unemployed. Forty two percent among IDUs of Kolkata could not read or write: it was nearly 50 per cent among the non-injectors. Delhi also showed near identical result, although in Mumbai it was little better. However, in Meghalaya among drug injectors and non-injectors, it was determined abysmally low i.e. three percent (Tellis, E. et al 2000).

The legal case of a person when convicted of involvement in production, manufacturing, possession, transporting, importing or exporting an amount equal or in excess of 10 kilograms (kg) of opium, one kg of heroin or 20 kg of hashish can be sentenced to death although the death penalty has yet to be carried through. Those convicted of possession or consumption of a small quantity of drugs for their own use are allowed to be released as long as they attend a de-addiction centre and within one year provide the court evidence of their medical follow up. Section 64 A of the Act allows for no prosecution to be imposed for a first time offender if the offence is related to possession of a small amount of drugs and the person agrees to seek drug treatment on a voluntary basis from a recognized institution.

As a general rule the criminalization of drug use has forced many drug users to choose drug treatment in order to evade imprisonment. As per the record of the Ministry of Social Justice and Empowerment in 1992 there were 145 counseling centres, 86 de-addiction centres and 14 after-care centres and over three million registered drug addicts in the country. The approach adopted by the Ministry is to recognize drug use as a psychosocial-medical problem and involve as much NGOs as possible in care and cure of the druggies. Community participation has been encouraged by the government as part of the process of care and cure, as it is not only cheaper but also maintains the link between the drug users, their families and the community. A large number of youth, both male and female, have succumbed to the use of drugs and eventually become drug addicts.

Globalization and modernization are the two undeniable aspects that contribute to the menace of drug abuse. The changing life styles, hectic schedule of the parents, the rat race for material gains at the cost of one's peace, lack of proper implementation of Laws, availability of more options to the young etc are the major things that prompt the youth of the world to go for drugs. India is no exception to this phenomenon. In the twenty-first century many vistas are open for development. The question is how the government of India responds to this alarming scenario of the youth. Reported to functionaries, the administration has place into performance a multi-pronged strategy taking motivational counseling, social-reintegration and building consciousness about the ill results of drug abuse. The administration is besides considering in terms of training the people on the ill effects of drug insult over appropriate comments in the educate curricula and services concentrate the factor of risk of succumbing to this vice, the references. To harness the menace, the Ministry has also taken a two-pronged scheme-supply and need step down approach.

The spell of supply reduction is below the view of the Enforcement Authorities the demand simplification strategy as revealed in the purview of the Ministry. The Scheme for Prevention of Drunkenness and Means of Drugs Abuse must be strictly implemented through 350 Non Government Organisations for going 387 De-addiction Centers and 52 Counseling Centers all over the nation for providing facilities like drug intervention, renewal peer helps and constant awareness and advocacy of knowing drug programmes for victims of meaning dependency. Now the challenge is to make people aware of the menace and encourage them to join in the battle once more this malady that endangers the country, and provides concrete actions of lease of living to make a collective effort to eradicate the numerous addicts in Indian society!

REFERENCES

Ahmad Nadeem, Bano Rubeena, Agarwal V.K and Kalakoti Piyush (2009). "Substance Abuse in India". Pravara Medical Review 4, (4).s, India.

Andrew Cherry, Mary E.Dillon and Douglas Rugh (Eds.) (2002). "Substance Abuse: A Global View". Greenwood Press, Westport, USA.

Angus Bancroft (2009). "Drugs, Intoxication and Society". Polity Press, Cambridge, UK.

Ashok Sahni (2005). "Stresses and Distresses in the Youth". Health Administrator. 17, (1).India.

Azad India Foundation (2010). "Drug Abuse in India".

Barker P. ed. (2003). "Psychiatric and Mental Health Nursing: The Craft and Caring". London: Arnold. p. 297.

CDC Newsroom Press Release (2010). June 3, 2010 (http://www.cdc.gov/media/pressrel/2010/r100603.htm)

Copeman M. (2003). Drug Supply and Drug Abuse. CMAJ, 168(9): 1113.

Damayanti Dutta. (2010). "Drug Addiction". India Today, 30 August 2010, India.

Dr. Ashok Sahni (2005). "Stress and Health of Managers, Professional and the Youth". Bangalore; Indian Society of Health Administrators, India.

Dr. Ashok Sahni. Stress and Health of Managers, Professional and the Youth. Bangalore; Indian Society of Health Administrators, 2005.

E-medicine Health Experts for Everyday Emergencies. Drug Dependence and Abuse Overview (http:// www.emedicinehealth.com/drug_dependence_and_ abuse/ article_ em.htm)

Health Administrator Vol. XVII, Number 1: pp. 75-77.

Hornik, R., Maklan, D., Judkins, D., Cadell, D., Yanovitzky, I., Zador, P., Southwell, B., Mak, K., Das, B., Prado, A., Barmada, C., Jacobson, L., Morin, C., Steele, D., Baskin, R., Zanutto, E., (2001). "Evaluation of the National Youth Anti-Drug Media Campaign". Third Semi-Annual Report of Findings. Westat, Rockville, MD. (eds.), USA

(a) http://www.azadindia.org/socialissues/Drug-Abuse-in-India.html

(b) http://www.unodc.org/unodc/en/frontpage/2011/August/north-east-india-a-ray-of-hope-for-female-injecting-drug-users.html?ref=fs2)

Isidore S. O. and Robin Room (Eds). (2005). "Alcohol, Gender and Drinking Problems: Perspectives from Low and Middle Income Countries". Geneva: Department of Mental Health and Substance Abuse, WHO, Switzerland.

Jayapalan, N. (2002). "Urban Sociology". Atlantic Publishers and Distributors, New Delhi, India.

Joan Axelrod-Contrada. (2008). "The Facts about Drugs and Society". Marshall Cavendish, New York, USA.

Johnston, L.D., O'Malley, P.M., Bachman, J.G. (2002). "Monitoring the Future National Results on Adolescent Drug Use: Overview of Key Findings", NIH Publication No. 03-5374. National Institute on Drug Abuse, Bethesda, MD (ED), USA

Juyal, R. et al. (2006). "Substance Use among Inter College Students in District Dehradun". Indian Journal of Community Medicine. 31, (4), October-December 2006 Issue, India.

Karmakar RN (2006). Forensic Medicine and Toxicology. 1st Ed. Kolkata: Bimal Kumar Dhur of Academic Publishers. p. 375.

Khokhar A. (2008). "A Study on Substance Abuse among Women from an Urban Locality of Delhi". Indmedica5, (5) (2008-11 - 2008-12).

Knight JR, Wechsler H, Kuo M, Seibring M, Weitzman E.R. (2002). "Alcohol Abuse and Dependence among U.S.College Students". Journal of Studies on Alcohol, Published by Harvard Medical School Vol. 63, (3), PP. 263 -270.

Kumar, C and Prabhu, G.R. (2006). "Prevalence of Drug Abuse among Male Youth in Tirupathi, AP". Indian Journal of Community Medicine. 31, October-November 2006 Issue, India.

Kumar, M.S., and Sharma, M. (2008). "Women and Substance Use in India and Bangladesh". Substance Use, Misuse 43, (8-9):pp. 1062-77, Bangladesh.

Lal Singh (2007). "Anatomy of Social Problems". Cyber Tech Publications, New Delhi.

Le Bon O, Basiaux P, Streel E. Tecco J, Hanak C, Hansenne M.

Mandira Moddie (2005). "Health Care Dealing with Drug Abuse". Frontline. 22, (17), 13-26 August 2007, India.

National Institute on Drug Absue (2006). NIDA Community Drug Alert Bulletin: Stress and Substance Abuse (http://www.nida.nih.gov/StressAlert/StressAlert.html)

National Institute on Drug Abuse (2006). "Stress and Substance Abuse". NIDA Community Drug Alert Bulletin (http://www.nida.nih.gov/StressAlert/StressAlert.html)

Pable Feliciano, Lorie Broom Hall, Jean J. Schensul, Cristina Huebner, Merrill Singer and Marvin Snow (2000). "The High, the Money, and the Fame: The Emergent Social Context of 'New Marijuana' Use among Urban Youth". Medical Anthropology, 18, pp. 389-414, Overseas Publishers Association.

Pruitt, Lisa R. (2008). "The Forgotten Fifth: Rural Youth and Substance Abuse". Stanford Law & Policy Review. 20 October 2006.

Ravneet Kaur and Dr. (Mrs.) Jatinder K.Gualti. (2007). "Drug Abuse: Trends and Issues". Published by Agricultural University, Ludhiana, Punjab, India.

Rotimi Alagbe (2004). "Dangers of Drug Abuse Among Youths-Nigeria". 28 August 2004, Taking IT Global. Published by Washington University, USA.

Selvan, M. S and Kurpad, A.V. (2004). "Primary Prevention: Why Focus on Children and Young Adolescents?" Indian Journal of Medical Research, 120, India, December 2004.

Srinath Reddy, K., Perry, C.L., Melissa. H.S., Monika Arora (2006). "Differences in Tobacco Use among Young People in Urban India by Sex, Socio-economic Status, Age, and School Grade: Assessment of Baseline Survey Data". The Lancet, 367, (9519), 18 February and 24 February.

Supriya Bezbaruah (2001). "Addiction: Tripping On Medicine". India Today 25 June 2001 Issue, India.

UNDCP -ROSA (2002). "Women and Drug Abuse: The Problem in India". Ministry of Social Justice and Empowerment, Government of India and the United Nations International Drug Control Programme, Regional Office for South Asia, India.

UNODC (2010) "World Drug Report, 2010 by United Nations Office On Drugs and Crime Report

Wadgaonkar, Sangita; Nimale, N.E; Ankushe, R.T. (2000). National Institute of Health and Family Welfare (NIHFW), New Delhi, India.

Yolanda, C.P, Cathedrine Crisp and Donna Lynn Rew (2010). "Parental Acceptance and Illegal Drug Use among Gay, Lesbian and Bisexual Adolescents: Results from a National Survey". National Association of Social Workers (NASW), Social Work, July 55, (3) pp. 265-275.

11

Health Conditions and Public Health Measures of Tribes

– R.S.Varahala Dora
– N.V.S. Surynarayana
– Goteti Himabindu

Introduction

Tribes in India have their own way of living within social and cultural moorings, purely governed on the basis of local conditions and ethos. The term "tribe was first included in the Government of India Act 1935. Tribal communities in India mainly consist of forest dwellers who have accumulated a rich knowledge on the uses of various forests and forest products over the centuries. According to Article 342 of the Indian Constitution, the Scheduled Tribes are the tribes or tribal communities or part of or groups within these tribes and tribal communities which have been declared as such by the President through a public notification. India possesses a total of 427 tribal communities, of these more than 130 major tribal communities live in North East India, which is comprised of the 8 states Meghalaya, Mizoram, Manipur, Tripura, Sikkim, Assam, Nagaland and Arunachal Pradesh. The major tribal communities of the North East India have been categorized into sub-tribes and if these sub-tribes are taken into account the total number of tribal groups reach up to 300.

Article 342 of the Constitution of India defines 'tribes' as "an endogamous group with an ethnic identity; who have retained their traditional cultural identity; they have a distinct language or dialect of their own; they are economically backward and live in seclusion, governed by their own social norms and largely having a self-contained economy."India has the world's second largest concentration of the tribal population, next to Africa. The Scheduled Tribe (ST) population in India is 84,326,246 constituting about 8.2 per cent of country's total population of 1,026,103, 289 belonging to over 550 tribal communities which includes 93 Primitive Tribal Groups (PTGs) and 227 ethnic groups. There are 325 languages spoken by different communities with a large number of dialects. The tribal sub-plan areas is spread over nine districts and consists of about 33 tribes in Andhra Pradesh. The total population of Andhra Pradesh according to 2001 census is 76,210,007 of which tribals constitute 5, 024,104 accounting for 6.59 per cent of the total population.

Public health is the science and practice of protecting and improving the health of a community though health education, control of communicable diseases, application of sanitary measures, and monitoring of environmental hazards. It is distinct from clinical medicine in that it focuses on the health of populations rather than individuals. Public health practice can take many forms including the assessment and monitoring of the health of populations to identify health problems and priorities; the formulation of public policies designed to solve identified local health problems; and the design of programmes to prevent or control disease. Epidemiology is an aspect of public health practice that deals with the study of the causes, distribution and control of disease in population.

Climatic Conditions

The climate of the agency area is classified as Sub-tropical with high seasonal variation in rainfall and wide extremes of temperature. The average minimum temperature ranges from 3°. to 4°.C in November/December while average maximum temperature ranges from 35°. to 40°.C in May/June. Regarding rainfall and seasonal conditions usually the southwest monsoon starts from 3rd week of April every year and northeast monsoon starts from October. The climate conditions are very cool in the area on account of elevation, green vegetation and thick forest. The temperature gets down with the onset of South West Monsoon and tumbles to a mean minimum of 17.5°.C by January after which there is reversal trend till the temperature reaches mean maximum of 34°.C by the end of May, that is April to June are Warmest Months. The Agency Zone is different in agro-climatic conditions compared to the other zones of the state.

Availability of Potable Water

Plenty of water resources available in the form of rivers, springs and streams in this area. Some villages were provided with open wells, bore wells and Kundi's (spring water storage device). Natural springs (Ooota) are the only source available for drinking water as well as utility purpose in remote villages. According to the survey in the villages, they have been facing severe scarcity of drinking water in spite of good rainfall over the region. Every year people die due to drinking contaminated water and water borne diseases like malaria, dengue, typhoid, diarrhoea, and cholera in rainy season.

Health is one of the vital indicators reflecting the quality of human life. World Health Organisation (WHO) describes health as a state of complete physical, mental, social and spiritual well-being and not merely as absence of diseases or infirmity. Today majority of Indian indigenous (Trible's) people are facing various communicable and non communicable diseases. It is found that positive correlation between the health status of tribal people and their socio-economic development. Tribes considered as socially and economically backward and disadvantaged. Tribal poverty has come into sharp focus since their food sources from the forest have started dwindling. Also, widespread poverty, illiteracy, under nutrition, absence of safe drinking water and sanitary living conditions, poor maternal and child health services and ineffective coverage of national health and developmental services have been identified by several studies, as possible contributing factors to the dismal health conditions prevailing among the tribal population in India.

Majority of Indian tribal's are living in the remote forest. Available evidence suggests that poverty is the prime cause for ill health, persistent morbidity and early death. However, lack of access to right foods: iron, protein and micro-nutrients such as iodine and vitamins, is the principal cause for the very high incidence of nutritional deficiency diseases: anemia, diarrhea, night blindness, goiter, etc., The normal diet of the tribals consists mainly of Nagli. It may sometimes be Accompanied by rice and tur/urid dal. Vegetables are eaten seasonally. Consumption of eggs, meat, fish and milk is negligible. During the summer, they survive mainly on Kadu Kand' (a bitter root) and a thin gruel made out of Nagli. There is no special diet for pregnant and nursing mothers, or children, and there is no special weaning diet either. Due to inadequate intake of food, especially during the lean months, they generally remain undernourished. Since most of the tribals work in the fields, it is hardly possible for them to carry boiled water wherever they go. Tribals refuse to drink water purified by potassium permanganate, as they do not like its taste and smell. They also believe that if milk is kept in pots washed with such water it curdles. In view of the strong association of Tuberculosis (TB), malaria, AIDS, Sexually Transmitted Diseases (STD) to reproductive health, the policy framework falls short in not assessing the operational inadequacies for improving the programme implementation .of these public health programmes - for example, data shows that most malarial deaths are on account of delayed treatment.

The average time taken in tribal areas for a blood slide to be examined and results informed is six weeks to six months. On account of inadequate budgets for travel allowances, workers tend to wait for 10-15 days till enough number of slides are collected before handing them in for testing by when the slides get spoilt and fixed. traditional medicine, which was found to be acceptable, and proved over time, to be efficacious, affordable and easily acceptable. In India, the blind adoption of the high cost western medicine system has resulted in the danger of destroying our own strengths, without having the money to sustain this new technology. In tribal areas, the Girijan Co-operative Corporation and the department of ayurveda have done commendable work in listing and identification of herbal medicinal plants - this research work should be fully utilized and exploited for the benefit of the tribal, as herbal medicine is acceptable, affordable, accessible and most importantly found to be capable of curing several ailments such as malaria fevers, STDs, etc, very effectively. Such an integration of systems of traditional medicine - nature cure, herbal cure, ayurveda, etc, which are less dependent on the MBBS doctor and more familiar to the tribals needs to be consciously built into the package. But then the establishment of such a health system would require massive re-training of the health providers in integrated medicine.

Malaria is the foremost public health problem of Tribal areas contributing 23 per cent of malaria cases, 40 per cent of Plasmodium falciparum cases and 50 per cent of malaria deaths in the country15. More than 60 per cent of tribal population of Andhra Pradesh lives in high-risk areas for malaria. Though the tribal communities constitute nearly 8 per cent of the total population of the country, they contribute 25 per cent of the total malaria cases and 15 per cent of total P.falciparum cases. Various epidemiological studies and malariometric surveys carried out in tribal population including primitive tribes reveal a high transmission of P.falciparum in the forest regions of India, because malaria control in such settlements has always been unattainable due to technical and operational problems.

- NGOs mapping should be carried out in the tribal areas and credible NGOs especially with clinical services backup should be encouraged to take the total responsibility of managing the RCH and health services in the sub-centre/PHC/CHC where public health system is deficient/inadequate.

- NGOs and corporate sectors should be encouraged to take up CBD projects covering minimum a block population and could coordinate mobile health services, counseling, referral transport, awareness creation and social mobilization.
- NGOs and private nursing homes/hospitals may be involved in the programme including service delivery through a frame work of partnership.
- Accreditation methods can be followed for private and NGO operated facilities. All facilities within the framework should follow uniform reporting system and referral system.
- Outsourcing/franchising of discrete services (such as diagnostics) to NGOs/Private Sectors.

Cases of health problems in tribal areas are:

1. Every year there are epidemics in the Scheduled Areas and loss of life occurs in large numbers. However, they are dealt with only as an emergency situation but not addressed in a more holistic manner. There are endemic diseases that are not being adequately addressed like malaria and T.B.
2. Drinking water, which is a significant cause for most of the health problems of the tribal's, is not a primary focus of the ITDAs. Potable drinking water should be a priority for all ITDAs so as to tackle gastro-enteritis and other preventable illnesses.
3. There is no proper link between the district public hospitals, the PHCs and the field level medical staff to follow-up on cases.
4. The PHCs in Scheduled Areas are too distant, are inadequately staffed and have few medical supplies. They have very few tribal staff; most staff are non-resident and are irregular in their work and are not

sympathetic to tribal people. The PHCs and sub-centers should be increased and quality of services should be improved.

5. At present the training given to CHWs is poor, the medical equipment and the medicines given are inadequate and so is the stipend, which is meager and irregular. There should be strong thrust to improving the Para-medical teams in the tribal areas. However, it should also be understood that they cannot totally be a replacement or a solution to the professional and qualified medical doctors and hence there is a need to appoint more number of qualified doctors at the PHCs.
6. The budget allocations to health sector are poor and priorities are misplaced. While there is emphasis on funds allocation to higher education in medicine, there is barely any provision for community level health practitioners especially in the tribal areas which are considered punishment posting. For example, there is a severe criticism on RMPs as quacks and demand to ban their practice. However, they are the only source of health services to most of the tribal areas. Instead of terminating their services, the quality of medical knowledge and practice should be improved for RMPs and the Community Health Workers, so that primary health can be addressed properly.
7. The immunization programmes undertaken in the agency areas is highly flawed. The ANMs who have to administer vaccinations within a few hours do not have adequate transport facilities; have to walk long distances to their villages of work. So they either throw away the medicines or do not administer when the vaccine is potent. Vaccinations programme has to be better planned.
8. The only tangible responsibility given to the health department working in the scheduled agency areas is Family Planning, where they are given specific numerical targets. This drive should be stopped, as tribals are

vulnerable to disease and death and should not be a priority for Family Planning programmes.

9. There is no emphasis given to the indigenous health practices, or to the Indian forms of medicine like Ayurveda. There are very few Ayurveda hospitals in the Agency areas. This is a cause for concern. Ayurveda medical course for scheduled areas should be introduced.
10. There have been moves towards privatizing the health sector which is most recently visible in the G.O 90†††. The PHCs, or any part of the health services in the Scheduled areas should not be privatized as it is the fundamental duty of the government towards the tribal population in providing free public health and education services.
11. Some tribal's have complained against the culturally humiliating practice of identifying certain illnesses, even officially, with some tribes. For example, Yaws, which is locally termed as "Koya-rogam".

Conclusion

Tribes are most neglected people who are also living with us in our country. Even though, the government is spending more money towards the welfare of the tribes they are not properly reaching the beneficiaries. Tribal health is main problem out of all the problems which caused big loss of human recourses in the country. Hence, the government, NGOs, politicians, People who are interest in the welfare of tribals should improve the budget allocation for tribal health, education, facilities and amenities for their better living and better productivity.

REFERENCES

A Report to the Scheduled Areas and the Scheduled Tribes Commission.

Banerjee, B. G., and Kiran Bhatia. *Tribal Demography of Gonds*. Delhi: Gian Pub. House, 1988. ISBN 81-212-0237-X

Beine, David m. 1994. A Sociolinguistic Survey of the Gondi-speaking Communities of Central India. M.A. Thesis. San Diego State University. 516 p.

Devajana C. Nanjunda* and P.T. Dinesha** Role of Non-governmental Organisations (NGOs) Interventions on Tribal Health: Some Annotations from Grass Root Level.

Dr. J.Koswara Rao. Ethno botany Thisess work. Lambert Publication Germane in 2011.

Elwin, Verrier. *Phulmat of the Hills; A Tale of the Gonds*. London: J. Murray, 1937.

Fürer-Haimendorf, Christoph von, and Elizabeth von Fürer-Haimendorf. *The Gonds of Andhra Pradesh: Tradition and Change in an Indian Tribe*. London: George Allen & Unwin, 1979. ISBN 0-04-301090-3.

John Kuriyan* Tribal Health Programme In June 1978, the Department of Social Welfare, Government of Maharashtra, Commissioned the Centre for Development Studies and Activities (CDSA).

Kaufmann, Walter. *Songs and Drummings of the Hill Maria, Jhoria Muria and Bastar Muria Gonds. And, the Musical Instruments of the Marias and Murias*. 1950.

Mehta, B.H. *Gonds of the Central Indian Highlands: A Study of the Dynamics of Gond Society*. New Delhi: Concept, 1984.

Museum of Mankind, Shelagh Weir, and Hira Lal. *The Gonds of Central India; The Material Culture of the Gonds of Chhindwara District, Madhya Pradesh*. London: British Museum, 1973. ISBN 0-7141-1537-1, pp. 481-486.

Pagdi, Setumadhava Rao. *Among the Gonds of Adilabad*. Bombay: Popular Book Depot, 1952.

Perry, William James, *The Children of the Sun: A Study in the Early History of Civilization*, London: Methuen, 1927.

Pingle, Urmila, and Christoph von Fürer-Haimendorf. *Gonds and Their Neighbours: A Study in Genetic Diversity*. Lucknow, India: Ethnographic & Folk Culture Society, 1987.

Policy Perspective. Economic and Political Weekly. 33(9). Feb 28 - March 6, 1998.

Rao, K Sujata.: Heath Care Services in Tribal Areas of Andhra Pradesh: A Public.

Russell, R. V., *The Tribes and Castes of the Central Provinces of India*, London, 1916.

Sharma, Anima. *Tribe in Transition: A Study of Thakur Gonds*. India: Mittal Publications, 2005. ISBN 81-7099-989-8

Singh, Indrajit. *The Gondwana and the Gonds*. Lucknow, India: The Universal Publishers, 1944.

12

A Study on Health Profile of Koya (Tribal) Women in Khammam District

– S.Thulasamma
– V.Sreedevi
– D.Usha Rani

ABSTRACT

The Tribals are the autochthonous people of the land who are believed to be the earliest settlers in India peninsula. They are generally called the Adivasis implying original inhabitants. The well being of the body, mind and emotions are all part of good health and are all closely tied together. The study was carried out in Khammam District of Andhra Pradesh. The respondents of the study were Koya tribal women. A sample of 150 tribal women was selected randomly from two villages namely Gangelanacharam and Medipalli of Khammam District. The interview schedule and observation method was used for collecting of data Statistics like percentage and frequencies were used for interpretation of the data. Data revealed that a high percentage (89%) of the respondents was married and livings with their spouses three-fourth of the respondents were married at the age of 10-15 years. None of the respondents were married after 21 years of age. Most of them (96%) were ill iterated, 67 per cent of the respondents were taking proper care of their health. Majority (76.0%) of the respondents were resorting to self medication when they fell sick. A very low proportion (7%) of deliveries took place in hospitals. A high (88%) percentage of the respondents stated that they went to an indigenous doctor (RMP) for their treatment. 71 per cent of the respondents immunized their children. An over whelming proportion (44%) of women had other problems like body pains, joint pains, cold & Cough. In the case of infections, a higher percentage (47%) of children had cold & Cough. It is concluded that majority of the respondents were resorting to self medication when they fell sick. An overwhelming proportion of deliveries were carried out with untrained experienced Dai at home. Implementation of various welfare programmes with a human resource development approach would improve the quality of life of the tribals.

Introduction

India is the natural abode of hundreds of Tribal communities and their population according to 2011 census is 84,326,240 constituting nearly 8.15 per cent to the total population of the country. Tribals as the name implies, are "Adivasi" or original dwellers, living in the subcontinent from un-recorded time and possibly driven in to the forests by more aggressive new comers: Aryan groups being among the earliest to socially subjugate them. In order to escape complete domination, tribals evolved their distinct identity through endogermy and their particular practice of shifting agriculture. Health has always been a major concern of community development. "It is a basic requirement, not only for the fulfillment of human aspiration, but also for the enjoyment of all mankind of a better quality of life. It is also indispensable for a balanced development of the individual within the family and as a part of the community and the nation (Mohlar1990). Every culture, irrespective of its simplicity and complexity has its own notion regarding health and health seeking behaviour, and this is after referred to as "Health culture" it is an integral component of the overall culture of the community".

Tribal's traditionally enjoyed good health. They were able to extract medicinal herbs, roots and leaves and apply these to local medication. They had a vast instinctive knowledge of natural medication. In the concept of health of the Tribal people there are two components which are present almost universally. Firstly, the individual may be committing or omitting certain acts which may bring upon the individual or the household some affliction. But this individual's action may also cause some affliction to be harmful for the whole village, clan or larger group. This is very clear in the context of bringing smallpox or any other epidemic to the family and to the village as a whole. But such conceptualization is not mediated through an intervening variable like sanitation. Normally any group of tribal people do not associated certain diseases or epidemics with in sanitary conditions of community living. This does not mean that some specific tribal people do not like or create clean or sanitary settlement. Where the earthen pitchers are used for carrying water or cooking, meticulous care. Cleaning them may be observed similarly the tribal people clean their cloths and their body regularly. Secondly all Tribal People at all levels of existence know and practice some herbal remedies or message or some other physical manipulation of the body, shows very clearly that, if not explicitly, at least implicitly, they believe in physical factors producing better health or diseases under certain conditions. That is why; invariable one comes across the faith of the tribal people, irrespective of educational levels, socio-economic conditions or cultural milieu, in the efficacy of surgical operations of treatment.

Health is a function, not only of medical care, but of the overall integrated developed of society – cultural, economic, educational, social and political. Each of these aspects has a deep influence on health which in turn influences all these aspects. Hence, it is not possible to raise the health status and quality of life of the people unless such efforts are integrated with the wider effort to bring about the overall transformation of society. Good health and good society go together (Basu, 1992). This is possible only when supportive services such as nutrition, environment and education reach a higher level. The common beliefs, customs and practices connected with health and disease have been found to be intimately related to the treatment of disease it is necessary to take holistic view of all the culture dimensions of the health of community. In most of the Tribal communities, there is a wealth of folklore related to health. Documentation of this folklore available in different socio-cultural systems may be very rewarding and could provide a model for appropriate health and sanitary practices in a given eco-system. Maternal and child care is an important aspect of health seeking behaviour which is largely regulated among the Tribal groups. Health and treatment are closely interrelated with the environment particularly the forest ecology. Many Tribal groups' use different parts of a plant not only for the treatment of disease, but for population control as well (Chaudhari, 1990). It has been noted by many that tribal's living in remote forest areas have a better overall health status and eat a more balanced diet than tribals living in less remote forest free areas. The mode of utilization of available natural resources after determines the long term impact on health.

The backward and underprivileged population in the century includes about 65 million Tribals. Efforts of the Government of India and the people have led to some significant progress and development in the country. However, Tribals at large still remain far below the national standers of all aspects of quality of life.

Following are some important facts about the Tribal population of India:

- There are over 400 Scheduled Tribes which constitute about 7.8 per cent of our population.
- About 65 per cent Tribals have a percapita monthly income of less than Rs. 40/- and more than 82 per cent have an income less than Rs. 60/- compared to corresponding National average of Rs. 70/-.
- The literacy rate in Tribal areas is still dependent on livestock. Forestry and agricultural activities. More than 90 per cent of Tribals involved in such activities compared to 73 per cent of the corresponding national estimate. Also compared to 15 per cent of rural population, more than 17.8 per cent of Tribals are agricultural labourers.
- Most of the Tribals live in nuclear family setup and early age at marriage (Below 15 Years) is their tradition. However, an average family size of 5.7 per house hold as been recorded in Tribals compared to the National figure of 6.0
- Though the exact estimates on vital indices in Tribal population of our country not know, it may be interesting to note that during the year 1978, a lower Infant mortality rate (IMR) of 113 in Tribal population was observed against 125 of the National estimate in general and 136 in rural areas including the Tribals.

Profile of Koyas

The Koyas are a Telugised Tribe of the gords and speak Telugu. They are divided in to a number of sub-tribs such as Raj Koyas, Mana Koyas, Thumma Koyas, Basa Koyas, Mooso Koyas, Gutta Koyas, Chitti Koyas, Banda Koyas, Chenchu Koyas and Koyanaiks. Among the Koya sub castes, there were many occupational groups such as kammori Koya (Blacksmith), Musura Koyas (Brassoniths), Vaddi Koyas (Stone cutters) etc. However all these Koyas mostly depend upon forest and agriculture for their livelihood?

The Koyas are the most numerous Tribes in Andhra Pradesh. Most of them are found in the areas of East Godavari, Srikakulam, Visakha and Khammam Districts. They are generally medium in structured with dark complexion. They have broad nose, full lips, small chin and low for head apart from worshipping their own deities the Koyas also observe Hindu festivals. The Koyas organize a number of Jataras and propitiate aspires to protect their crops from infects and bless them with abundant harvest. Human scarifies are also offered by the Koyas which has now been giving up. Among the Jataras, the Medaram Jataras has a special significance where Samakka, Saralamma and Saddamma are worshipped once in two years in the Hindus month of Magha Shudda Poornima. Besides Medaram, Yeturnagaram (Warangal Dist) also attracts thousands of devotes of the Koya community where innumerable animals are scarified to propitiate. Like other Tribes, the Koyas also have many beliefs and superstitions and observe them fastidiously on various occasions. They also have belief in sorcery and witch craft widely practiced even today.

Powerful social organisation function at various levels arrange the Koys mainly in observe the social norms and to maintain harmonious inter-tribal relations of the community. Their social organisation is highly democratic which is managed by Kula Panchayats. Kula Panchayat is headed by a Kulapedda (Chieftain). Above him is the Kuladora, the chieftain of a group of ten or fifteen villages organized in the form of a Samithi (Council), who presides over the meetings. Kula panchayat meetings are attended by all able bodies Men and Women of the respective areas. Persons suspected of crimes are given due punishment in the form of penalties. Any defaulter who refuses to pay the fine is socially boycotted. This way, Kula Panchayat exhibits a strong sense of social solidarity among the Koya.

Methodology

The following are the objectives of the study:

(a) To know about the health profile of Koya (Tribal) Women in Khammam District.

(b) To assess the health care of Koya (Tribal) Women in Khammam District.

(c) To examine the health seeking behaviour of Koya (Tribal) women in Khammam District.

They study was conducted in Enkur Mandal of Khammam District of Andhra Pradesh. Two stages random sampling procedure was followed in the selection of the respondents. Enkur mandal consists of 11 villages. In the first stage, out of the 11 villages, two villages namely Gangulanacharam and Medipalli were purposively selected because of the high rate of habitation of Koya Tribal population. In the second stage, 75 Koya Tribal women from each village were randomly selected. Thus the total sample for the study consisted of 150 Koyas Tribal women. The interview schedule, observation method was also used for data collection. The date thus collected was subjected to statistical tests to enable easy interpretation of the data. Frequencies and percentages were used for interpretation of the data.

Results and Discussion

General Profile of Respondents

Age: It is one of the important variables in the understanding of an individual's location and status in the society. Distribution of the respondents according to their age is presented in Table 12.1.

Table 12.1: Distribution of the Respondents by their Age Levels

Age in Years	Number	Percentage
15-20	21	14.00
21-30	62	41.33
31-40	29	19.33
41 and above	38	25.33
Total	**150**	**100.00**

From table 12.1 it is evident that majority of the respondents (41%) belonged to the age group of 21-30 years, followed by the next higher percentage (25%) of respondents were in the age group of 41 and above. 19 per cent of the respondents belonged to the age group of 31-40 years and only 14 per cent belonged to the age group of 15-20 years. On the whole it may be stated that the selection of respondents were fairly representative of all the age group.

Age at Marriage

Age at marriage is an important variable which is generally influenced by many social and cultural factors viz., education, Occupation, Kinship, Family type, customs, social control, bride price etc.

Table 12.2: Distribution of the Respondents by their Age at Marriage

Age at Marriage	Numbers	Percentage
10-15 Years	109	72.66
16-20 Years	41	27.33
21-25 Years	–	
26 and above		
Total	**150**	**100.00**

From table 12.2, it was clear that a high percentage (73%) of the respondents were married at the age of 10-15 years. The remaining 27 per cent of respondents were married in the age of 16-20 years. None of the respondents were married after 21 years of age.

Marital Status

The family is the institution and it is antecedent to marriage. Marriage has always been an elastic variable in usage. It is vaguely used for wedding, nuptials of matrimony etc. As a social institution marriage is a part and parcel of the family.

From data in table 12.3 it was clear that a high percentage (89%) of the respondents were married. A small (9%) per cent were widowed, while 2.0 per cent ware separated. Name of the respondents were divorced by and large the sample consisted of married responded.

Table 12.3: Distribution of the Respondents by their Marital Status

Marital Status	Numbers	Percentage
Married	134	89.33
Widowed	13	8.66
Divorced	0	–
Separated	3	2.0
Total	**150**	**100.00**

Educational Status

The education of women is very essential for happy and healthy homes, improvement of society, economic property and solidarity. Above all education is the means which would improve the status and position of women in general. Literacy is the obvious instrument which would improve the present status of women in the society.

Table 12.4: Distribution of the Respondents by their Educational Levels

Educational Levels	Numbers	Percentage
Illiterates	144	96.00
Primary	006	04.00
Secondary	0	–
Higher	0	–
Total	**150**	**100.00**

It is evident from the above data that majority of the respondents (96.00%) were illiterates. Only 4.0 per cent had primary education. None of the respondents were found to have had secondary & higher education. The data revealed that illiteracy among women was still prevailing at a high rate. This was due to poverty and indifference towards girls, negligence of girl's education. Social values and norms and strong felt work needs also contributed to low levels of education among women. A number of measures have been taken up to raise women's literacy and educational level. The new education policy was also paving the way for increasing literacy levels among women, especially those belonging to SC, ST and other minority groups.

Health Care of Koya Women

The healthy individual has a quiet mind, is tranquil, at peace with himself/herself, his/her neighbour and with the universe at large, he/she is well adjusted to the circumstances, conditions and concept of his/her external world being able to maintain an even temper, an alert intelligence, a happy disposition and to display socially considerate behaviours. The following tables reveals that health care of Koya (Tribal) women.

Table 12.5: Distribution of the Respondents according to their Health Care

Item	Respondents	Respondents	Total
Taking care of proper health	67.33 (101)	32.66 (49)	100 (150)
Self medication	76 (114)	24 (36)	100 (150)
Observation of menarchy	100 (150)	–	100 (150)
Self eleanliness	100 (150)	–	100 (150)
During menustration restriction is helpful from the rest point of view	100 (150)	–	100 (150)
Taking rest during menustration period	6 (9)	94 (141)	100 (150)
Taking rest during prenatal period	10.5 (14)	89.47 (119)	100 (133)
Taking rest during post-natal period	100 (133)	–	100 (133)
Immunization to children	71.4 (95)	25.33 (38)	100 (133)

N.B: Figures in parenthesis indicate number of respondents.

It was clear from the table 12.5, that 67 per cent of the respondents were taking proper care of their health. Majority

(79.0%) of the respondents was resorting to self medication and the remaining was consulting the doctors when they fell sick. Cent per cent of the respondents observed menarche. Among 85 per cent of the women had menstrual flow for about 3-5 days followed by 9 per cent who had 6-7 days and rest (6%) had more than eight days. All of them insisted on cleanliness. About 68 per cent of the tribal women expressed that menarche may not be observed about they keep themselves clean. All most all respondents expressed that restrictions during menstruation was helpful to them as rest could be taken however, only a few (6%) of them took rest during menstruation period. Maximum (89%) of the respondents did not take rest during pre-natal period. Only 10 per cent took rest and out of them only 22 per cent rest for about 15 days, 57.0 per cent for one month and the rest (27%) for 3 months. Cent per cent of the respondents look rest during post-natal period. Majority (60.1%) of them took rest for one month followed by 16 per cent for two months, 14 per cent for 3 months & above and the remaining (10.0%) for 15 days. 71 per cent of the respondents have immunized their children. While 25 per cent didn't get their children immunized. The reasons stated were their apprehension and ignorance about immunization.

Type of Delivery Attendance

The types of delivery attendant assumed greater importance in relation to mortality and survival chance of infants for the following reasons:

(a) Poor hygiene
(b) Low rate of immunization of expectant mother
(c) Unscientific methods practiced for deliveries at home.

Koyas believe that pregnancy of women was the result of god's gift. Usually the first delivery took place in parent's house only. When the days of delivery drew nearer, the parents brought their daughter to their house. The pregnant women were not allowed to attend any hard work. When labour pains started, one of the aged women of the village, who knew the process of delivery, attended her during labour period. She cleaned the baby, cut the umbilical cord and attended on her for the entire day. The woman was not allowed to attend any work after delivery till the purificatory bath on 9th or 11th day was over. The data regarding the type of delivery attendant was presented in Table 12.6.

Table 12.6: Distribution of the Respondents according to Type of Delivery Attendant

Type of Delivery Attendant	No.	Percentage
Doctor at Hospital	10	7.51
Experienced Dai at home	123	92.48
Elderly women at home	–	–
Total	**133**	**100.00**

The above data revealed that a very low proportion (8%) of deliveries took place in hospitals. On the contrary an overwhelming proportion (92%) of deliveries was carried out with untrained experienced dai at home. One of the reasons for conducting a higher proportion of deliveries by untrained experienced Dai was due to lack of proper health guidance before delivery and non-availability of health centers/sub-centers or non availability of ANM.

Health Consultant

Further analysis of data on health consultant was presented in Table 12.7.

Table 12.7: Percentage Distribution of the Respondents in Relation to their Health Consultants

Consultant	Number	Per cent
Doctor	26	17.33
Nurse	13	8.6
M.P.H.W	–	–
R.M.P	131	87.33
Total	**150**	**100.00**

As shown in Table 12.7 a higher (87.33%) percentage of the respondents said that they would go to an indigenous doctor (R.M.P) for their treatment when they fell sick while a (17%), (9%) of the respondents consulted qualified Doctors and nurses respectively for treatment.

In the present study area the primary health centre was 7 kms, away from the village, and as such very few of the respondents were utilizing the facility of primary health centre.

Immunization

Immunization refers to the provision of resistance power against the disease in children. It was very important to reduce infant mortality by means developing certain anti-bodies in the children. It was the most effective measure to control communicable disease such as small pox, diphtheria, Tetanus, polio, whooping cough, tuberculosis, typhoid measles etc., some of the diseases commonly occurred during child and so can be prevented by means of immunization.

Table 12.8: Per cent Distribution of Immunization Among Children

Immunization	Number	Percentage
Immunized**	95	71.4
Not Immunized	38	25.33
Total	**133**	**100.00**

** Any kind of immunization given to the child is considered as immunized.

Data showed that a higher (71%) percentage of children were given immunization by one or the other immunizing agents. One fourth of children were not immunized against the communicable disease that usually affected children.

It was clear from the table 12.9 that cent per cent of the children of the respondents were immunized against polio. Immunizations like B.C.G and D.T.P was given to 94 per cent and 97 per cent respectively. Only a few per cent (9%) got immunized against measles. The date high lights the poor rate of immunization of children in the tribal areas.

Table 12.9: Percentage Distribution of Children by Type of Immunization

Type of Immunization	No.	Percentage
B.C.G	89	93.68
D.T.P	92	96.84
Polio	95	100.00
Measles	18	18.95

Common Ailments of Mother and Children

Data on common ailments of children and mothers was presented in the Tables 12.10 and 12.11.

Table 12.10: Percentage Predominance of Health Problems in Women

Ailment	No.	Percentage
Anemia	81	54.00
Malnutrition	56	37.33
Warm infection	–	–
Sexually transmitted disease	–	–
Spontaneous abortions	8	5.33
Fungal infection	–	–
Molted teeth	30	20.00
Malaria	4	2.67
T.B	4	2.67
Ecozoma	–	–
Boils	21	14.00
Scabies	–	–
Diarrhoea	3	2.00
Jaundice	1	0.67
Others	66	44.00

N.B.: Some women suffered from more than one ailment, so they occur under different ailments.

It was clear from data in Table 12.10 that majority of the respondents are suffering from anemia (54%) and malnutrition followed by 20.0 per cent who had molted teeth and 14 per cent who suffered from boils and 5 per cent from spontaneous abortions. The other infectious diseases like T.B, Malaria, and Diarrhea were negligibly seen. The per cent incidence of all these infections was in the range from 0.67 per cent to 2.67 per cent. On the contrary, an overwhelming proportion (44%) of women had other problems like body pains, joint pains, cold, fever etc. Which were a sign of general weakness, mostly due to poor nutritional and imbalanced diet.

Table 12.11: Per cent of Children Suffering from Health Problem

Ailments	No.	Percentage
Scabies	–	–
Eye Disease (Vit A Deficiency)	7	3.93
Caugh and cold	84	47.19
Fungal Infection	6	3.37
Boils	7	3.93
Measles	14	7.87
Dental caries	5	2.81
Pneumonia	5	2.81
Fever	49	27.53
Diarrhoea	21	11.80
Dysentery	9	5.06
Worm infection	–	–
Malnutrition	87	48.88
Others	–	–

N.B: Some children suffered from more than one ailment, so they occur under different ailments.

A total of 178 children were observed. The findings were given in table 11 of the various clinical manifestations of nutritional deficiency diseases, a higher percentage (49%) of children were suffering from protein energy malnutrition. However, severe cases of protein deficiency with edema and Marasmic symptoms were identified in a small group of children. The diet of the children was low in proteins. A small proportion (4%) of children had vitamin A Deficiency symptoms.

In the case of infections, a higher percentage (47%) of children had cold, cough, followed by fever (27%), diarrhea (12%) and measles (8%). In the case of other aliments observed, fungal infections, dental caries, pneumonia and dysentery were negligible. The per cent incidence of all these infections was in the range of 2.81 to 5.06 only. It indicated that, lack of personal hygiene and sanitation was contributing to these conditions.

Sum Up

It was concluded that a high percentage of the respondents were married and living with their spouses. Three fourths of the respondents were married at the age of 10-15 years. None of the respondents were married after 21 years of age. 67 per cent of the respondents were taking proper care of their health. Majority (76.0%) of the respondents were resorting to self medication when they fell sick. Cent per cent of the respondents observed monarchy. All of them insisted on cleanliness during that project that period. Al most all respondents expressed that restriction during menstruation was helpful from the point of view of rest. Only a few (6%) of them took rest during menstruation period. Maximum (89%) of the respondents did not take rest during pre-natal period. Cent per cent of the respondents took rest during post natal period. Avery low proportion (7%) of deliveries took place in hospitals. On the contrary an overwhelming proportion (92%) of deliveries was carried out with untrained experienced Dai at home. This is due to the lack of proper health guidance and non-availability of health centers, ANM ect. A higher (87%) percentage of the respondents stated that they went to an indigenous doctor (R.M.P) for their treatment, when they fell sick. With regard to immunization, 71 per cent of the respondents immunized. With regard to type of immunization cent per cent of the children of the respondents were immunized against polio. While a few per cent (19%) of children were get immunized against measles.

Majority of the respondents were suffering from anemia (54.0%) and malnutrition (37%). Infectious diseases like T.B., malaria, diarrhea were namely seen. On the contrary an over whelming proportion (44.0%) of women all other problems like body pains, joint pains, cold, fever, etc, In children higher percentage (49%) of them were suffering from protein energy malnutrition. In the case of infection, a higher percentage (47%) of children had cold, cough. In the case of other aliments fungal infections, dental caries pneumonia, dysentery was negligible.

Implication of the Study

- Education facilities both formal and non formal are meager. These need to be provided by better schools for children and by organizing adult education programmes and functional literacy programmes of a functional nature for women and children.
- Regular visits of health workers need to be facilitated with regard to prenatal and postnatal care and immunization programmes for children. By training the indigenous persons and attending deliveries the incidence of infant deaths can be reduced.
- Immunization is to be systematized to cover all the children and to protect dam from childhood diseases.
- Encourage the concepts of small family norm and adequate spacing. Improved pre-natal and post-natal care will be provided to ensure safe mother hood. The population in the reproductive age group shall be empowered, through education, to be responsible for their own family size
- Implementation of various welfare programmes with a human resource development approach would improve the quality of life of the tribals.

- Constant contact and repeated efforts are to be recommended rather than sporadic Intensive efforts in all developmental activities inclusive of the activities to improve nutritional and health status should be taken up.

REFERENCES

S.K. Ksthriya (1992) Health and Culture Among the under Privileged Groups in India (In) State of India's Health (ed.Alok Mukhopadhyay). Voluntary Health Association of India, pp. 175-186.

Chaudhari, Buddhadeb (1990) Social and Environmental Dimensions of Tribal Health (In) Cultural and Environmental Dimensions of Health (ed. By B. Chaudhari. Inter-India Publications).

Chowdary S.S. G.C Ghosh (1984) Indigenous Health Practice Among the Idu Mishimi of Arunachal Pradesh, Human Sciences, 33: 24-33.

Guru S.S and Koshy, A.K (1997) "Maternal Nutrition, Antenatal Care and Infant Mortality", Man and Life, Vol. 23, No. 1 & 2, pp. 57-65.

Reddy, S (1990) "Disease and Curing Patterns Among Yerukulas – A Study of Indian Village", Vanyajathi, Vol. 38, No. 3.

SECTION – III

YOUTH AND NATION BUILDING

13

Youth the Fabricators of the Nation

– B.Praveena Devi

Youth sounds ambiance in the minds of the citizens of a country. In our country, this sound in more than any other in the world. And we are proud to say that utmost youth are Indians. This is the real wealth of our country. They should be part of every activity along with the adults. Deem this as a vision for our society. A country where all citizens, young and old, are informed about and engaged in all major issues that affect their lives. A place where adults and young people are together at the table; debating, grappling with problems, crafting solutions and jointly deciding on how resources should be allocated. A robust democracy where all people, including youth, exercise their right to select those who should speak and act on their behalf and hold them accountable. Where young people have an equal opportunity to have a sustainable livelihood. Imagine adults and young people working together to build a thriving a society from the ground up – contributing to nation building from the community level up to the national level.

Nation building is a dream of every citizen. The term nation building is used here to refer to a constructive process of engaging all citizens in building social cohesion, economic prosperity, and political stability in an inclusive and democratic way. It is important to note that the priceless resource of any country is its human resource. There is no other resource that matches the human being, because mankind is the foundation or the corner stone of any development and civilization. Out of the human intellect a nation is built. This can be confirmed by the fact that many countries are able to attain steady growth and development with limited natural resources through the intelligence of their people and the labour force. Young people are a crucial segment of a nation's development. Their contribution therefore is highly needed. Young people are social actors of change and as the saying goes "youth are not only the leaders of tomorrow, but also the partners of today."

The government and society at large have equal responsibility to provide the youth with suitable grounds and thereby bringing about a matured and responsible population for the coming generation to lead a better life. As such the establishment of the Department of State for Youth, the development of a comprehensive National Youth Policy, the establishment of National Youth Service Scheme.

It is a process through which all people have access to and control of structures and mechanisms that govern their lives. Admittedly, the vision sounds unattainable and lofty for below reasons:

- Few societies have found adequate ways to ensure that all adults fully participate in the political process.
- Even fewer have found adequate ways to ensure that young people share in the burdens and benefits of citizenship.
- Youth prefers entertainment than interest in administrative activities.
- Society is the real scenario for youth to be a generous, hopeful, studious, sincere and real hero in the nation

development. However, he was excluded from all the roles in the society.

- Parents always think about the future of his/her children but they never consider them as the future of the nation. Their success results nations beauty. But the scenario is different their success is for other nation where they will get more remunerations.

Role of youth needed in major sectors of Nation:

- Education;
- Administration;
- Political participation;
- Science & Technology;
- Corporate sector; and
- Research organisations (eg. ISRO, NTRA, CRA, AIAER).

Great experts head these, if a youth wants to be a part he has to cross many levels where the hurdles like money, race, socio economic statuses, goodwill of the officers, hereditary what not every step is hurdle which many of them can't bare and drop their ideas to be a part of above sectors. Out of all sectors political sector never encourages to be main role. There are three frequently cited reasons for why young people are excluded from political participation.

1. Young people are perceived as lacking the skills and qualities.
2. Young people are not afforded the opportunities to share power with adults.
3. Young people are portrayed as lacking the motivation.
4. Young people are not daughter/son of any politician (hereditary).

Young people are often viewed as lacking the skills needed to become part of the political process. These perceptions are often backed by popular theories on childhood development and adolescence, many of which define youth as social group that is in the 'stage of becoming adults. Young people are the last group we are allowed to systematically exclude. Young people are not afforded the opportunities to share power with adults in part because they are viewed as lacking the requisite skills. Consequently, they are not invited to the table. The very idea of "youth citizenship" – young people participating as equals – is a stretch for many adults. The irony is, however, that once at the table, young people are often viewed as a threat to adult power. Rather than work with young people to build the skills, adults either abdicate power or work to control it. This tendency to exclude young people has been well-substantiated in international. Therefore 'youthfulness' has become a major justification for excluding young people from decision making. It is also important to emphasize that these ideas are also present all major social institutions; from the family, the school, the community; religious institutions etc. It is not a surprise that there are not expectations, and processes that facilitate the political participation of young people within their communities as well as at the national level. One of the more frequently used justifications excluding young people is the entrenched myth of youth apathy - young people are frequently portrayed as lacking motivation to become involved. This myth is captured most aptly in the media hype about Generation X syndrome, which describes young people as a socially inert, self-absorbed group with little or no interest in the political process.However, recent research reveals that young people are far from apathetic. Yet young people are showing great interest in political issues and are constantly searching for different ways of expressing themselves. It would be a grave mistake to assume that youth do not participation in the political process at all.

Activities Needed to Muster Young People

There are innumerable activities that seek to mobilize young people politically in neighborhoods and cities across the nation - activities initiated by young people and some initiated and supported by adults committed to youth empowerment. These initiatives cover a very broad spectrum.

- Organising young people in their communities;
- Educating young people to use the democratic process;

- Advocating for and training young people to be part of governance structures of civil society organisations and through local government;
- Monitoring and advocating for changes in the legislation at city and state level and many other such areas; and
- The central idea of making social welfare work compulsory for the students is to make them realize its importance in future life and also Nation Building role in society and Nation Building.

These initiatives are unique because young people play a central role in the determination and execution of strategies. Many agree that this rich tapestry of localized youth action holds the promise of expanding the possibility for young people as equal and active stakeholders in the political process. However, such initiatives tend to be limited to the micro level and rarely transcend the neighborhood and city level. The idea of tackling this subject arose at the International Development Conference: Global Meeting of Generations held in Washington DC in January 1999. At this forum, young people from across the world grappled with the role young people should play in the governance process of their societies as well as international bodies such as the United Nations. Young people must be ready and willing to take advantage of any opportunity that comes his way. It is important to note that we cannot all work in offices; therefore some of us would have to train ourselves to be welders, plumbers, electricians, carpenters, craftsmen, farmers and so on.

REFERENCES

http://observer.gm/africa/gambia/article/youth-and-national-development-challenges

Rajan Y S, Mission India: A Vision for Indian Youth, Penguin Books India, ISBN: 0143334999.

Rajesh Shukla , Indian Youth Demographics and Readership, ublished by the Director, National Book Trust, India, Nehru Bhawan.

14

Impact of Youth Culture and Intergenerationality in the Society

– N.V.S.Surynarayana
– R.S.Varahala Dora
– Goteti Himabindu

Introduction

There is debate within the scientific community about whether or not youth culture exists. Some researchers argue that youth's values and morals are not distinct from those of their parents, which means that youth culture is not a separate culture. Others note that we must be cautious about extrapolating a current effect to other periods of history. Just because we see the presence of what seems to be a youth culture today does not mean that this phenomenon extends to all generations of young people. Additionally, peer influence varies greatly between contexts and by sex, age, and social status, making a single "youth culture" difficult, if not impossible, to define. Others argue that there are definite elements of youth society that constitute culture, and that these elements differ from those of their parents' culture. Janssen et al. have used Terror Management Theory to argue for the existence of youth culture.

Terror Management Theory is a psychological concept that hypothesizes that culture originates from an attempt to cope with the knowledge of our mortality. We do this by adopting a worldview and developing self-esteem. Researchers test TMT by exposing people to reminders of their mortality. TMT is supported if being reminded of death causes people to cling more strongly to their worldview. Janssen et al. tested the following hypothesis: "If youth culture serves to help adolescents deal with problems of vulnerability and finiteness, then reminders of mortality should lead to increased allegiance to cultural practices and beliefs of the youth." Their results supported their hypothesis and the results of previous studies, suggesting that youth culture is, in fact, a culture.

Youth culture is "the sum of the ways of living of adolescents; it refers to the body of norms, values, and practices recognized and shared by members of the adolescent society as appropriate guides to actions" This definition includes two elements. The first is culture, which can be defined as the symbolic systems, and processes of maintaining and transforming those systems, that people share. The second part of this definition is that youth culture is specific to adolescents, and differs at least partially from the culture of older generations.

Elements of youth culture include beliefs, behaviors, styles, and interests. An emphasis on clothes, popular music, sports, vocabulary, and dating set adolescents apart from other age groups, giving them what many believe is a distinct culture of their own. Within youth culture, there are many distinct and constantly changing youth subcultures. These subcultures' norms, values, behaviors, and styles vary widely, and may differ from the general youth culture. Schwartz and Merten used the language of adolescents to argue for the presence of youth culture as distinct from the rest of society. Schwartz argued that high school students used their vocabulary to create meanings that are distinct to adolescents. Specifically, the adolescent status terminology (the words that adolescents use to describe hierarchical social statuses) contains qualities and attributes that are not present in adult status judgments. According to Schwartz, this reflects a difference in social structures and the way that adults and teens experience social reality. This difference indicates cultural differences between adolescents and adults, which supports the presence of a separate youth culture.

Theories of Youth Culture

The presence of youth culture is a relatively recent historical phenomenon. There are several dominant theories about the emergence of youth culture in the 20th century. These include theories about the historical, economic, and psychological influences on the presence of youth culture. One historical theory credits the emergence of youth culture to the beginning of compulsory schooling. James Coleman argues that age segregation is the root of a separate youth culture. Before compulsory schooling, many children and adolescents interacted primarily with adults. In contrast, modern children associate extensively with others their own age. These interactions allow adolescents to develop shared experiences and meanings, which are the root of youth culture. Another theory posits that some types of cultures facilitate the development of youth culture, while others do not. The basis of this distinction is the presence of universalistic or particularistic norms. Particularistic norms are guidelines for behavior that vary from one individual to another. In contrast, universalistic norms apply to all members of a society. Universalistic norms are more likely to be found in industrialized societies.

Modernization in the last century or so has encouraged universalistic norms, since interaction in modern societies makes it necessary for everyone to learn the same set of norms. Modernization and universalistic norms have encouraged the growth of youth culture. The need for universalistic norms has made it impractical for young people's socialization to come primarily from immediate family members, which would lead to significant variation in the norms that are communicated. Therefore, many societies use age grouping, such as in schools, to educate their children on societies' norms and prepare them for adulthood. Youth culture is a byproduct of this tactic. Because children spend so much time together and learn the same things as the rest of their age group, they develop their own culture.

Psychological theorists have noted the role of youth culture in identity development. Youth culture may be a means of achieving identity during a time when one's role in life is not always clear. Erikson theorized that the major psychological conflict of adolescence is identity versus role confusion. The goal of this stage of life is to answer the question, "Who am I?" This can be difficult in many societies, in which adolescents are simultaneously expected to behave like children and take on adult roles. Some psychologists have theorized that the formation of youth culture is an attempt to adopt an identity that reconciles these two conflicting expectations. For example, Parsons (1951) posited that adolescence is a time when young people are transitioning from reliance on parents to autonomy. In this transitory state, dependence on the peer group serves as a stand-in for parents.

Burlingame restated this hypothesis in 1970. He wrote that adolescents replace parents with the peer group, and that this reliance on the peer group diminishes as youth enter adulthood and take on adult roles. Fasick relates youth culture as a method of identity development to the simultaneous elongation of childhood and need for independence that occurs in adolescence. According to Fasick, adolescents face contradictory pulls from society. On one hand, compulsory schooling keeps them socially and economically dependent on their parents. On the other hand, young people need to achieve some sort of independence in order to participate in the market economy of modern society. As a means of coping with these contrasting aspects of adolescence, youth create independence through behavior—specifically, through the leisure-oriented activities that are done with peers.

Impact of Youth Culture on Adolescents

For decades, adults have worried that youth subcultures were the root of moral degradation and changing values in younger generations. Researchers have characterized youth culture as embodying values that are "in conflict with those of the adult world", Common concerns about youth culture include a perceived lack of interest in education, involvement in risky behaviors like substance use and sexual activity, and engaging extensively in leisure activities. These perceptions have led many adults to believe that adolescents hold different values than older generations and to perceive youth culture as an attack on the morals of current society. These worries have prompted the creation of parenting websites such as theyouthculturereport.com and the Center for Parent Youth Understanding (cpyu.org), whose goal is to preserve the values of older generations in young people. Despite the attitudes of many adults, there is not a consensus among researchers about whether youth subcultures hold different beliefs than adults do. Some researchers have noted the simultaneous rise in age segregation and adolescent adjustment problems such as suicide, delinquency, and premarital pregnancy.

Perhaps the increased prevalence of age segregation contributed to the problems of modern youth, and these problems represent a difference in values. However, most evidence suggests that these youth problems are not a reflection of different morals held by younger generations. Multiple studies have found that most adolescents hold views that are similar to their parents. One study challenged the theory that adolescent cohorts have distanced themselves from their parents by finding that between 1976 and 1982, a time when rates of adolescent problems increased, adolescents became less peer-oriented. A second study's finding that adolescents' values were more similar to their parents' in the 1980s than they were in the 1960s and '70s echoes Sebald's findings. Another study did find differences between adolescents' and parents' attitudes, but found that the differences were in the degree of belief, not in the attitude itself. There may also be pluralistic ignorance on the part of youth regarding how their attitudes compare to peers and parents. A study by Lerner et al. asked college students to compare their attitudes on a number of issues to the attitudes of their peers and parents. Most students rated their attitudes as falling somewhere between their parents' more conservative attitudes and their peers' more liberal attitudes.

The authors suggested that the reason for this is that the students perceived their friends as more liberal than they really were. If adolescents' values are similar to their parents', then why do adults insist that adolescents inhabit a separate world with different values? One reason may be that the similarities between adolescent and adult values are relatively invisible compared to the differences between these two groups. The way young people dress, the music they listen to, and their language are often more apparent than the values they hold. This may lead adults to overemphasize the differences between youth and other age groups. Adults may also falsely believe that youth's assertion of independence in exterior aspects of their life represents a manifestation of a different value system. In reality, sports, language, music, clothing and dating tend to be superficial ways of expressing autonomy—they can be adopted without compromising one's beliefs or values. Of course, there are some areas in which adolescents' assertion of autonomy can cause long-term consequences. These include behaviors involving substance use and sexual activity. The impact of youth culture on deviance and sexual behavior is debatable. Drinking alcohol is normative for adolescents in the United States, with more than 70 per cent of high school students reporting ever having had a drink. Similarly, about 2/3 of teenagers have engaged in sexual intercourse by the time they leave high school. Because they are ubiquitous in adolescence, many researchers include drinking and having sex as aspects of youth culture.

Engaging in these activities can definitely have harmful consequences for adolescents, although the majority of adolescents who engage in these risky behaviors do not suffer long-term consequences. The possibilities of addiction, pregnancy, incarceration, and other negative outcomes are some potentially negative effects of participation in youth culture. However, youth culture may also have benefits for the adolescent. We have already discussed how youth culture may facilitate identity development in the teenage years. Peer influence can also have a positive effect on adolescents' well-being. For example, most teens report that their friends pressure them not to use drugs or engage in sexual activity.

Intergenerationality

Intergenerationality is interaction between members of different generations. Sociologists study many intergenerational issues, including equity, conflict, and mobility:

- **Intergenerational equity** is the concept or idea of fairness or justice in relationships between children, youth, adults and seniors, particularly in terms of treatment and interactions.
- **Intergenerational conflict** is either a conflict situation between teenagers and adults or a more abstract conflict between two generations, which often involves all inclusive prejudices against another generation.
- **Intergenerational cycle of violence** is a pattern of violence or abuse that is passed from one generation to the next. Generally, an individual who witnesses domestic violence as a child is much more likely to be an abuser or a victim of domestic abuse in adulthood.
- **Intergenerational mobility** is a measure of the changes in social status which occurs from the parents' to the children's generation.
- **An Inter-generational contract** is a dependency between different generations based on the assumption that future generations, in honoring the contract, will provide a service to a generation that has previously done the same service to an older generation.

- **Intergenerational policies** are public policies that incorporate an intergenerational approach to addressing an issue or have an impact across the generations.
- **Intergenerational shared sites** are programmes in which children, youth and older adults participate in ongoing services and/or programming concurrently at the same site, and where participants interact during regularly scheduled planned intergenerational activities, as well as through informal encounters.
- **Inter-generational ministry** is a model of Christian ministry which emphasizes relationships between age groups and encourages mixed-age activities.

Conflict

An intergenerational conflict is either a conflict situation between teenagers and adults or a more abstract conflict between two generations, which often involves all inclusive prejudices against another generation. Intergenerational conflict also describes cultural, social, or economic discrepancies between generations, which may be caused by shifts in values or conflicts of interest between younger and older generations. An example change to an inter-generational contract that may be necessary to reflect a change in demographics. It is associated with the term "generation gap".

Contract

An inter-generational contract is a dependency between different generations based on the assumption that future generations, in honoring the *contract*, will provide a service to a generation that has previously done the same service to an older generation. The most common use of the term is in statutory pension insurance provisions and refers to the consensus to provide pension for the retired generations through payments made by the working generations. The use of the word *contract* is not entirely accurate as the next generation implicitly enters the agreement without consent.

Cycle of Violence

Intergenerational cycle of abuse is violence that is passed from father to son or daughter, parent to child, or sibling to sibling. It often refers to violent behaviour learned as a child and then repeated as an adult, therefore continuing on in a perceived cycle.

Equity

Intergenerational equity, in the sociological and psychological context, is the concept or idea of fairness or justice in relationships between children, youth, adults and seniors, particularly in terms of treatment and interactions. It has been studied in environmental and sociological settings. In the context of institutional investment management, intergenerational equity is the principle that an endowed institution's spending rate must not exceed its after-inflation rate of compound return, so that investment gains are spent equally on current and future constituents of the endowed assets. This concept was originally set out in 1974 by economist James Tobin, who wrote that, "The trustees of endowed institutions are the guardians of the future against the claims of the present.

Their task in managing the endowment is to preserve equity among generations." Conversations about intergenerational equity occur across several fields. They include transition economics, social policy, and government budget-making. Intergenerational equity is also explored in environmental concerns, including sustainable development, global warming and climate change. Conversations about intergenerational equity are also relevant to social justice arenas as well, where issues such as health careare equal in importance to youth rights and youth voice are pressing and urgent. There is a strong interest within the legal community towards the application of intergenerational equity in law.

Intergenerational Policies

An intergenerational policy is a public policy that incorporates an intergenerational approach to addressing an issue or has an impact across the generations. Approaching policy from an intergenerational perspective is based on an understanding of the interdependence and reciprocity that characterizes the relationship between the generations. An intergenerational approach to public policy recognizes that generations share basic needs including adequate income, access to quality health care and social services, educational and employment opportunities, and a safe place to live. Further, policies that are supportive of any age group must build on the common concerns of all generations.

REFERENCES

Bronfenbrenner, U. (1974). The Origins of Alienation. *Scientific American, 231,* pp. 53-61.

Burlingame, W.V. (1970) The Youth Culture. In E.D. Evans (Ed.), *Adolescents: Readings in Behaviour and Development.* Hinsdale, Ill: Dryden Press, pp. 131-149.

Coleman, J. (1961). *The Adolescent Society.* Glencoe, IL: Free Press.

Fasick, F. (1984). Parents, Peers, Youth Culture and Autonomy in Adolescence. *Adolescence, 19(73),* pp. 143-157.

Gecas, V., & Seff, M. (1990). Families and Adolescents: A Review of the 1980s. *Journal of Marriage and the Family, 52,* pp. 941-958.

Harrison, Benjamin T. (2000)' Roots of the Anti-Vietnam War Movement,' in Hixson, Walter (ed) the Vietnam Antiwar Movement. New York: Garland Publishing.

Janssen, J., Dechesne, M, & Van Knippenberg, A. (1999). The Psychological Importance of Youth Culture: A Terror Management Approach. *Youth & Society, 31(2),* pp. 152-167.

Lerner, R.M., Meisels, M., & Knapp, J.R. (1975). Actual and Perceived Attitudes of Late Adolescents and Their Parents: The Phenomenon of the Generation Gaps. *Journal of Genetic Psychology, 126,* pp. 195-207.

Meyer, David S. (2007).The Politics of Protest: Social Movements in America. New York: Oxford University Press.

Parsons, T. (1954). Age and Sex in the Social Structure of the United States. In *Essays in Sociological Theory,* New York: Free Press, pp. 89-103.

Parsons, T. (1951) *The Social System.* Glencoe, Ill: Free Press.

Rice, F. (1996). *The Adolescent: Development, Relationships and Culture* (7th ed.). Boston: Allyn & Bacon.

Schwartz, G. & Merten. D. (1967). The Language of Adolescence: An Anthropological Approach to the Youth Culture. *The American Journal of Sociology, 72(5),* pp. 453-468.

Sebald, H. (1986). Adolescents' Shifting Orientation Toward Parents and Peers: A Curvilinear Trend Over Recent Decades. *Journal of Marriage and the Family, 48*, pp. 5-13.

Steinberg, L. (2008). *Adolescence.* New York, NY: McGraw-Hill.

Sugarman, Barry. Involvement in Youth Culture, Academic Achievement and Conformity in School: An Empirical Study of London Schoolboys. 1967. *The British Journal of Sociology, 18*. pp. 151-164.

http://www.crmvet.org/disc/mfdp.htm

http://www.encyclopedia.com/topic/Youth_culture.aspx

15

Substance Abuse Among Student Youth

– Mande Suresh

Drug Addiction and Drug Abuse is a chronic or habitual use of any chemical substance to alter state of body or mind for other than medically warranted purposes. Addiction is more often now defined by the continuing, compulsive nature of the drug use despite physical and/or psychological harm to the user and society and includes both licit and illicit drugs, and the term "substance abuse" is now frequently used because of the broad range of substances include alcohol and inhalants that can fit the addictive profile. Psychological dependence is the subjective feeling that the user needs the drug to maintain a feeling of well-being. Physical dependence is characterized by tolerance and the need for increasingly larger doses in order to achieve the initial effect and withdrawal symptoms when the user is abstinent. The author conducts a study on the impact of substance abuse among student youth, as it is the major problem of the modern life style.

The paper highlights the historical profile of the substance abuse. The study clearly mentions how the effect of urbanization, modernization and globalization and encouraging the student youth to take drugs for momentary pleasures and intoxication. The paper deals with various issues and aspects of substance abuse in this particular age group. The present scenario has been clearly presented. The paper describes the various problems of the society has to face due to this problem. The paper suggests various means to eradicate this problem.

Definition of Substance Abuse

Drug Addiction and Drug Abuse is a chronic or habitual use of any chemical substance to alter state of body or mind for other than medically warranted purposes. Addiction is more often now defined by the continuing, compulsive nature of the drug use despite physical and/or psychological harm to the user and society and includes both licit and illicit drugs, and the term "substance abuse" is now frequently used because of the broad range of substances include alcohol and inhalants that can fit the addictive profile. Psychological dependence is the subjective feeling that the user needs the drug to maintain a feeling of well-being. Physical dependence is characterized by tolerance and the need for increasingly larger doses in order to achieve the initial effect and withdrawal symptoms when the user is abstinent.

Definition of Student Youth

As a category, youth are a transient population in demographic terms, sandwiched between childhood on the one and adulthood on the other, experience transitional social and mental and physical changes. It is not easy to reach a consensus as to where the period of youth starts and ends. The United Nations Organisation (UNO) defines youth as a group that falls in the 15-24 years category whereas for Commonwealth Youth Programmes it is between 16 and 24 years. According to the Government of India, youth is the sum of individuals falling in 15-35 years age group. However, despite its limitations the definition of age is useful in forming statistical details and offers the practical convenience of a definitive social group with it own specific needs and problems.

Historical Profile of Substance Abuse

World Drug Report 2006 of United Nations has given a figure of 16 million opiate addicts world-wide. This figure is not inclusive of other addictives or alcoholics. *Opiate is the prime drug of abuse. According to a 2004 United Nations Office on Drug* and Crime (UNODC) and Government. of India report, India alone has nearly 9 million cannabis users, followed by 2 million opiate users and 0.3 million sedative hypnotic users. Besides, 62 million alcoholics as much size of the population of France were reported in India.

The drug addicts and drug users buy heroin and pharmaceutical mixes after pooling money, sharing not only the same common solution but the same needle. Drug users range on an average from between two to five people while sharing the substance mixture. While heroin pushers may use the addictive two to four times a day, buprenorphine users and the pharmaceutical mixes tend to inject less often as a result of lasting kick. Drugs would be commonly administered intravenously but occasionally intra muscular injection is also seen. Injectable drug users were noted to pull and push the blood several times in the syringe before the final administration. Addictives are often used in India in open public places without any hesitation. While, those who are hesitant or apprehensive of enforcement authorities prefers abandoned or under construction buildings, public toilets, at home, offices, railway yards, and burial grounds.

Methodology

Significance of the Study

For fashion or getting solace youth begin the habits of using nicotine, taking alcohol and drugs and very soon get addicted to them. Of late, the prevalence of addiction to these substances has been very high among students and non-students of the age group 15-30. The growing trends in urbanization, modernization and globalizations open many vistas not without their negative implications. The potentials and energies of the youth are wasted in pursuit of momentary pleasures and intoxications that make them slaves to substance abuse. Hence focus on the menace of Substance Abuse among the Student and the Non-student youth in the city of Visakhapatnam is significant in order to find out possible solutions to deal with this problem.

Objectives of the Study

- To ascertain socio-economic and demographic characteristics of the respondents of the Student and the Non-student youth of Greater Visakhapatnam Municipal Corporation limits.
- To examine the causative factors of substance abuse.
- To record the feelings of the substance abuse among student and non-student youth.
- To recommend to policy makers to initiate stern implementation of laws that prevents drug abuse and innovate policies to rehabilitate the drug dependents.

Nature of the Sample

The investigator, with the help of identified substance abusers tried to identify such abusers who fall in the age groups specified earlier. As such, the investigator followed Snowball sampling method in identifying the subject for the study.

Research Tools

In order to gather valuable data from the respondents, a structured interview schedule is devised. The Schedule is broadly divided into five major sections. The first section deals with the demographic data of the respondents. The second section contains queries aimed at collecting the details of various types of substance abuse such as smoking, alcohol and drugs. The opinions of the respondents about the use of substance and their self-consciousness were elicited in section three. The fourth and the fifth sections cover the feelings and repercussions of the respondents on their substance abuse and the effects of substance abuse on the individual and the family, respectively.

The Present Scenario of Drug Use and Abuse Among Youth in India

India ranks second to Afghanistan in production of illicit opium and probably the only country producing gum as found by the Indian Central Bureau of Narcotics. Opium poppy is grown in the central Indian state of Madhya Pradesh (Mansaur), Rajasthan (Kota, Jodhpur, etc.) and Uttar Pradesh (Gazipur). By the turn of the century the Indian government licensed nearly 160,000 farmers to cultivate opium on 35,000 hectares. In the year 2000 over 1,300 metric tons of opium was harvested, the largest amount in many decades. In 1999 an estimated 300 metric tons of illicit opium was diverted to the black market, converted into heroin 'brown sugar' and being sold in international markets. Ten per cent of the diversion of opium gum would make India the world's fourth largest producer of illegal opiates

Interpretation of Data and Major Findings

I. Social characteristics:

Table 15.1: Age-wise Distribution

Age (in years)	Student Youth (n=100)	Non-student Youth (n=100)
< 20	32	8
20-25	68	37
> 25	0	55
Mean	20.90	24.85
Standard Deviation	2.33	3.198

From the table 15.1, it is found that a majority of the substance abusers are males who are in the age group of 20-29, which is very productive, phase in one's life. The mean age of student and non-student youth was 20.9 and 24.8 respectively.

Table 15.2: Education wise

Education	Student Youth (n=100)	Non-student Youth (n=100)
Education < 10th standard	0	34
Intermediate & vocational technical courses	7	19
Degree	34	29
Bachelor of Technology (B.Tech)	49	7
Post Graduation	10	11

From the above table 15.2, it is observed that a majority of the respondents (49%) among student youth were B. Tech holders while 34 per cent of the non-student youth respondents were having less than 10th standard.

Table 15.3: Religion wise Distribution

Religion	Student Youth (n=100)	Non-student Youth (n=100)
Hindu	71	81
Muslim	7	9
Christian	22	10

From the above table 15.3, it is inferred an overwhelming majority of the respondents (71%) and (81%) in student and non-student youth respondents belong to Hindu religion followed by Christians and Muslims in that order.

Table 15.4 : Caste wise Distribution

Caste	Student Youth (n=100)	Non-student Youth (n=100)
Scheduled Castes	10	21
Scheduled Tribes	0	2
Backward Classes	26	44
Other Castes	42	15
Minorities	22	18

From the table 15.4, it is found that a majority of the respondents (42%) in student youth category belong to other castes, which are not notified as reserved categories by the Government.

Table 15.5: Marital Statuses

Gender (Sex)	Student Youth (n=100)		Non-Student Youth (n=100)	
	Married	Unmarried	Married	Unmarried
Male	1	87	39	59
Female	0	12	0	2

From the above table 15.5, it is observed that except one respondent, all the student youth respondents were unmarried. Most of the respondents (61%) from non-student category were also bachelors while 39 per cent of them were married.

Details of Addictions

Table 15.6: Period of Smoking

Period of Smoking (in year)	Student Youth (n=100)	Non-student Youth (n=100)
< 3	33.0	5.0
3-5	43.0	28.0
> 5	24.0	67.0

From the table 15.6, it is found that a majority (43%) stated that they started smoking three years before.

Table 15.7: Reasons for Smoking

Reasons for Smoking	Student Youth* (n=100)	Non-student Youth* (n=100)
Influence of Friends	78.0	69.0
Financial Problems	6.0	41.0
Domestic Problems	17.0	38.0

The above table 15.7 shows that a majority of the respondents of the student (78%) and the non-student youth

(69%) categories were influenced by their friends for becoming addicted to smoking.

Table 15.8: Number of Cigarettes

Number of Cigarettes (per day)	Student Youth (n=100)	Non-student Youth (n=100)
5	17.0	4.0
10	41.0	27.0
> 10	42.0	69.0

From the above table 15.8, it can be seen that a majority of the student youth respondents (42%) smoke more than 10 cigarettes a day while their counter-parts topped the table with (69%).

Nicotine Products

Table 15.9: Period of Nicotine Addiction

Period of Nicotine Addiction	Student Youth (n=100)	Non-student Youth (n=100)
< 6 months	2.0	7.0
6-1 year	26.0	27.0
1-3 years	7.0	40.0
Cannot say	7.0	2.0
Not Applicable	58.0	24.0

From the above table 15.9, it is reflected that the beginning of consumption of nicotine products (Khainy, Gutkha etc) by the respondents. Out of (42%) of the users among the student youth respondents, (2%) stated that they started it six months back followed by (26%) since one year.

Table 15.10: Frequency of Consumption Of Nicotine Products

Frequency of Consumption	Student Youth (n=100)	Non-student Youth (n=100)
Once in a day	6.0	3.0
Three times a day	12.0	30.0
Often	19.0	38.0
Not sure	5.0	5.0
Not Applicable	58.0	24.0

From the above table 15.10, as it can be seen that a nineteen per cent of student youth consume them often while (12%) reported that they take three times a day.

Non-student youth top the data with an alarming majority of (38%) out of a total (76%) reported to have been using nicotine products often.

Alcohol Consumption

Table 10.11: Age-Wise of Alcohol Intake

Age (in years)	Student Youth (n=100)	Non-student Youth (n=100)
< 17	4.0	18.0
17-20	25.0	23.0
> 20	3.0	55.0
Don't drink	68.0	4.0

From the above table 10.11, it is learnt that one-fourth of the student youth respondents of the sample started taking alcohol between the ages of 17 and 20 while more than half of the non-student youth respondents stated that they started taking alcohol when they attained 20 years and after.

Table 15.12: Reasons for Consuming Alcohol

Reasons of Consuming Alcohol	Student Youth* (n=100)	Non-student Youth* (n=100)
Love Failure	9.0	32.0
Domestic Problems	2.0	36.0
Peer Pressure	20.0	49.0
Frustration	4.0	29.0
Not Applicable	68.0	4.0

From the above table 15.12, it is found that the reasons for getting addicted to the habit of taking alcohol were mainly due to peer pressure in both the categories.

Drugs

Table 15.13: Age at which Drugs Used

Age of Drug Users	Student Youth (n=100)	Non-student Youth (n=100)
Before Twenties	26.0	16.0
After Twenties	74.0	84.0

From the above table 15.13, it is stated that a nearly three-fourths of the sample of student youth respondents and more than four-fifths of the non-student youth took drugs after they attained twenty years.

Table 15.14: Frequency of Usage of Drugs

Frequency of Usage of Drugs	Student Youth (n=100)	Non-student Youth (n=100)
Daily Once	56.0	25.0
Daily 2 or 3 Times	44.0	75.0

From the above table 15.14, it is found that the student youth respondents (56%) take drugs at least once in a day.

Table 15.15: Reasons Associated Usage of Drugs

Associate Person	Student Youth (n=100)	Non-student Youth (n=100)
Relatives	2.0	34.0
Siblings	4.0	10.0
Friends	90.0	89.0
Alone	9.0	23.0

From the above table 15.15, it can be observe that most of the respondents in both the categories associate themselves with their friends, while using drug.

Table 15.16: Place at which Drugs are taken

Place where Drugs are taken	Student Youth* (n=100)	Non-student Youth* (n=100)
At Lonely Places	62.0	74.0
Pubs	28.0	10.0
At Friends' Room	72.0	65.0
In And Around Grave Yards	40.0	41.0

From the above table 15.16 it is found that the student youth respondents take drugs in friend's room (72%) and lonely places (62%). On the other, the places used for non-student youth respondents were lonely areas (74%), friends' room (65%); grave yards (41%) and Pubs (10%).

Table 15.17: Uses of Sharing Needles to Inject Drugs

Usage of Sharing Needles	Student Youth (n=100)	Non-student Youth (n=100)
Sometimes	0	17.0
Never	100	83.0

From the above table 15.17, it is found that a majority of the non-student youth respondents (17%) were found to have used needles or syringes used by others.

Table 15.18: Dangers by Driving under Drug Influence

Danger by Driving	Student Youth (n=100)	Non-student Youth (n=100)
Yes	58.0	33.0
No	42.0	67.0

The table 15.18, shows that more than half of the student youth respondents (58%) and (33%) of the non-student youth respondents created problems to themselves/others with their driving under drug influence.

Major Findings and Recommendations

This life is a precious gift anyone can get but only once. Therefore, it should be properly utilized to make the maximum benefit – for oneself and for society. As the maxim 'Health is wealth' exhorts, being healthy is the greatest wealth one can possess in this world.

1. There will be a sound mind in a sound body. Keeping oneself spiritually, mentally and physically fit is the secret of one's success.
2. Once one gets access to substances beyond the prescribed limit by way of medication.
3. The use of cough syrup by youth as an alternative to alcohol is on the rise due to its easy availability.
4. Liquid substance like cough syrup, injections like morphine, phidine, fortwin etc are Schedule drugs and cannot be sold over the counter without a proper prescription.
5. Doctors should also clearly indicate the number of bottles/ampoules that can be given to a patient and chemists should make a note on the prescription at the time of issuing the drugs. This would prevent the misuse of the drugs to some extent.
6. There must be greater awareness among the people about the dangers of using habit-forming prescription drugs. People with very bad habits die-hard and relying on drugs for 'temporary relief' can prove to be a costly bet for youth.
7. Treatment and rehabilitation are essential components of demand reduction. They should be seen as a means to help persons overcome addiction and not a form of punishment.
8. Research has indicated that treatment, carried out under proper conditions, does change behaviour, in which it occurs (community-based, clinic, workplace, prison or other) may be less important than the skills of persons involved, the processes used and the type of treatment.
9. In planning to prevent relapse, many services are needed, including rehabilitation, community services and active follow-up.

It is noted that successful programmes require qualified staff, constant management, adequate resources, and the flexibility to adapt to changing circumstances. Hundreds of psychotherapy outcome studies have demonstrated that people successfully change with the help of professional treatment. Similar results are found in the literature on addictive behaviours. ... These studies demonstrate that intentional modification of addictive behaviours occurs both with and without expert assistance.

REFERENCES

Ahmad Nadeem, Bano Rubeena, Agarwal V.K., Kalakoti Piyush. (2009). "Substance Abuse in India". Pravara Medical Review 4, (4).

Ahmed, S. (1982). Trends in Abuse of Narcotic Drugs and Resulting health Hazards. International Conference on Demand and Supply of Opiates in Pakstan, (pp. 5-14). Pakistan.

Andrew Cherry, Mary E. Dillon and Douglas Rugh (Eds.). (2002). Substance Abuse: A Global View. Westport: Greenwood Press.

Bajerot. (1977). "The Nature of addiction" In Drug dependence: Current and Social Issue Problems.

Bansal Raj, K and Banerjee, S. (1993). Substance Use by Child Labourers in Surat City. The Indian Journal of Psychiatry 35, (3): pp. 159-161.

Centre on Addiction and Substance Abuse. (1994). The Cost of Substance Abuse to American's Health Care System. Report 2: Columbia University Medicare Hospital Costs.

Charles L. Winek (1974). Everything You Wanted to Know About Drug Abuse...but were Afraid to ask. New York: Marcel Dekker Inc.

Denise Kandel, (1973). "Adolescent Marijuana use: Role of Parents and Peers", Science 181: 1067-1081.

Don Des Girls, and Samuel Friedman, (1994). "AIDS and the use of Injected Drugs", Scientific American, February.

Douglas Anglin. M and George Speckard, (1988). "Narcotics Use and Crime: A Multi Sample, Multimethod Analysis", Criminology, 26, (2).

Gerry V. Stimson, (1992). "The Global Diffusion of Injecting Drug Use: Implications for HIV Infection", London Presentation for VIII International Conference on AIDS/III-STD World Congress, 22, July.

Gupta R, Narang R.L, Verma, S, Panda, J.K, Garg, D, Munjal, A, Gupta KR, Gupta A, Kumar A, and Singh S. (1989). Drug Abuse Among Non-Student Youth Labour in Ludhiana. The Indian Journal of Psychiatry. 29, (4), pp. 559-362.

Juyal. Ret al. (2006). "Substance Use Among Inter College Students in District Dehradun". Indian Journal of Community Medicine. 31, (4), October-December.

Khokhar A. (2008). "A Study on Substance Abuse Among Women from an Urban Locality of Delhi". Indmedica 5, (5) (2008-11 - 2008-12).

Knight JR, Wechsler H, Kuo M, Seibring M, Weitzman ER, (2002). "Alcohol Abuse and Dependence Among U.S.College Students". Journal of Studies on Alcohol, Published by Harvard Medical School Vol. 63, (3), pp. 263-270.

SECTION – IV

TRIBAL EDUCATION AND EMPOWERMENT

16

Tribal Education and Their Empowerment in Tamil Nadu

– K.Nachimuthu

Introduction

India is a welfare State, committed to the welfare and development of its people and of vulnerable sections in particular. The preamble, Directive Principles of State Policy, Fundamental Rights and specific sections, viz., Articles 38, 39 and 46 in the Constitution of India, stand testimony to the commitment of the State to its people. Socially disadvantaged groups of Scheduled Castes/Scheduled Tribes have received special focus over the years for their social and economic advancement. Government has taken several steps for framing appropriate policies needed to design and implement various welfare programmes for achieving the objective of creating favourable environment to ensure speedy socio economic development of SCs/STs. For the well being of these communities, special target-oriented programmes are being implemented by earmarking funds, providing subsidies, offering reservations in employment and educational institutions etc.

There are as many as 573 tribes and sub tribes in India. They have been broadly classified into different classes, groups depending upon their present state of development and factors namely, mode of living in forest, shifting villages, forest villages, community villages and revenue villages. They have got a heterogeneous cultural pattern with variegated economic condition and activities largely based on ecological settings and ethnic environment. The basic economic activities of the tribal's may be classified under the following heads:

1. Food gathering;
2. Pastoral;
3. Shifting hill cultivation;
4. Handicrafts;
5. Cultivation;
6. Trade and Commerce; and
7. Labour.

According to the 1991 Census, the population of Scheduled Castes in Tamil Nadu was 107.12 lakhs, constituting 19.18 per cent of the total population. The Scheduled Tribes numbering 5.74 lakhs constitute 1.03 per cent of the total population. The major ameliorative activities for these communities are grouped as educational development, economic development, housing and other schemes, Special Component Plan and Tribal Sub Plan.

The implementation of the Special Component Plan (SCP) for Scheduled Castes and the Tribal Sub Plan (TSP) for Scheduled Tribes has received special attention since their inception, as these programmes are effective instruments to ensure proportionate flow of funds for SCs and STs from other general development sectors.

Literacy Rate of SC/ST

As per 2001 census the literacy rate Scheduled Castes and Scheduled Tribes was 54.69 per cent and 47.10 per cent respectively. Literacy rate of SC females compared to general population was much lower in the states of Bihar (15.58%), Jharkhand (22.55%), Uttar Pradesh (30.50%) and Rajasthan (33.87%). Literacy rate of ST females is extremely low in Bihar

(15.54%). As per 2001 census the literacy rate was lowest for SCs in Bihar (28.47%) and highest in Mizoram (89.20%) and for STs it was lowest in Bihar (28.17%) and highest in Mizoram (89.34%). Literacy rate of STs was more than the SCs in the states of Jharkhand, Meghalaya, Mizoram and Sikkim and in general the SCs were ahead of the STs in literacy. But in urban areas the STs are ahead of SCs. The percentage of learners of SCs and STs under literacy Campaigns are 23 per cent and 12 per cent respectively. The share of expenditure in implementation of literacy campaigns between the centre and states in tribal areas is 4:1 instead 2:1 in other area.

Scheduled Tribes of Tamil Nadu

The growth rate of ST population in the decade 1991-2001 at 13.4 per cent is higher than the overall growth rate of 11.7 per cent of the state. As per the 2001 Census, among the numerically large STs, Kurumans have reported the highest growth rate of 43 per cent, followed by Malayali (24.2%), Irular (12.1%) and Kattunayakan (5.8%). The overall sex ratio of the ST population in Tamil Nadu is 980 females per 1000 males, which has recorded improvement from 960 in 1991 Census. Among the district, Thanavur has recorded the highest sex ratio of the ST population (1054) and Perambalur the lowest (936). Majority of the ST population of the state are Hindus (99.2 per cent). There are only 3,497 (0.5 per cent) Christians and 453 (0.1 per cent) Muslims ST populations in the state.

Literacy and Educational Level of STs

Literacy and level of education are two basic indicators of the level of development achieved by a group/society as literacy results in more awareness besides contributing to the overall improvement of health, hygiene and other social conditions. According to 2001 Census, percentage of ST literate (those who can read and write with understanding) persons aged 7 years and above is 41.5 per cent in the state, which is lower than 73.5 per cent reported for the state as a whole. The literacy rate (41.5 per cent) has however increased from 27.9 per cent recorded in 1991 Census.

Scheduled Castes of Tamil Nadu

The growth rate of SC population in the decade 1991-2001 at 10.7 per cent is lower in comparison to the overall growth rate of 11.7 per cent of the state. Among major SCs, Paraiyan have recorded the highest growth rate of 38.6 per cent, followed by Arunthathiyar (33.2%) and Pallan (18.5%) during 1991-2001. The overall sex ratio of the SC population in Tamil Nadu is 999 females per 1000 males, which is higher than the national average of 936 for the SC population in 2001. The sex ratio of SC population has registered improvement over 978 reported in 1991 Census. Among the districts the highest sex ratio (1059), is recorded in Tirunelveli district and the lowest in Salem district (947). At the individual caste level, all the major SCs, except Pallan and Paraiyan, have registered overall lower sex ratio as compared to the state average.

Literacy and Educational Level of SCs

Literacy and level of education are two basic indicators of the level of development achieved by a group/society. Literacy results in more awareness besides contributing to the overall improvement of health, hygiene and other social conditions. According to 2001 Census, percentage of SC literate persons (those who can read and write with understanding) aged 7 years and above is 63.2 per cent, which is lower than 73.5 per cent reported for the state as a whole. The literacy data show that the SC population of the state has made significant improvement during the decade 1991-2001. The literacy rate, which was 46.7 per cent in 1991, has increased by 16.5 percentage points in 2001.

Schemes in Tamil Nadu

1. Land purchase scheme
2. Self help group - economic activity assistance
3. Self help group - revolving fund assistance
4. Financial assistance to individual beneficiaries
5. Collector's discretionary fund scheme
6. Self employment programme for youth(SEPY)
7. Vocational training programme

8. Entrepreneurship development programme (EDP) for self help group members

Social Welfare Department

As Per Tamilnadu Government Order No.1773, dated on 23.06.1984 referred the G.O numbers 709, Social Welfare dated the 7th October 1977 and the Government Memo No.65226/HW.VIII/77-3, Social Welfare, dated the 2nd November 1977 there are 36 SC and 76 ST communities are available in Tamilnadu. In order to improve the living conditions of Scheduled Castes/Scheduled Tribes by improving the income earning capacities through Income Generating Programme and improving human skills through training programmes, TAHDCO provides financial assistance to both the programmes.

TAHDCO schemes have been decentralized and formulated at the district level for the economic development of Scheduled Caste and Scheduled Tribes under the dynamic leadership of District Collectors, in the form of District Action Plans in accordance with the local needs, local potential and availability of resources. The amount for this plan is allocated to the districts based on Scheduled Castes/Scheduled Tribes population, so as to ensure that there is no unbalance and there is rational distribution of selection of beneficiaries throughout the state.

All the schemes in the District Action Plans have categorized into the following nine activities for the purpose of monitoring. They are: *(i)* Land Purchase Scheme; *(ii)* Agricultural Activities including Land Purchase Scheme; *(iii)* Agricultural Allied Activities; *(iv)* Mining and Quarrying; *(v)* Manufacturing/Processing/Services/Repairs; *(vi)* Construction Activities; *(vii)* Trade and Commerce; *(viii)* Transport, Storage and Communication; and *(ix)* Other services.

National Schemes

TAHDCO acts as a State Channelizing Agency in implementing the National Schemes of the Ministry of Social Justice and Empowerment, Govt. of India. The Schemes are

1. National Scheduled Caste Finance & Development Corporation Scheme (NSFDC)
2. National Scheduled Tribes Finance & Development Corporation Scheme (NSTFDC)
3. National Safari Karamacharis Finance & Development Corporation (NSKFDC)
4. National Scheme for Liberation & Rehabilitation of Scavengers & Dependents (NSLRS) Scheme

Many tribal youth, after their school final education finds it difficult to pursue their higher education for want of the right guidance and finance. Tamilnadu Tribal Welfare Association (TWA) takes effort in helping them choose the right course, assisting them in admissions and also by giving them educational loans and scholarships. There are instances where a tribal girl has been helped to undergo nursing course and also of a tribal student who with the assistance of TWA completed his MBBS course. It is a pride for the tribal community that a tribal boy could join medical college and complete his course with the assistance of TWA. TWA also offers legal assistance whenever required for the tribal community.

Education for All

'Sarva Shiksha Abhiyan' - "Education for All" scheme is sometimes referred to as "each one, teach one". The aim of Sarva Shiksha Abhiyan is to provide useful and efficient elementary education to all children in the age group of 6 to 10 by 2010. There is also another goal to bridge the social, regional and gender gaps with the active participation of all the communities in the management of schools. Interesting news which caught my eye on January 16th, 2010 was "Human Resource Department's internal appraisals of 'Sarva Shiksha Abhiyan' showing most of its physical target's for 2009-10 are set to be fully achieved." – With 85 per cent schools opened of set target, 78 per cent teachers, 92 per cent schools with drinking water, providing free textbooks to 92 per cent school students.

Education

Literacy status is one of the key indicators of socio-economic development and the relative employment opportunities largely depend on the level of education. At present 1017 ADW schools and 247 Tribal Residential Schools are run mainly for the benefit of these communities. Totally 2,23,762 Children are studying in AD schools and 38,656 children in Tribal Residential Schools. Out of 1017 ADW schools, 29 schools are still in rented buildings and out of 247 GTR schools, 37 are in rented buildings. Though nearly 70 per cent of the total allocation has been spent on educational development, the literacy level of the Scheduled Castes (46.74%) and Scheduled Tribes (27.89%) was less than the overall literacy level (62.66%). The difference in female literacy level (for SC 34.81 per cent and for Tribals 20.23%) is still more pronounced.

The pass percentage in X and XII standards in Adi dravida (AD) Welfare schools was 57 per cent and 73 per cent in 1997-98 and during 2000-01 it was 54 per cent and 59 per cent respectively. Hence major thrust was laid on educational schemes and specific measures were taken to improve the quality of education in AD and Tribal schools. Special coaching was given to the entire X and XII Std students, special guides were prepared and distributed to them so that they could perform well in the public examination. Special training was imparted through the Department of Teachers Education Research and Training (DTERT) to the teachers working in Adi Dravidar and Tribal schools by using modern methods of teaching and new techniques. Secondary grade teachers training programme was started since 1997-98 in 17 DIET centres exclusively for Adi-dravidars and Tribals. So far, 850 students including 85 tribal students had undergone training and the first batch completed two years course in 1999.

Besides sanction of regular educational concessions, the other measures taken include strengthening of infrastructural facilities like construction of school buildings, additional classrooms, laboratory buildings, provision of lab equipments, computers, furniture and play materials, up gradation of schools at all levels, opening of residential schools, construction of vocational training centres, provision of basic amenities like toilets, drinking water etc. So far 92 high/higher secondary ADW schools and 11 GTR high/higher secondary schools were provided with computer facilities. Computer education was introduced in 87 high/higher secondary schools and computer training was imparted to the teachers in high and higher secondary schools.

With a view to ensuring 100 per cent enrolment and reducing the dropout rates among girls, an incentive of Rs. 500/- at the rate of Rs. 50/- per month for 10 months for 60,000 girl students studying in III to V was provided in the educationally backward districts. Similarly to encourage their continuous schooling, an incentive of Rs. 1000/- at the rate of Rs. 100/- p.m. was provided to 30,000 girls entering VI Std., in the entire State. In order to encourage girl students for pursuing higher studies, free bicycles were provided to all SCs/STs/SC converts studying in XI and XII standards in Government/aided schools. Free education programme up to post graduation level for SC/ST girl students was introduced.

Special Area Programme for Rural Development

Most of the schemes implemented by Rural Development Department have separate allocations to provide basic amenities in the habitations of Adi-dravidar/Tribal communities. These schemes also envisage the upliftment of the socio-economic conditions of the rural Adidravidar/Tribal Communities. The schemes implemented for the welfare of the Adi-dravidar/Tribal communities are:

(a) Swarna Jayanthi Gram Swarozgar Yojana (SGSY)
(b) Indira Awaas Yojana (IAY)
(c) Sampoorna Grameen Rojgar Yojana (SGRY)
(d) Restructured Central Rural Sanitation Programme (RCRSP)

The biggest mistake in the tribal development planning in India has been the clubbing together of all tribes, as if they constitute a homogenous cultural group. Nothing can be farther from the truth. The scheduled tribes (ST) exhibit a whole spectrum of human and cultural evolution – from hunter-gatherer-fisher (foragers) through shifting cultivation, pastoralism, marginal farming, to agriculture based on irrigation. It is naïve to think that they all have similar problems and that same or similar development or welfare schemes will be useful to them all equally.

Conclusion

Unless the forces of destabilization are checked and corrective measures applied, the provision of social and economic services will not have any significance. The levels of socio-economic development vary considerably between nontribal and tribal population, between one tribe and another tribe and even among different sub-groups of a tribal group. The disparities and diversities make tribal development and micro level planning for tribal's at grass root level imperative.

Everywhere in the country the tribes show a great variation in the economic, social, political, educational, and health spheres. They are also subject to differential treatment from the government, NGOs and social scientists. As a consequence they have differential opportunities of development which affects their probability of survival in the present circumstances – the probabilities and circumstances that are not natural but man-made. It is important, therefore, to reclassify the Indian tribes, and institute new perspective and strategy for tribal development.

Both Central and State Governments and NGOs take continuous efforts to improve their way of life by providing basic infrastructural facilities such as educational institutions, health care facilities, laying roads, building houses and co-operative societies. Awareness camps, medical camps and training camps are frequently organized. Women empowerment is also aimed through starting of Self Help Groups by providing micro credit. Though these activities are continuing since 1951, yet these have not achieved major goals. It is pointing towards the inefficiency in the current trend, which needs a re-thinking, a different strategy for tribal development.

REFERENCES

Mohan, G. and Stokke. K. 2000. *Participatory Development and Empowerment: the Dangers of Localism in Third World Quarterly,* Vol. 21., No. 2., pp. 247-268.

Nachimuthu, K & Vijayakumari, G (2007) Development and Welfare Programmes: Role of Universities and NGO's, Universities and NGO's, Discovery Publishers, New Delhi, pp. 200-207.

Om Mehta (1976). Tribal Development: The New Strategy, Government of India, New Delhi, 1976, p. 2.

Pradip Kumar Singh (2004) Tribal Development in India: What went Wrong?, Journal of Social Research, Department of Anthropology, Ranchi., Vol. 26, No. I & II.

Raha, M.K & Coomar, P.C. (1989). Tribal India: Problems Development Prospect, Vol. II, Gian Publishing House, New Delhi, 1989, p. 90.

Tamil Nadu Goverenment Website Publications. (2012), SC and STs of Tamil Nadu, http:// www. tn.gov.in.

Watts, M. J. 1993. Development I: Power, Knowledge, Discursive Practice in *Progress in Human Geography,* Vol. 17., No. 2., pp. 257-272.

17

The Role of NGO's in Tribal Education in India

– G.Sundharavadivel

Introduction

The non-governmental or the voluntary organisations have been playing a crucial role in all the socio-economic spheres, including that of the tribal peoples, in India. At one level, they can be termed as the 'means' by which the nation makes optimum use of its human resources. However, the mushrooming of voluntary organisations working in the field of rural development in recent years has generated widespread debate about their role, structure, programmes and performance.

A unique feature of voluntary organisations is that they stimulate voluntary action among the target community and involve the progressive elements of that community. In the present context of human resource development, voluntary organisations, in their functioning, have demonstrated the freedom and flexibility of working with a personal touch, a capacity for initiative and experimentation with novel programmes. Thus, voluntary organisations exercise full freedom in selecting localities for programme implementation and are free of bureaucratic hassles. In the Indian context, the attributes of a tribe are that they live in relative isolation of hills and covered forests, and often in geographical areas inaccessible to the mainstream population. Tribes generally are groups without a written letter or script. Their sense of history is shallow or mixed with mythology, and in terms of their cultural ethos, language, customs, institutions and beliefs, they stand out from other sections of society.

In India, tribes have different names such as vanyajati, vanavasi, pahariya, adimajati, janajati, anusuchit jati and scheduled tribes — all of which mean the 'aboriginal'. India stands second in terms of tribal population after Africa in the world. According to the 2001 Census, the total population of the tribal's is 84.2 million, and accounts for 8.2 per cent of the country's population. There are about 689 scheduled tribes speaking about 105 languages and 225 subsidiary languages. They have traditionally lived in about 15 per cent of the nation's geographical area, mainly forests, hills and the undulating inaccessible terrain in plateau areas that are rich in natural resources. They have lived mostly as isolated entities for centuries together and this explains their politico-socio-economic backwardness.

However, we have to acknowledge that even before the freedom struggle a few voluntary organisations were active in the sphere of tribal welfare. They also played a significant role in the field of rural development and nation building and continued to do so. Many great personalities took initiatives to form such organisations, which at present, are performing a key role at the grassroots level in implementing various developmental works. Until such time that a genuinely democratic machinery of governance evolves, there will remain a strong urge for voluntary organisations to play a mediating role between the State and the people.

As early as 1871, the Bhil Seva Mandal came up in Gujarat. At that time, A.V. Thakkar was the moving spirit behind voluntary organisations committed to tribal development. By the time India got independence, he could establish more than 20 voluntary institutions in different parts of the country. Some other leaders in the Indian National Congress were also involved in tribal development activities. Dr. Rajendra Prasad's Bharatiya Adim Jati Sevak Sangh helped a lot in shaping the tribal policy when the Indian Constitution at the drafting stage. Various approaches have been evolved in the country in the domain of tribal affairs; prominent among them are the voluntary agency approach, the political approach and the anthropological approach. These three approaches find support in three important policies:

1. Policy of Isolation;
2. Policy of Assimilation; and
3. Policy of Integration.

After Independence, the policy of integration was found to be the most suitable one. Also, Nehru's concept of tribal integration was reflected in the successive five-year plans. The policy of integration is the outcome of serious research activities undertaken by many social anthropologists in India. Its main objective is 'social integration and cultural assimilation'. It was in the fifth five-year plan that the tribal sub-plan (TSP) approach was adopted. In order to fulfill the sub-plan objectives nearly 198 ITDAs and 257 MADA pocket, 78 clusters and 75 micro projects for primitive tribal groups (PTGs) were set up all over the country. Consequently, various strategies came into being. With the passage of time, it has widely been noted that the programmes and activities related to tribal development cannot be implemented by the governments alone. Thus, the significance of participation of the community and the role of voluntary organisations/NGOs was realized in this all-important sphere.

Objectives

- To study the role of NGO's/voluntary organisations in tribal development.
- To study the budgetary allocations for tribal welfare.

- To analyze the amount spent for various developmental programmes like vocational training centres and literacy programmes.
- To study the tribal participation in the NGO sector.

Methodology

The present study used the literature available in different tribal welfare departments, government of India source on tribal welfare, its budgetary allocation and their analysis. A detailed analysis was made using budgetary allocations and their expenditure on the literacy rate improvement, vocational training and other welfare activities. An interpretation was made from the financial year 2001-02 to 2006-07 on the different developmental programmes.

Voluntary Organisations are Necessary

A voluntary organisation can easily adapt itself to the needs of the people. A sensitive worker can assess each specific situation with sympathy and personal care. Thus, the gulf that arises between what should be done and what is being done as a result of some what inflexible operation of the administrative apparatus, can be bridged.

Objectives of NGOs/Voluntary Organisations

Whatever the nature of NGOs/voluntary organisations, they play a key role in the upliftment of the weaker sections of society. The objectives of voluntary or non-governmental agencies include some or all of the following:

- To create an awareness regarding participation in socio-economic development
- To create an able and efficient local leadership
- To assist in the planned efforts to create socio-economic infrastructural facilities
- To facilitate the process of expanding employment opportunities
- To induce appropriate persons to set up small scale productions and
- To make the tribal's give up the pre-agricultural technology and seek better education.

Role of NGOs/Voluntary Organisations

NGOs/voluntary organisations have a long history of active involvement in the promotion of human welfare and development. They come up with a mission to serve a human cause, spontaneously-voluntarily and without any compulsion or control, to fulfill certain needs of specific groups of people. These organisations are flexible and possess the virtue of humanitarian service with concern. Voluntary action is the soul of social action as this medium secures active involvement of the people from policy making to implementation of programmes. Their activities cover a diverse range of functions in the welfare sector. The programmes of voluntary organisations are strictly service-oriented, professional in nature and specialized in functions. The essential feature of voluntary action is that it fixes the problem. It starts to not only to solve a problem but also to prevent the occurrence of it. Voluntary action, thus, ultimately aims at creating a situation conducive to the development of potentialities in individuals, groups and communities so they can find solutions to their problems and realise their ultimate goals.

Regarding the role and nature of voluntary organisations, there appears to be two different views. Some are happy with the functioning of such organisations and plead for their increasing role. According to them, these organisations should be given ample scope to serve people. For, the government agencies, crippled as they are with bureaucratic complications and rigidity, have failed to work satisfactorily. Others hold that it is undesirable to give undue importance and authority to voluntary agencies as there is a great possibility of institutionalizing the chances.

In this context, the suggestion is that the voluntary organisations should be given ample scope to work in collaboration and co-operation with the government agencies and subject to strict government scrutiny and monitoring. The need for involving the NGOs in rural development was highlighted and acknowledged by various official committees set up by the Government of India. One of these was the

Balwant Rai Mehta Committee (1957) which in its report emphasized that during the implementation of community development schemes more and more emphasis should be laid on NGO's/VOs. The Dhebar Commission in its report on the scheduled areas and Scheduled Tribes opined that the principle of active and purposeful participation of people at all levels could best be served by assigning an important role to non-official organisations. It is necessary in any democratic framework to take up some of the nation-building activities under non-official auspices.

The report of the committee on Panchayat Raj Institutions (1973) appreciated the role of voluntary organisations in the development of rural and interior areas. The committee reiterated that these organisations could be particularly involved in conceiving projects and schemes. They can be of great help in creating strong public opinion in support of measures of social change. The Sivaraman Committee set up by the Government of India also recommended involvement of voluntary organisations in planning and implementation of the integrated rural development programmes. Thus, there exists a widespread agreement among all the concerned that voluntary organisations have an important role to play in the overall development of the rural areas.

Grant-in-Aid to Voluntary Organisations for the Welfare of the Scheduled Tribes

The Ministry of Tribal Affairs is the key governmental agency with respect to the welfare and development of the tribal peoples all over the country. It is the responsibility of the ministry to reach the target groups, particularly the tribals living in remote and inaccessible areas. The objective is to bring them into the mainstream of development by assisting them to overcome their social, psychological and educational backwardness. Capacity building is the key factor here. Such training would equip them to employ their capabilities to their fullest potential thereby reducing their reliance on others and achieving self-sustenance to the maximum extent possible – which is the ultimate goal of the government.

The NGOs supplement the efforts of the State in ensuring that the benefits reach the maximum number of people. In certain cases, voluntary organisations are in a better position to implement the governmental schemes in a more efficient manner than the administrative machinery. This is primarily attributable to the highly committed and dedicated human resources that are available with the voluntary organisations. The role of NGOs was in the reckoning since the first five-year plan. Many organisations have done commendable job in tribal areas and are still active. Since the last two decades, there has been an exponential growth in the number of NGO/VOs approaching the ministry of tribal affairs for financial assistance.

It has been felt that along with few very dedicated and committed voluntary organisations/non-governmental organisations a large number of other organisations have also come up that want to grab public funds for their narrow and selfish interests. The ministry would take all the possible steps to curb the entry of such voluntary organisations/non–governmental organisations in the field of tribal welfare. The Ministry of Tribal Affairs feels that some organisations solely depend on aid from the government. This situation has to change. The voluntary organisations should aim to expand their effort on the support from the government and thereafter establish other support systems that could free them from financial constraints.

It should be the intention of the organisations to obtain support of other sources for their work. This can happen after they establish themselves with the support of the government and prove their usefulness to society, at large. If the impression that NGOs can support themselves financially gains ground, then the support of corporate houses and even the community would follow as a natural consequence. Contribution, both in kind and cash, would come easily once their credentials are firmly established. Additional resources, if necessary, could also be mobilised. Voluntary organisations should make all possible efforts to involve the community in their work.

Community participation helps in building confidence among the people and in providing feedback for further improvement and reorientation of the programmes. Thus, the long-term interests of the tribal communities can be served. The Ministry of Tribal Affairs endeavors to provide full advantage of all schemes to the non-governmental organisations/voluntary organisations that have absolute credentials in the field of tribal welfare. It also wants to promote new groups with brilliant ideas and new strategies for the speedy development of the targeted people.

It has been the constant endeavor of the ministry to identify the voluntary organisations/non-governmental organisations which have an all India character and known for their selfless service and facilitate them with some preferential treatment with regard to sanction of new proposals and relaxation of certain norms and conditions relating to release of annual grants. In this direction, the ministry has identified a few such organisations and categorized them as "Established Voluntaries Agencies (EVAs)"

The following organisations have been identified as the EVAs by the ministry:

- Ram Krishna Mission and its affiliated organisations
- Akhil Bharatiya Banavasi Kalyan Ashram
- Bharat Sevashram Sangh and its affiliates
- Bharatiya Adim Jati Sevak Sangh
- Seva Bharati & its affiliated organisations
- Vidya Bharati and its affiliated organisations
- Swami Vivekanand Youth Movement

Schemes in the Voluntary Sector

There are three on-going schemes with the ministry, which are open to participation of the voluntary and non-governmental organisations. The schemes are:

- Grant–in–aid to voluntary organisations working for welfare of scheduled tribes (GVWST).

- Educational complex in low literacy pockets for the development of women's literacy in tribal areas (ECLP)
- Vocational training centers (VTC)

In addition to the said schemes, the ministry has an exclusive programme for non-governmental organisations with regard to the development of primitive tribal groups (PTGs)

Scheme of grant-in-aid to voluntary organisations working for the welfare of the scheduled tribes (GVWST)

Objective: The prime objective of the scheme is to provide for an overall improvement and development of the target group i.e., the scheduled tribes though voluntary efforts in the fields of education, health & sanitation, environment, drinking water and legal services as well as the need-based socio-economic upliftment efforts. It also supports other relevant activity deemed appropriate and having a direct impact on the target group. The scheme is under implementation since 1953-54.

Salient features: The grants are provided to the non-governmental organisations on their application in prescribed formats, in the form of supporting projects that meet the objectives of the scheme. The NGO's are required to maintain separate accounts in respect of the grants released to them, which are open for inspection by all appropriate officers/ agencies of the government. The NGO is also required to maintain separate accounts of Grant-in-Aid audited by the Government Auditor or a Registered Chartered Accountant and submit complete set of copies of Audited Statement of Accounts as prescribed by the Ministry. The grants are generally made in two installments every year subject to satisfactory performance of the NGO. Activities of the NGOs are monitored as per the established provisions of the Financial Rules besides field inspection by the Ministry or the State Government officials or by any other agency designated by the Ministry.

Funding Pattern: Funds are granted – to the extent of 100 per cent – directly to the Non-Governmental

Organisations working in the Scheduled Areas based on the recommendations of the State Governments and the Union Territories. The non-governmental organisations are supported to the extent of 90 per cent of the project cost for projects in areas other than Scheduled Areas. However, the Ministry of Tribal Affairs has the discretion to assist even up to hundred per cent.

Schemes of Educational Complex in Low Literacy Pockets

The Scheme was introduced in 1993-94 in 136 districts with less than 10 per cent literacy rate among tribal women. It is being implemented through:

- Non-Governmental Organisations
- Institutions set up by the Government as Autonomous Bodies and
- Registered Co-operative Societies.

Objectives: The primary objective of the scheme is the promotion of education among tribal girls in the targeted districts of the country. The secondary objective is to improve the socio-economic status of the economically backwards and the illiterate tribal masses.

Coverage: The scheme covers 136 districts with less than 10 per cent literacy among ST women spread over 14 States namely Andhra Pradesh, Bihar, Chattisgarh, Gujarat, Jharkhand, Madhya Pradesh, Orissa, Rajasthan, Tamil Nadu, Uttar Pradesh, Uttaranchal and West Bengal.

Procedure for Release of Grant-in-aid and Funding Pattern

The extent of assistance under the scheme would be 100 per cent in all cases.

- In the event of the Ministry of Welfare itself executing any element of the programme i.e. engagement of consultants, for project formulation, monitoring and evaluation, as well as expenses towards cost of training of NGO functionaries, etc, full cost shall be borne from the budgetary provision of the scheme.
- Under the programme, while predefined cost heads are stipulated at the project formulation stage, each

implementing agency shall submit a detailed project proposal clearly bringing out the programme modalities and individual expenditure heads. Ministry of Welfare while approving the project shall indicate the extent of support to the project as a whole as well as to each component of the project against which re-appropriation to the extent 20 per cent of the total grant shall be permissible.

Salient Feature: Educational complexes can be set up in rural areas in the notified districts and can have classes up to V with provision for up-gradation up to Class XII provided they have sufficient accommodation for classrooms, hostels, kitchen, and garden and for sporting facilities. These educational complexes impart not only formal education to tribal girls but also train students in agriculture, animal husbandry and other vocations and crafts as to make them skilled for leading a better life. The teaching from classes I to III is imparted in tribal dialects of the area and women with proficiency in tribal dialect are engaged as teachers. The strength of students for each class is fixed at 30, however a maximum of 10 more students, if available, in the locality are admitted as day scholars.

Establishment of Ashram Schools

The Ashram schools have played an important role in raising the literacy levels of the scheduled Tribes. They provide the necessary environment conductive to learning. The schedule is in operation since 1990-91.

Construction of Girls Hostel for Scheduled Tribes

The main objective of the scheme is to ensure adequate enrolment of scheduled Tribes girls in educational institutions, particularly at the school stage. The scheme of girls' hostels for scheduled tribes has been in operation since the Third Five Year Plan.

Construction of Boys Hostel for Scheduled Tribes

The main objective of the scheme is to ensure adequate enrolment of Scheduled Tribes boys in educational institutions, particularly, at the high school level. The scheme of Boys Hostel for Scheduled Tribes has been in operation since 1989-90 under the Centrally-sponsored scheme of Establishment of Boy's Hostel in Tribal Sub-Plan areas.

Schemes for Primitive Tribal Groups (PTGs)

Objective: There are certain tribal communities that are having low levels of literacy, declining or stagnant population, and pre-agriculture level of technology and are economically backward. There are 75 such groups in 15 States/UTs that have been identified and categorized as the Primitive Tribal Groups (PTGs). Each of these groups is small in number, differentially developed with respect to one another, of remote habitat with poor administrative and infrastructure back up. Therefore, they are in urgent need of support from the government as well as the non-government agencies. Their protection and development at par with other tribal groups has to be accorded utmost priority.

Scope: Such provisions/activities should not be identified only at the central level as they may differ from State to State and within a State from project to project (ITDA). However, funds under the scheme could be used for helping the beneficiaries of the project to cope with extremely adverse situations that threaten their very survival and protect them against various forms of exploitation thereby bringing them to a stage from where they can demand and receive specific assets and services. The activities under the scheme may include measures such as awareness generation and confidence-building, training for skill development of tribal youth, self help groups and provision of services/inputs not covered by any existing scheme. In terms of beneficiaries, the scheme can cover maximum number of the PTGs.

Implementing agency: The scheme will be implemented through integrated tribal development projects (ITDP)/ Integrated Tribal Development agencies (ITDAs), tribal research institutes (TRI) and non governmental organisations having requisite skills and determination. The State government concerned will be responsible for proper execution, implementation, supervision and coordination of the scheme, including selection of NGOs.

Vocational Training Centers

Objectives: There is a great need for vocational training centers in tribal areas where the Left wing extremism is on the rise. Large-scale unemployment has been stoking rebellious tendencies among the tribal youth in such areas. The extremism is manifestation of frustration and lack of faith in the present pattern of development. It is necessary that both the State and Central governments should make efforts to wean away the tribal youth from disruptive activities. Establishing vocational training institutes and creating a wide range of employment opportunities can be the way forward. Non-governmental organisations shall meet the following requirements:

- It is a registered body under an appropriate Act so that it gets a corporate status. A legal personality and a group liability have to be established for its activities.
- It has an appropriate administrative structure and a duly constituted managing/executive committee.
- The aims and objects of the organisations and programmes in fulfillment of those aims and objects are preciously laid down.
- The organisation is initiated and governed by its own members on democratic principles without any external control.

Conclusion

In India, we have a pluralistic society as opposed to a monolithic culture. The voluntary organisations cater to the needs of our cultural plurality. If we would like to avoid concentration of power in the hands of a few, we must retain this multi-ethnic character of a free society and make full use of it. Voluntary organisations can serve as 'power breakers'. Efforts should be made to prepare people for a new kind of society through voluntary work. When the State's resources are limited, voluntary action would bring forth additional resources and cover the areas hitherto uncovered by the State. In view of their flexibility in operation, ability at experimentation and innovation, pioneering spirit and other such qualities, voluntary organisations can continue to work for better standards, better methods and better forms of organisation. There is an argument that at the empirical-existential level voluntary agencies are nothing but the stooges of the ruling elite and the corporate sector, mainly of the capital finance variety. In this new role, voluntary organisations have created a crisis that begs a comprehensive solution.

However, given the circumstances in terms of administrative or governmental reach, especially in the implementation of welfare schemes for the tribal peoples, we for once cannot deny the positive role of the non-governmental organisations. There are many areas yet to blink the state's radar. They are either very remote or inaccessible. In such a situation, the concerned and committed civil society groups have no other alternative but voluntary approach. The role of NGOs in the fields of education, health, sanitation, housing and particularly agriculture has not been a wide ranging one. We shall hope they would expand their area of action.

REFERENCES

Dhebar, Commission Report on Scheduled Areas and Scheduled Tribes, Delhi, 1961.

Dude S.C., "Approaches to Tribal Problems in India, Kitab Mahal, Allahabad, 1968.

Franda, Marcus, Voluntary Associations and Local Development in India: The Janta phase, New Delhi, Young Asia Publications, 1983.

Ghurye G.S., The Scheduled Tribes, 2nd Edition, 1958.

Gore, M.S., 'Relative Roles of State and Voluntary Agencies in the Organisation of Social Services", Proceedings of the Seminar on 'So Administration in Developing Countries', New Delhi, India International Centre, New Delhi, 1964.

Kulkarni, V.M. Voluntary Action in a Developing Society, New Delhi, Indian Institute of Public Administration, 1969.

Methe D.R., "Legal Protection to Tribals and Tribal Development A New Deal for Tribals and Tribal Development" in S.G. Deogaonkar (ed), Problems of Development of Tribal Areas, 1980.

Shah, Ghanshyam and Chaturvedi, H.R. Gandhian Approach to Rural Development: The Valid Experiment, Delhi, Ajanta Book International, 1983.

Verrier Elwin, A New Deal for Tribal India, 1963.

Verghese, B.G., "Voluntary Action: A New Mission for the New Missionaries", Voluntary Action, XIV: 1, January-October, 1977.

Windey, M.A. "A Rural Reconstruction Movement in India" Voluntary Action, XVIII: 3-4 March-April , 1976.

18

Socio-Educational Status of Tribal Students of Yercaud Block in Tamil Nadu

– M. Vetrichelvan
– A. Jahitha Begum

The tribal people are economically the poorest people of India. Majority of them live below the poverty line. The tribal economy is based on agriculture of the crudest type. The innocence, illiteracy and helplessness of the tribals are exploited by the outsiders (Sharma.K Yogendra, 2001). The British policy, in particular, had led to ruthless exploitation of the tribals in various ways as it favoured the zamindars, landlords, money-lender, forest contractors and excise, revenue and police officials. A large number of tribal young men and women are either unemployed or underemployed. They are unhappy for they are not able to get jobs that can keep them occupied throughout the year (Rath Govind Chandra, 2006). They need to be helped in finding secondary source of income by developing animal husbandry, poultry farming, handicrafts, handloom weaving, etc. This study has been undertaken to know the educational status of students in 10 tribal schools of Yercaud Block with the following objectives.

Objectives of the Study

The study was conducted in 10 tribal schools of Yercaud Block with the following objectives:

- To know the Socio Economic Status of the students.
- To identify the Educational Status of the Parents of Tribal students.
- To know the Food Habits of the Tribal Students.
- To find out the Hostel Facilities of the Tribal Students.
- To find the Availability of Teaching Aids and Usage Education. Technology in Class rooms.
- To know the Educational Awareness of the Parents.

Research Questions

- What about the socio-economic status of Tribal students?
- How far the parents of Tribal school students educated?
- What are the food habits of tribal students?
- What are the facilities available in hostel for tribal students?
- What about the availability of teaching aids in the Tribal schools?
- How far the teachers using the equipments of education technology in tribal schools?
- What is the level of educational awareness amount the parents of Tribal students?

Descriptive research studies are designed to obtain pertinent and precise information concerning the current status of phenomena and, whenever possible, to draw valid general conclusions from the facts discovered. They are restricted not only to fact findings but may often result in the formulation of important principles of knowledge and solution of significant problems. Concerning local, state, national and international level issues (Best J.W, 1998).

This present study is a qualitative descriptive study of the school. Totally 56 schools are there and the researcher selected 10 schools only. The researcher personally visited the Tribal schools observed the educational conditions in the Tribal schools. The area of the study is Salem District Yercaud

Taluk of Tamilndau State. The investigator selected any 10 schools by purposive sampling technique.

Variables of the Study

The following are the variables of the study:

1. Socio economic status of students.
2. Educational status of parents.
3. Food habits of tribal students.
4. Hostel facilities.
5. Available the teaching aids.
6. Education technology-uses.
7. Educational awareness of parents.

Instrumentation

In the present study investigator constructed checklist to assess the educational status of students in tribal schools. This study used check list and observation schedule as the tools.

The observation schedule used in the present study was validated with experts opinion.

Data Analysis

In the present study qualitative analysis and percentage analysis were carried out to find the educational status of the tribals students and schools in Yercaud block.

Findings and Discussions

Socio-economic Status of Students

Findings

- 30 per cent of students' socio economics status is good.
- 60 per cent of students' socio economics status is average.
- 10 per cent of students' socio economics status is below average.

Discussion

- The parents whose annual income is above 50000 is good.
- The parents whose annual income is below 50000 is average.

- The parents whose annual income is below 50000 is below average.
- More or less this area peoples economics status middle level.

Bar Chart – 1

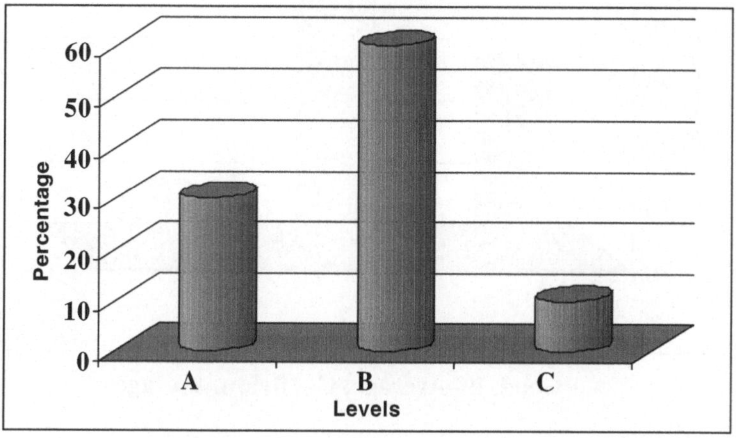

A – Good, B – Average, C – Below Average

Educational Status of Parents

Findings

- 30 per cent of parents education is good.
- 60 per cent of parents education is average.
- 10 per cent of parents education is below average.

Discussion

- Education level of the parents degree and above is good.
- Education level of above school level is average.
- Illiterate people are coming under below average.
- Most of the Parents of Tribal students studied upto 5th standard.
- 10 per cent of the parents are uneducated.
  Food Habits of Tribal Students

Bar Chart – 2

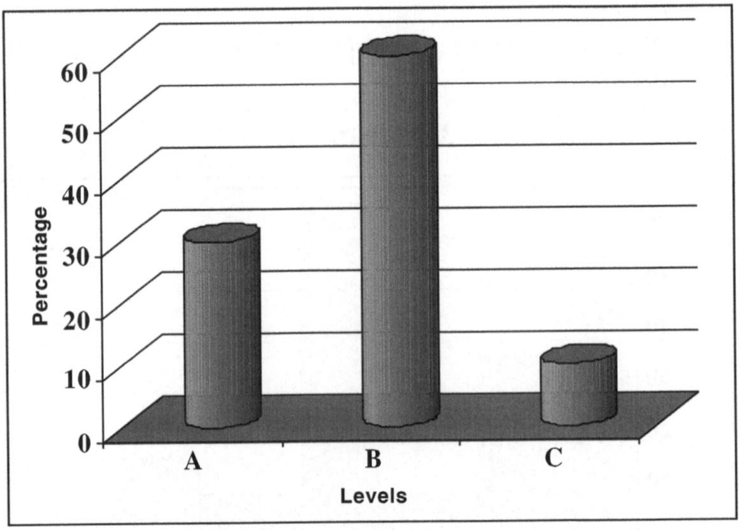

A – Good, B –Average, C – Below Average

Findings

- 10 per cent students have good food habits.
- 70 per cent students have average food habits.
- 20 per cent students have below average food habits.

Discussion

- Good food habits include a nutrition foods, fruits and all other aspects.
- Average food habits include midday meals and hostel meals available during the school time.
- Below average food habits include food not available 3 times per day.

Hostel Facilities

Findings

- 30 per cent Schools have good facilities in Hostel.
- 60 per cent Schools have average facilities in Hostel.
- 10 per cent schools have below average in Hostel.

Bar Chart – 3

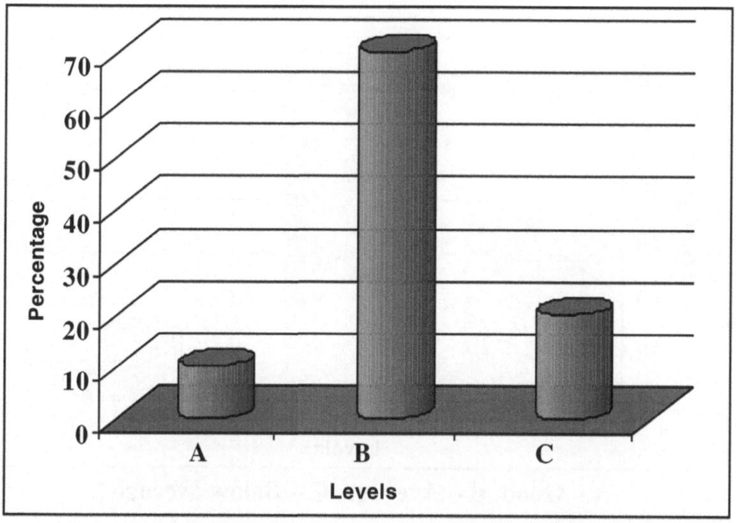

A – Good, B – Average, C – Below average

Discussion

- Good facilities includes good type of accommodation such as pakka concrete buildings, availability of cots etc. and water facility, good food good bathroom, toilet etc.
- Average facilities includes medium level facilities and accommodation.
- Below average includes low level facilities, water facilities, no bathroom etc. food facilities and accommodation.

Available of Teaching Aids

Findings

- 30 per cent of schools possess good teaching aids.
- 50 per cent of schools possess average teaching aids.
- 20 per cent of schools possess below average teaching aids.

Discussion

- Good teaching aids means availability of Working models, Non-working models, graphs, true things, flash cards, rotation charts, match charts etc.

Bar Chart – 4

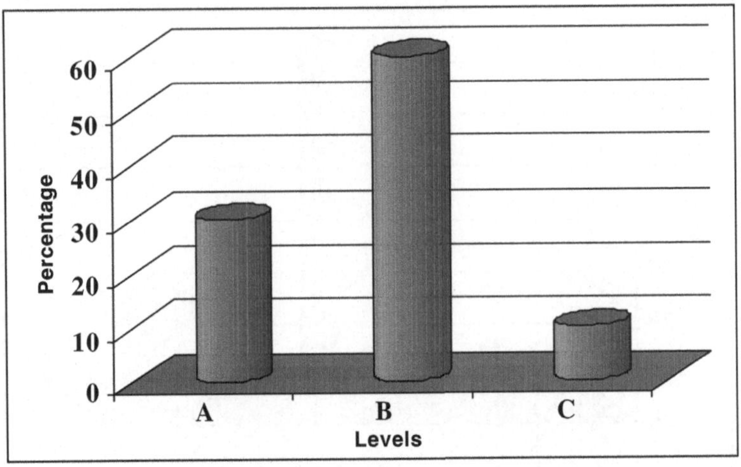

A – Good, B – Average, C – Below average

- Average teaching aids means flash cards, charts, black board only.
- Below average teaching aids means available black board only.

Bar Chart – 5

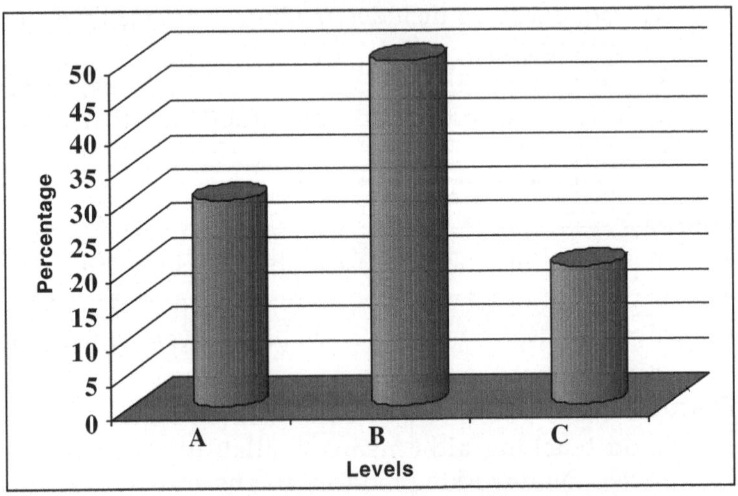

A – Good, B – Average, C – Below average

Education Technology-Usage

Findings

- 10 per cent of teachers only use Education Technology in their classroom effectively.
- 80 per cent of teachers use Education Technology at average level.
- 10 per cent of teachers not at all using Education Technology.

Discussion

- 10 per cent of the teachers use education technology effectively and utilized the teaching technologies in the class room
- used the computer, TV and CD player.
- 10 per cent of the teachers did not use any of the educational technologies teaching and worry about their teaching learning process.
- 80 per cent of the schools got the facilities to make use of technical equipments.
- Electric facilities are available for most of the schools. Recently Computer, television with CD Players have been distributed for all schools.

Bar Chart – 6

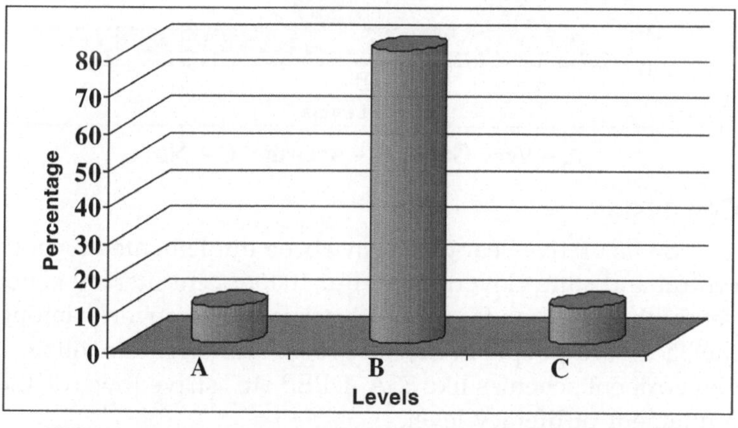

Effectively , B –Average Level, C – Not at all using E.T

Educational Awareness of Parents

Findings

- 80 per cent of parents have very good awareness towards education.
- 20 per cent of parents have average awareness towards education.

Discussion

- Good awareness means aware of the importance of education for human development.
- Average awareness means whole parents literacy level is low, but parents are motivating their children for studies.

Bar Chart – 7

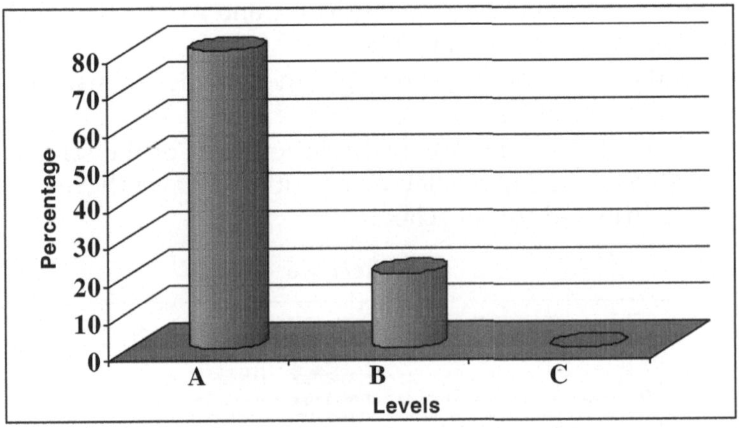

A – Very Good, B – Average, C – No

Conclusion

So far 10 five year plans have been implemented by both central and state Government. But 100per cent literacy is not yet reached. Reason for this illiteracy is due to poverty among the backward people in the hilly regions and remote villages. Government schemes like SSA, DPEP etc., strive towards the implement of literacy level.

REFERENCES

Best J.W (1998), Research in Education. Prentice Hall of India Pvt. Ltd., New Delhi.

Research Methodology, Sumith Enterprises, New Delhi.

Rath Govind Chandra (2006), Tribal Development in India, Sage Publications, New Delhi.

Sharma.K Yogendra (2001), History and Problem of Education, Vol. 2, Kanisha Publications Distributors, New Delhi.

19

Need of Education for Tribal Empowerment

– N. Sony Havilah
– K. John Sudheer

Introduction

Education is the basic instrument for fulfillment of the rights and responsibilities of an individual and is considered as embodiment of social justice. But the educational opportunities for tribal people much less than that of advantaged groups. Only few people have been able to reap the fruits of development and pass them on to their offsprings. In the same way, the cycle of inequalities remains perpetuated by the educational institutions itself. India has a large number of primitive tribes that lives in different parts of the country. The life of these people is characterized by the substandard housing, highly insanitary conditions, grossly inadequate civic amenities, grinding poverty, perpetual struggle for existence, segregated insecurity and instability etc. To overcome all these difficulties they need education. The purpose of education is to prepare the people for life by imparting the necessary knowledge and skills and at the same time people need to be developed holistically to make a right use of the knowledge and skills. So, the education has to promote every person to feel the situation to think independently, critically and even creatively to take right decisions and solve their problems. This paper discusses the following aspects:

- How these educational opportunities need to accomplish these problems?
- What are the educational problems that generally occur in tribal areas?
- What are the provisions to be enhanced for enhance the quality of tribal education?

Educational Opportunities

- To remove inequalities and create egalitarian society, the education plays a crucial role not only for human being to enlighten and empowerment but also to achieve better quality of life. Hence, education serves the following purpose.
- To raise the standards of living.
- To alter the present hierarchical society into truly democratic based on the principles of freedom, equality, social justice and fraternity.
- To develop knowledge, skills and attitudes necessary
- Economic development.
- To achieve social and national integration by fostering a feeling of oneness.
- To provide opportunities for social contacts so that student can acquaint with the ideals and values of national culture.

Educational Problems in Tribal Areas

Recognizing the importance of education in tribal areas and adopting appropriate policies and operational strategies towards empowering the tribal masses, government has made progress in education during the last six decades; Still there is a need to be done in terms of reducing geographical and social disparities in access to educational opportunities. Though the facilities for educating the scheduled tribes have been provided, yet it can be said that quality of tribal education has improved.

(a) **Lack of educational facilities**: School plays a crucial role in shaping the individuals into physically strong, mentally alert, emotionally stable, culturally sound and socially efficient citizens. But tribal people cannot make use of education because there are only limited number of schools and colleges.

(b) **Poverty of large sections**: Most of the people in tribal areas are under the below poverty level and the children from those families do not have the same chance of education as those who come from higher grade.

(c) **Difference in standards of schools and colleges**: There is an extreme form of educational inequalities when a student got admission into an institution such as university or professional college is made on the marks obtained at the public examination because the students from urban areas attending a good school having an advantage over the students from tribal areas where the schools are ill equipped.

(d) **Difference in home environment**: There are apparent cultural differences and location practices among the life style of tribal people so that the child from tribal house have their own difficulties to get education than that of children from urban home with highly educated parents.

(e) **Disparities between the education of boys and girls**: At all stages and all sectors there has been disparities exists between boys and girls. The parents are reluctant to send their children especially girls to the schools and colleges because of ignorance, traditions and customs that prevailed in the tribal community.

(f) **High private cost of education**: The cost of books, lab equipments, electronic equipments like television, computers and goods for co curricular activities have increased substantially in recent years and these amounts are several times that of tuition fee. The students and staff of these tribal areas cannot bear these expenses.

The provisions are needed to be enhanced

The following actions are helpful for strengthening the outcomes of education:

- The above problems can be overcome by the widest dispersal of educational institutions by instituting an adequate scholarship programme or by providing the needed hostel facilities or by making suitable transport arrangements.
- Encourage trained educated tribe youth to take-up teaching in tribal areas because they can understand the different circumstances.
- It is desirable to provide free books, stationary and even school means and uniforms. In additions to it necessary to develop a large programme of scholarships.
- Follow more reliable and egalitarian methods of selection for admission into higher educational institution.
- Difference in home environment is obviously the most difficult to overcome and here progress generally depends on the improvement in the standards of living. But sometimes this can be ensured by establishing day study centers or boarding houses.
- Special incentives should be provided to encourage girls from tribal areas.
- The school education is completely free in advanced countries and our country should also gradually work towards a stage that all education should be tuition free mainly in tribal areas.

Keeping in full view, the key importance of education for tasks of reconstruction and strengthening of tribal people, the government has to enshrine certain above educational provisions for the people who are living in tribal areas.

Conclusion

Equality in education is most vital because it can serve as a potential instrument for bringing about economic and social equality in long run. Moreover, besides providing universal primary education to every child, the government has to establish secondary schools and colleges and also other educational institutions like libraries, learning centre, recreational centers for tribal people which help them to overcome many difficulties in their life.

REFERENCES

Das, S.T., (1989); *Life Style: Indian Tribes (Locational Practices),* Jain Publishing House, New Delhi.

Government of India (1986); *Programme of Action,* NPE, 1986 Ministry of Human Resource Development, Dept of Education, New Delhi.

Sarason, S (1991); *The Predictable Failure of Educational Reform,* Jossey Publishers, San Francisco.

Talesra, Hemlata (1989); *Tribal Education,* Himanshu Publications, Udiapur.

Vir, Dharan (1990); *Tribal Women: Changing Spectrum in India,* Classical Publishing Company, New Delhi.

20

Non-formal Education Opportunities for Hill Tribes in Northern Thailand

– Santosh Kumar Mishra

Key Words: Tribe, Northern Thailand, non-formal education, rural population, Hill Tribe Welfare and Development Centre, and Department of Non-formal Education (DNFE).

Introduction

Among the rural population of Thailand, hill tribes are a disadvantaged and vulnerable group of society, largely dependent on agriculture for income and employment. While their socio-economic situation has improved in many aspects in recent years, modernization and influence from the lowlands have led to rapid changes in life patterns within highland communities, where traditional self-sufficiency can no longer be sustained. Lacking skills and means to cope with these changes, highland communities suffer from deterioration in such key areas as agriculture, employment and socio-cultural values.

Given this background, increasing attention is paid to the need of addressing a wide range of issues concerning hill tribe people, not only in the areas of citizenship and land settlement but also in terms of quality of life and welfare. Accordingly, the role of education in improving socio-economic conditions through human resource development is well recognized. In fact, a large number of governmental and non-governmental organisations, civilian and military, national and international, provide support to enhance educational opportunities for hill tribe people. It is expected that enhanced education opportunities, whether formal or non-formal, would engender sustainable socio-economic development for hill tribe communities. This research note is as an attempt to analyze the impact of support activities by the Royal Thai Government in promoting non-formal education opportunities for hill tribe people.

Thailand: Non-Formal Education Project

The *"Non-Formal and Continuing Education Project"* of the Thai Association of University Women aims to improve the quality of life of women and children. It provides training in the form of seminars and workshops for many different groups of women in the areas of:

- health care;
- income generation;
- culture;
- literacy;
- numeracy; and
- Information technology.

The project is wide-reaching providing training for professional and career women to develop their careers, identifying and training local women leaders to serve their communities, and providing basic education courses for those who have missed out on a formal education. A network of teachers has been formed to cooperate with the non-formal and continuing education committee of the Thai Association of University Women. 2008 activities included:

- Five workshops on nursery education for teachers, nursery owners and child carers. The workshops were held in Bangkok and covered management and teaching skills, as well as providing training for those wishing to run their own child care centres.

- Five study visits to award-winning schools in Bangkok for teachers and administrators. This was organised with the collaboration of the Ministry of Education and the Ministry of Social and Human Devlopment and has provided valuable in-service training that would not otherwise be available.
- Publication of 3,000 copies of a cookbook entitled, *"Thai Cooking & Thai Culture"*. Many women collaborated in the production of this book, collecting and trying out traditional recipes and demonstrating how to cook typical Thai dishes. The sale of the book will generate enough income to allow this project activity to continue and will also help to preserve Thai culture and traditional cuisine.

Non-formal Education in Thailand

The Department of Non-Formal Education in Thailand plays important roles for the out-of-school youth and adults. All programmes provided by the Department of Non-formal Education can be classified into three main categories: basic education, vocational education and skills training, and information services. The duration of programmes can be vary from thirty hours to two years. The target groups include:

- prison inmates,
- Thai Muslims,
- laborers,
- farmers,
- people with disability,
- hill tribes,
- local leaders,
- slum residents,
- minority groups, and
- people who have no opportunity to continue in school.

Literacy and Numeracy Programmes

These programmes help adult learners learn basic skills in reading, writing, calculating, and problem solving. The curriculum of this programme is designed to meet the needs of learners. There are specific curricula for various non-formal education target groups, such as for the southern Thai Muslims and northern hill-tribes. The literacy programmes are equal to grade four of the formal schooling system. The Main objectives of literacy programme are to help people to be able to read, write, and make them realize duties of the citizens in the constitutional monarchy system

Equivalency Programme (Non-formal Education Basic Curriculum)

This programme is designed for youth and adults over 15 years old, who did not have access primary education. It is a basic education use as a foundation for further education. There are three levels of Equivalency Programmes compared to each level of formal education. They are:

(a) Primary education adults;
(b) Secondary education; and
(c) Upper secondary education.

Life-skills Training Programme

The programme is designed to increase problems solving skill by using the combination of knowledge, positive thinking, and other skills. They are:

(a) HIV;
(b) Drug;
(c) Family problems;
(d) Social problems;
(e) Health, etc.

Non-formal Occupational Training

This programme is designed to promote the public welfare and upgrade the quality of life through occupational development by providing following three types of vocational education and skills training:

(a) First, interest groups provide specific occupational skills for various groups of people.
(b) Second, short-term occupational training designed for people who are interested can register with minimum expense for training materials.
(c) Third, a vocational certificate programme is a 3 year programme provided for those who completed primary education and would like to improve for knowledge and working skills.

Hill Tribes in Thailand – General Background

In Thailand, the term "hill tribes" designates ethnic minorities, most of whom live in the remote highland areas of the country. There are in total 3 527 hill tribe villages in 20 provinces of Thailand, comprising 133 070 households and 751 886 persons. The largest tribal group is Karen (46.18%), followed by Hmong (16.32%) and Lahu (11.21%). Of all the provinces, Chiang Mai has the largest hill tribe population; i.e. 1 072 villages with 33 573 households and 190 795 persons. Hill tribe people are among the most disadvantaged groups of the country, due largely to a lack of infrastructure, limited access to Thai citizenship and delayed land settlement (partly because of their traditional way of living in small communities and migrating frequently). Living in relative cultural isolation and with distinctive linguistic and cultural backgrounds, hill tribe people lack a sense of national identity. Although the majority of the first-generation hill tribes have obtained Thai identification, the Ministry of Interior is cautious about granting Thai identity to newly immigrated hill tribes, because of their alleged involvement in illegal trafficking. With the variety of laws involved, the legal status of hill tribes fluctuates between "naturalized", "alien" and "illegal". Besides, aggravated by cultural misunderstandings, they have often been associated with political infiltration and insurgency.

Hill tribe people face a higher degree of poverty than other groups in Thailand. The majorities are engaged in agriculture as their main economic activity, and household-based handicraft production and wage employment as secondary sources of income. Production inputs are limited, they lack access to basic social services (including education and health) and they also lack opportunities for systematic skill development, income and employment. Population growth at an annual rate of 2.9 per cent (compared with the national average of 1.2%) is also an issue of concern, in addition to natural resource and environmental degradation.

Hill tribe people in Thailand originate from three linguistic stocks and can be categorized into two geographical groups, i.e. low hill (Karen, Lua, Khamu and H'tin tribes) and high hill (Meo, Yao, Lahu, Lisu and Akha tribes). They practise three principal forms of land use, i.e. pioneer swidden agriculture, land rotation and wet (paddy) rice. The former group tends to practise an ecologically informed mode of shifting cultivation based on, wherever possible, rice production. They are considered to be indigenous to Thailand and the adjoining areas of Myanmar and Laos. The high hill group, engaged in high-altitude agriculture, migrated to Thailand from Myanmar, Laos and Southern China within the last century.

In the past, highland communities have often been associated with problems such as shifting cultivation, watershed forest destruction and opium cultivation. Government assistance to hill tribe people therefore mainly focused on such areas as forest destruction, narcotics, and national security. Land settlement and granting of national identity were also priority issues. Providing assistance to remote and scattered highland communities has been difficult, in addition to communication barriers with people speaking distinctive languages. sIn recent years, in addition to citizenship and land settlement issues, promotion of quality of life and welfare in highland development has been drawing increasing attention. Closely knit hill tribe communities holding traditional values and beliefs are breaking apart and losing their identity. It is partly due to factors as the changing pattern of economic activities, growing acceptance of Thai language instruction in schools, exposure to modern knowledge and other religions like Buddhism and Christianity. Their traditional ways of life do not always fit in with the present socio-economic and political conditions of the rest of the country, and a sense of individualism is growing among youngsters. Communication between the Thai-speaking younger generations and the "illiterate" older generations is thus sometimes hindered.

There has been growing recognition of the role of education for children, youth and adults to contribute to sustainable rural development. While an increasing number of hill tribe children attend primary schools at the initiative of their communities and of the Thai government, access to higher education and to post-study employment are still limited. In terms of vocational knowledge and life skills learning, training programmes provided by various governmental and non-governmental organisations conventionally tend to be short-term in nature. Moreover, due to limited funds, non-correspondence with existing skills, and low market prospects, hill tribe people have difficulty in sustaining the skills acquired.

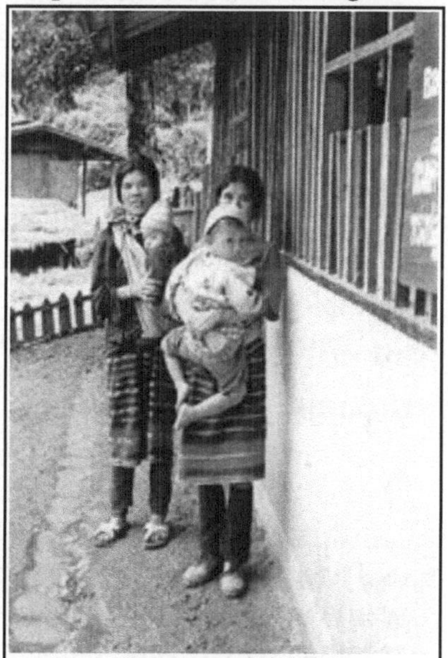

Lua Women and Children

Hill Tribes of Northern Thailand

Hill tribes can broadly be divided into two types: lowland and highland dwellers. The hill tribe people who live in the low valleys tend to be agriculturalists growing rice and corn. Tribes that live in the high altitudes of the mountains have traditionally relied on poppy cultivation for the production of opium to survive. There are a total of 6 main hill tribes that are indigenous to the hills of northern Thailand. These hill tribes have migrated to Thailand from neighbouring Burma, Laos, Vietnam and even China at various points throughout history. Brief description of six hill tribes is given below:

- **The Karen Hill Tribe of Northern Thailand:** There are a total of 250,000 Karen people living inside the borders of Thailand. The Karen, however, is a much bigger tribe in Burma where they number up to 4 million. The Karen are believed to be the most assimiliated of the hill tries into mainstream Thai society and as such it's often difficult to tell them apart from other ordinary Thais. The Karen tribe are by and large Buddhists; however, there has been a steady increase in conversions to Christianity in recent years due to missionary activities.
- **The Hmong Hill Tribe of Northern Thailand:** These tribes, also known as the Meo, are nomads who have communities present across South East Asia as well as China. There are believed to be a total of 65,000 Hmong living in Thailand, Chiang Mai, Chiang Rai and Phetchaban. There are about four million Hmong living in southern China and this tribe has strong cultural similarities with Chinese people. Apart from the cultivation of opium, the Hmong hill tribes are renowned animal breeders who produce good quality ponies.
- **The Akha Hill Tribe of Northern Thailand:** This tribe is also known as the Kaw. Ancestoral lineage plays a particularly important role among the Akha, many of whom are able to state their lineage back 1,000 years. The Akha migrated to northern Thailand from Burma at the beginning of the 20th century.
- **The Lahu Hill Tribe of Northern Thailand:** The Lahu are also known as the Mussur. There are about 40,000 Lahu living in the highlands around Chiang Mai and Chiang Rai. The Language of the Lahu which is called

Lahu Na serves as a lingua franca between other tribes. The Lahu are renowned musicians and are particularly known for playing the flute.

- **The Mien Hill Tribes of Northern Thailand:** There are believed to be about 30,000 Mien living in Thailand. The Mien, also known as the Yao are mainly found in Chiang Rai, Phayao and Lampeng provinces. Originally from China there are many Taoist elements incorporated into their religious belief system.
- **The Lisu Hill Tribe of Northern Thailand:** The Lisu are originally from Burma and came to Chiang Rai province in the 1920's. The Lisu intermarry regularly with the Lahu hill tribe of northern Thailand.

Government Policies

The first government initiatives for hill tribe development were taken in 1951 with the aim of providing general welfare services in remote, relatively inaccessible and poverty-stricken communities. To intensify development activities, the government established in 1959 the National Committee for the Hill Tribes as the first national-level organisation in charge of formulating policies focusing on hill tribe development. To date, the government policy towards the hill tribes is based on the Cabinet decision of 6 July 1976, which states the government's intention to integrate hill tribe people into the Thai state and to give them full rights to practise their religions and maintain their cultures as "first class", self-reliant Thai citizens. In addition, due to rapid environmental degradation in highland areas, the government now places further emphasis on natural resource conservation in its highland development policies. This has led to recent efforts to promote "*subsistence production*" (to achieve sufficient self-supply) and natural resource protection with further environmental considerations, rather than cash-crop production which depends on modern technology.

In the period when hill tribes were allegedly associated with communist insurgency, the Thai authorities endeavoured to improve relations with hill tribes and to promote permanent settlement where services could be concentrated and movements controlled. When the insurgency problem subsided in the early 1980s and international pressure on drug-abuse prevention and control grew, the focus shifted to curbing opium production by both local and international agents. With the growing environmental concern, the focus has shifted again, this time to natural resource conservation. Currently there are eleven government ministries involved in hill area development, namely the ministries of:

- Interior;
- Defense;
- Public health;
- Education;
- University affairs;
- Agriculture and cooperatives;
- Science;
- Technology and energy;
- Finance;
- Communication, and industry; and
- The Prime Minister's office.

Under the above ministries are 31 departments and 168 agencies with either a mandate or a commitment to support hill tribe communities. The national economic and social development plans and the Master Plan on Community Development, Environment and Narcotic Crop Control in Highland Areas are the key plans underlining the government's support activities to hill tribe communities.

Government Responses

Government initiatives on hill tribe development date back to 1951, with the objective to provide general welfare services in remote, relatively inaccessible communities affected by poverty. In 1959 the government established the National Committee for the Hill Tribes as the first national-level organisation in charge of formulating policies focusing on hill tribe development. To date, the government policy towards the hill tribes is based on the Cabinet resolution of 6 July

1976. The resolution states the government's intention to integrate hill tribe people into the Thai state as self-reliant Thai citizens. In addition, the Master Plan on Community Development, Environment and Narcotic Crop Control in Highland Areas provides the basis for the government's support of hill tribe people, with emphasis on natural resource conservation in highland development. Furthermore, the national economic and social development plans are the key plans underpinning government assistance to hill tribe communities.

Assistance to hill tribe communities has been facing a number of challenges, including geographical isolation (due partly to the hill tribe people's tradition of living in small communities), land settlement (delayed due also to continuous migration of hill tribe people) and communication barriers. Nevertheless, through the wide range of support provided by various governmental and non-governmental organisations, there have been tangible improvements in the socio-economic conditions of hill tribe people. Among these organisations, in order to examine how enhanced education opportunities would help improve agricultural production, employment and income generation, thus contributing to sustainable rural development, this research will look at the activities of the Department of Non-formal Education (DNFE) of the Ministry of Education, the Department of Agricultural Extension (DOAE) of the Ministry of Agriculture and Cooperatives, and the Department of Public Welfare (DPW) of the Ministry of Labour and Social Welfare. DNFE, under the theme of "Education for all", set a policy in 1998-99 to develop highland non-formal education based on the community learning centre model. The department provides educational services to promote literacy among the hill tribes through such programmes as the Hill Area Education project, the Somdet Ya project, and distance education. DOAE has been carrying out highland agriculture development since 1979. The highland agricultural policy of the Ministry of Agriculture and Cooperatives reflects the principles of the

Eighth National Economic and Social Development Plan. With the objective of supporting appropriate farmer occupational development for sustainable quality community life and environment, DOAE activities include, in addition to general extension services, Community Agricultural Services and Technology Transfer Centres and the Volunteer Hill Tribe Farmer project. Under the Cabinet resolution of 6 July 1976, DPW was designated as the main coordination agency for issues related to hill tribes. The development activities of DPW focus on human development, permanent settlement and sufficient food production, stressing coexistence between people and forest resources, participatory and grass-roots development, as well as promotion of indigenous knowledge. The department's wide range of support activities are carried out through the Hill Tribe Welfare and Development Centre, DPW mobile units and the Tribal Research Institute.

In the meantime, hill area development, while being considered increasingly important, has not been integrated into the mainstream development policies. Further, assistance to hill tribe people has faced insufficiencies in many respects, due largely to difficulties in physical access to, communication with and frequent migration by hill tribe people, delayed land settlement, and legal problems. In addition to lingering problems deriving from poverty, lack of infrastructure, delayed land settlement, legal status of hill tribe people in Thailand and illegal immigration, new concerns are recently emerging. One problem is the out-migration of the hill tribe labour force (influx of young people into lowlands and cities). Most of these people are unskilled and unprepared for a new environment, and thus susceptible to exploitation and unlawful conduct. HIV/AIDS, prostitution, drug addiction as well as degradation in agriculture and income are other serious problems.

To respond more effectively to the lingering and newly emerging problems, it would be important to improve the efficiency and complementarities of support programmes to supplement the limited budget and personnel. Issues that merit further attention would include participation of and communication with hill tribe communities in planning and implementing support activities; local curriculum development in formal and non-formal education corresponding to the community needs and realities; capacity-building of those engaged in the field-level implementation of support activities; and collaboration among governmental and non-governmental organisations concerned. In enhancing assistance to hill tribe people, integrated approaches to highland development would need to be emphasized as a means to address a wide range of problems. Particularly, quality of life issues that include education and health care would need to be given higher prominence, as they would contribute to the human potential and self-reliance of highland communities. Enhancement of education opportunities in such a way as to contribute to improved agricultural production, employment and income generation should be based on efforts to harmonize modern knowledge and technologies with local wisdom and practices. In supporting such efforts in Thailand, international development agencies would need to strengthen partnership in advocating sustainable highland development. FAO has the potential to promote such areas as sustainable highland agriculture, local curriculum development, capacity building of decentralized organisations, community resource management and small enterprise development.

Education, along with infrastructure, communication and health care, is an indispensable enabling factor for enhancing rural livelihood. It enables hill tribe people to take fuller advantage of employment and training opportunities, whether they choose to stay in their communities or decide to earn income in urban areas. Consequently, hill tribe people, based on the skills they acquired, would be in a position to reinforce their income-generating capacities and socio-economic potential, which will be the foundation of sustainable rural development.

The Department of Non-formal Education

The Department of Non-formal Education (DNFE) of the Ministry of Education aims at providing the public countrywide with access to lifelong education opportunities, particularly for the out-of-school and the underprivileged based on their readiness, needs and interests at any time. DNFE employs various strategies, such as decentralization, participation, network construction and mobilization, in such a way that the target groups at all levels can obtain basic and vocational education, skills training as well as up-to-date information through a variety of non-formal and informal education programmes.

DNFE has three main tasks:

- organise and promote non-formal education;
- render support to, cooperate with and encourage the formal schooling system; and
- organise and promote informal education, for which hill tribe people are one of the target groups.

The DNFE Hill Area Policy

"Education for all" is the underlying theme in DNFE activities. In compliance with the new national legislation for education reform, based on the 1999 National Education Act, DNFE emphasizes the following:

- Provide a variety of non-formal and informal education programmes responsive to the needs of the individuals, communities and particular areas.
- Put emphasis on lifelong education through various means, including distance education and all kinds of educational media.
- Consider the disadvantaged people as the most important target group of DNFE, including hill tribes, the disabled and street children, who should be served also by NGOs and private-sector entities. DNFE realizes the need of mobilizing the strength and services of all NGOs in order to supplement governmental organisations, which may not reach all the target communities.

The disadvantaged groups are supposed to be provided with basic education as well as vocational training for job opportunities.

- Decentralize the non-formal education administration system to the local level to manage, plan and operate educational programmes.

In order to enhance educational opportunities for hill tribes, DNFE in 1998-1999 set a policy to develop highland non-formal education based on the community learning centre (CLC) model. The centres provide educational services to promote literacy among the hill tribes. Hill tribes have opportunities via DNFE programmes for informal education such as learning from local wisdom, including culture and community-based knowledge. Local (folk) media plays an important role in passing on knowledge and social values through secular kinds of performances.

DNFE Support Activities

The Hill Area Education Project

Jointly organized in 1981 by DPW and DNFE, the Hill Area Education project (HAEP) aims at providing educational services responding to the needs and problems of hill tribe communities, through a flexible, low-cost, community-based learning model. HAEP uses an integrated approach combining support of governmental and non-governmental organisations with community participation. The HAEP philosophy is to reinforce already available knowledge and resources in the villages to implement participatory education for community development. In order to raise the sense of community ownership, a highland community learning centre (HCLC) is built by the villagers, using local materials. A volunteer teacher, as a community member, is sent to live in an HCLC, which any community member is welcome to visit.

Classes are conducted both for children and adults, based on a community-oriented curriculum which includes 35 per cent of basic skills (including Thai language and mathematics) and 65 per cent of life and social experience (consisting of 19 basic topics/units and a completely open-ended local curriculum). The curriculum is not graded. Completion of curricular objectives does not have to conform to fixed course duration. Children are required to spend some 6 000 hours to complete the entire course (see Annex VI for primary education for the hill area community curriculum) and adults about 1 200 hours. Learning achievements are assessed by teachers along with villagers or officials according to different methods and criteria including gender, age, ethnic group, etc. In addition to learning classes, HCLC offers radio and satellite programmes. Self-study by community members is also encouraged.

The Mae Fa Luang Hill Area Community Learning Centre

In commemoration and in honour of Her Royal Highness the Princess Mother, His Majesty conferred the name "Mae Fa Luang" to HCLC. Countrywide, by 2000 there were HCLC in 648 villages with 1 236 volunteer teachers and 97 000 learners. Currently Mae Fa Luang educational activities are divided into three categories:

- *Basic education*: general education programmes of pre-school, primary and secondary levels.
- *Information service*: provision of practical knowledge through mass media.
- *Vocational skill training*: focusing on developing skills, either to supplement existing skills or cultivating new ones.

Mae Fa Luang CLC in Chiang Rai (Lahu tribe community)

The Somdet Ya project

The Somdet Ya project, implemented on a pilot basis from 1999 to 2004 as collaboration between Her Majesty the King's Mother Project, the *Tambon* (sub-district) Chang Koeng Administrative Organisation and DNFE, is carried out in the vicinity of the Mae Chaem district centre in Chiang Mai province. The Somdet Ya project has four objectives:

- *provide* three-year education opportunities up to the ninth grade (M3), including life skills training (such as agriculture and traditional weaving) to hill tribe youths;
- *serve* as a suitable model for hill tribe education in accordance with the National Education Act 1999;
- *give* opportunities for disadvantaged children to be volunteer teachers in their communities; and
- *encourage* community participation in education and training. There are currently 30 students (18 boys and 12 girls, mainly Karen), who have completed six years of primary education under Mae Fa Luang, staying in the school compound (community learning centre) and sharing every aspect of life.

Distance Education

The Distance Education via Satellite project was initiated under the Seventh National Economic and Social Development Plan (1992-1996), which emphasized human resource development as an important means to guide the nation's development. In 1994 the Cabinet passed a resolution to grant the Ministry of Education permission to launch the Distance Education via Satellite project in collaboration with the private sector. The project was an attempt to apply advanced satellite communication technology to improve the education system. The purpose was to expand educational opportunities and to raise educational standards for students in remote areas to be able to receive quality education by satellite television broadcast. The Ministry of Education and the Thaicom Foundation signed a memorandum of assistance and collaboration for the use of a satellite in distance education management.

Distance education through television programmes via satellite has also become an alternative technology for the implementation of the government policy of expanding basic education from six to nine years. DNFE is designated to supervise the administrative organisation of the Thaicom project. For this purpose the Thaicom Distance Education Centre was established under DNFE. An educational television station has also been established to broadcast satellite distance education programmes, transmitting signals from the Thaicom-linked satellite. The Thaicom Distance Education Centre collaborates with the DNFE Centre for Educational Technology and the DNFE Development Division responsible for the production of distance education programmes and printed materials. The project planned to acquire a total of 6 000 sets of the equipment (a small satellite dish, an integrated receiver and decoder and a television set). So far, a total of 15 590 sets have been obtained and installed, including in remote areas.

Inter Mountain Peoples Education and Culture in Thailand Association (IMPECT)

IMPECT, which has been operating since 1991, is an indigenous and tribal non-governmental development organisation founded and staffed entirely by representatives of the indigenous and tribal peoples and communities involved with the association. It is today major non-governmental organisation acting on its own or on behalf of donor agencies in support of hill tribe communities. IMPECT registered with the government to obtain legal status on 16 March 1993. Representatives from six indigenous groups (Karen, Hmong, Meo, Lisu, Lahu and Akha) and tribal people were chosen from their own communities to form the executive committee of the association. Six indigenous groups are: (a) Karen; (b) Hmong; (c) Meo; (d) Lisu; (e) Lahu; and (f) Akha.

This committee set the policies and guidelines directing the association's work in order to ensure that the work was in line with the problems and needs of highland people and communities. IMPECT currently works with 190 indigenous and tribal communities in eight provinces in northern Thailand (Chiang Mai, Chiang Rai, Lampang, Mae Hong Son, Phayao, Nan, Tak and Kamphaeng Phet).

Being a forum of development for indigenous and tribal peoples in Thailand, IMPECT endeavours to ensure that indigenous peoples have the freedom and the right to preserve, revitalize and pass down to future generations their cultures and customs. IMPECT promotes greater self-reliance and mutual assistance among tribal people, who should maintain a sense of pride and dignity as distinct cultures, while having equal rights with other Thai citizens. Under this vision, the IMPECT objectives include development of local leaders, community organisations and networks, promotion of local wisdom in natural resource management, food security and alternative agriculture, protection of the rights and responsibilities of indigenous people as well as data collection and information dissemination. Donors include Netherlands, UNICEF, ILO and the National Cultural Committee. IMPECT activities are conducted on the basis of indigenous and tribal peoples' traditional knowledge and cultures along with an ethic of participatory and sustainable development. In addition to community development work (natural resource management and sustainable agriculture programme, social development and basic human rights promotion programme, basic education promotion and cultural revival programme, advocacy programme, community organisation and network strengthening programme), they carry out special projects including a centre for urban tribal youth, a local curriculum development project and an inter-tribal youth education and culture project.

The IMPECT Experience

IMPECT first implemented local curriculum development seven years ago in Mae Wang district (Chiang Mai province) as a pilot project. Since then IMPECT has been communicating the importance of local curriculum to government agencies.

The local curriculum development in Mae Lang Kam village (Hang Dong district, Chiang Mai province) started two years ago, through a participatory consultation process with the community and government representatives. Evaluation has been carried out at the closing of every semester. Currently two villages in Samoeng district (Chiang Mai province) have adopted a local curriculum, while it is under discussion in another village. Contents are on agriculture, tradition and customs as well as on livelihood. The proportion of local contents on each subject is decided in consultation with the community. The share of the local curriculum has been increasing, even in formal education.

IMPECT also supports a school in Nong Tao village, covering primary levels one to six, where 67 boys and 54 girls are enrolled, with eight teachers. Out of 26 grade six students in 2000, 24 pursued further studies. School activities are supported by children's savings, and DNFE provides textbooks. Subjects taught include life skills, social science, local habits and customs, occupations (including agriculture) and Thai language. Food processing, cooperatives and marketing are among the subjects taught. The local curriculum constitutes 20-30 per cent of the total curriculum. The head teacher suggested that skill training to improve product quality to meet market standards would be an important subject, contributing to enhanced quality of life for the community. The teaching skills of local people should also be promoted. According to the village chief, there has been some disagreement within the community about the idea of establishing a school, as the community does not understand its role. The community used to view the school as a source of problems (influx of new culture), not responding to real local needs. Upon implementation of the Education Law in 1999, things have developed more favourably. The village chief suggested that further collaboration between teachers (most of whom are from other villages) and communities be promoted.

Conclusion

Addressing the need for integrated approaches in development to contribute to improved quality of life for rural people is an important dimension. In Thailand, hill tribes are among the most disadvantaged and vulnerable groups of society. Most hill-tribe people engage in agriculture as their main economic activity and in household-based handicraft production as well as wage employment as their secondary sources of income. Their production inputs are limited; they lack access to basic social services, including education and health; and they also lack opportunities for systematic skill development, income and employment. *Furthermore,* closely knit hill tribe communities holding traditional values and beliefs are breaking apart and losing their identity. It is partly due to factors as:

- the changing pattern of economic activities;
- growing acceptance of Thai language instruction in schools; and
- exposure to modern knowledge and other religions like Buddhism and Christianity.

Communication between the Thai-speaking younger generations and the *"illiterate older generations"* is sometimes hindered. Given this recent trend, in addition to long-standing problems such as citizenship and land settlement, a wide range of issues related to hill tribe people are being addressed. Particular emphasis is on the promotion of quality of life and welfare through human resource development. Accordingly, the role of education in improving socio-economic conditions is further recognized. Education is a prerequisite to building a food-secure world, reducing poverty and conserving and enhancing natural resources.

REFERENCES

Bureau of Policy and Strategy, Office of the Permanent Secretary, Ministry of Education (2002). *"The National Educational for All Plan of Action for Thailand (2002-2016)"*. MOE, Bangkok.

Department of Non-Formal Education (Year of Publication not mentioned). *"A Study of Life Skill Activities of Non-Formal Target Population"*. Bangkok, DNFE. 2003:11

"Global IYM launch highlights Peace", IYM website: http://www.mountains2002.org/news/

National Statistics Office (2000). *"Population and Housing Census 2000"*. available from http://web.nso.go.th/eng/en/pop2000/report/adv_e.htm

Office of the Non-formal Education Commission (2006). *"Criteria and Method to Operate Non- Formal Education Basic Education 2001"* (revised in 2006). ONFEC, MOE, Bangkok.

Office of the Educational Council (1999). *"National Educational Act of B.E. 2542 (1999)"*. Available from http://www.edthai.com/act/index.htm#1

Office of the Non-formal Education Commission (2005). *"Non-formal Education Statistics, 2005"*. ONFEC, Bangkok.

Office of the Non-formal Education Commission (2006). *"Non-formal Education Statistics 2006"*. ONFEC, Bangkok.

Office of the Non-formal Education Commission (2007). *"Research on Equivalency Programme for Promotion of Lifelong Learning"*. ONFEC, Bangkok.

Shaeffer Sheldon, UNESCO Asia and Pacific Regional Bureau for Education. Available from http://www.unescobkk.org.

Tribal Research Institute website at http://www.chmai.com/tribal/.

http://www.fao.org/docrep/004/ak216e/ak216e05.htm, Accessed on July 8, 2012.

http://www.kwintessential.co.uk/articles/thailand/Hill-Tribes-of-Northern-Thailand/515, Accessed on July 7, 2012.

http://www.ifuw.org/what/brpid/2008-projects/thailand/, Accessed on July 8, 2012

Hill Tribe Welfare and Development in Thailand, Hill Tribe Welfare Division, Department of Public Welfare

http://www.fao.org/docrep/004/ak216e/ak216e07.htm#P584_100554, Accessed on July 03, 2012.

21

Development Measures of Tribals in India

– M. Vetrichelvan
– A. Jahitha Begum

The apparently wide fluctuation in estimates of South Asia's tribal population through the twentieth century gives a sense of how unclear the distinction between tribal and nontribal can be. India's 1931 census enumerated 22 million tribal people, in 1941 only 10 million were counted, but by 1961 some 30 million and in 1991 nearly 68 million tribal members were included. Since independence, however the special benefits available to Scheduled Tribes have convinced many groups, even Hindus and Muslims, that they will enjoy greater advantages if so designated. The schedule gives tribal people incentives to maintain their identity. By the same token, the schedule also includes a number of groups whose "tribal" status, in cultural terms, is dubious at best; in various districts, the list includes Muslims and a congeries of Hindu castes whose main claim seems to be their ability to deliver votes to the party that arranges their listing among the Scheduled Tribes.

A number of traits have customarily been seen as establishing tribal rather than caste identity. These include language, social organisation, religious affiliation, economic patterns, geographic location, and self-identification. Recognized tribes typically live in hilly regions somewhat remote from caste settlements; they generally speak a language recognized as tribal. Language is not always an accurate indicator of tribal or caste status. Especially in regions of mixed population, many tribal groups have lost their mother tongues and simply speak local or regional languages. Linguistic assimilation is an ongoing process of considerable complexity. In the highlands of Orissa, for example, the Bondos—a Munda-language-speaking tribe—use their own tongue among themselves. Oriya, however, serves as a lingua franca in dealings with Hindu neighbours. Oriya as a prestige language however, has also supplanted the native tongue as the language of ritual. In parts of Assam, historically divided into warring tribes and villages, increased contact among villagers began during the colonial period and has accelerated since independence.

Self-identification and group loyalty are not unfailing markers of tribal identity either. In the case of stratified tribes, the loyalties of clan, kin, and family may well predominate over those of tribe. In addition, tribes cannot always be viewed as people living apart; the degree of isolation of various tribes has varied tremendously. The Gonds, Santals, and Bhils traditionally have dominated the regions in which they have lived. Moreover, tribal society is not always more egalitarian than the rest of the rural populace; some of the larger tribes, such as the Gonds, are highly stratified (www.tribal.nic/index.html).

Definition of Tribe

There is no agreement among the sociologists and anthropologists regarding the definition of the term "tribe". Some of the definitions may be examined here:

D.N.Majumdar: A tribe is "a collection of families bearing a common name, members of which occupy the same territory, speak the same language and observe certain taboos regarding marriage, profession or occupation and have developed a well assessed system of reciprocity and mutuality of obligation".

Andre Beteille's revised definition of a tribe runs like this: "We have described the tribe as a society with a political, linguistic and a somewhat vaguely cultural boundary; further, as a society based upon kinship, where social stratification is absent" (www.tribal.nic.in).

Characteristics of Tribe

1. **Common Territory:** A tribe is a territorial community. It means the tribe has a definite territory in which its members reside.
2. **Collection of Families:** As the definitions of tribe cited above clarify, that tribals constitute a collection of families. These collections may have various sizes. These families which normally have blood relationship among themselves could be matriarchal or patriarchal in nature.
3. **Common Name:** Every tribe has its own name. Each tribe is known to other tribes by its distinctive name.
4. **Common Language:** The members of a tribe speak a particular language. Different tribes speak different languages. These languages are not only different from the language of the civilized people, but they themselves differ from one another. Common language contributes much to the development of community feeling. since these languages do not have a script of their own, education of the tribals has become problematic.
5. **Common Ancestor:** The triblas claim that they have a common ancestor. A major cause of the sense of communal unity in the tribe is "the tie of blood relationships" between its members arising out of common ancestry. The tribals are bound by kinship bonds.
6. **Common Culture:** Each tribe has a way of life of its own. Each tribe has its own way of behaving, thinking, feeling and acting. Each has its own customs, traditions,

morals, values, its own peculiar institutions in brief, its own culture. The very peculiarities of a tribe reveal that it has a distinctive culture of its own.

7. **Common Political Organisation:** Each tribe has its own political system. The tribal chief normally exercises authority over all the other members. The chieftainship is normally hereditary. He occupies an important position in the tribal society. The tribals do not possess a government in the modern sense of the term. But they do have their own tribal government, tribal council and tribal court or judicial system.
8. **Feeling of Unity:** The members of a tribe always feel that they are united. This sense of unity is essential for them to retain their identity. Tribals are normally cohesive and they fight against common enemies as one man. They are ever ready to avenge the injustice done to the group or the individuals (Sharma.K Yougendra, 2001).

Tribal Profile in Tamil Nadu

Tamil Nadu has 36 tribal communities spread over its 21 districts, concentrated largely in the hill areas of northwestern parts of the state. The prominent tribal-inhabited hill ranges are: Jawadhi and Elagiri hills of North Arcot district; Kalrayan hills of South Arcot; Kalrayan, Aranuthumalai, Neiyyamalai and shervaroy hills of Salem district; Sitteri hills of Dharmapuri district; Anamalai hills of Coimbatore district; and Palani hills of Madurai district. The Malaiyalis are the most numerically dominant tribe in Tamil Nadu, followed by the Irulars. Malaiyalis are primarily concentrated in the hills, and the Irulars live both in the hills and plains.

Although there are 36 tribal communities in Tamil Nadu, the strength of most of the communities is less than 1,000. In fact, the strength of many communities is less than 100. According to the 1971 Census, the population of eight tribal communities is less that 100, of 13 communities between 100 and 1,000 and of nine communities between 1,000 and 10,000. The tribal population is recorded as 311,515 (0.76%) in 1971,

520,226 (1.07%) in 1981 and 574,194 (1.03%) in 1991. According to the 55th round survey of the NSSO in 2000, there are 353 illiterates per 1,000 persons (age group of 15 and above), 11.10 per cent of rural households are landless, 78.20 per cent are marginal farmers and 0.20 per cent are big farmers. The average monthly per capita Expenditure (MPCE) is Rs. 384.46 in rural areas and Rs. 1,075.91 in urban areas of the state (www.tribaledu.com).

Economic Problems and Political Conditions of Tribals

The tribal people are economically the poorest people of India. Majority of them live below the poverty line. The tribal economy is based on agriculture of the crudest type. The main economic problems of the tribals are explained below.

1. **Exploitation:** the innocence, illiteracy and helplessness of the tribals are exploited by the outsiders. The British policy, in particular, had led to ruthless exploitation of the tribals in various ways as it favoured the zamindars, landlords, money-lender, forest contractors and excise, revenue and police officials.
2. **Unprofitable Agriculture:** About 90 per cent of the triabls are engaged in cultivation and most of them are landless and practice "Shifting Cultivation". They need to be helped in adopting new methods of cultivation. The tribals possess uneconomic holdings because of which their crop yield is very less. A very small percentage of the population participates in occupational activities in the secondary and tertiary sectors.
3. **Problems of Land Ownership:** A good portion of the land in the tribal areas has been legally transferred to non-tribals. Tribals demand that this land should be returned to them. In fact, the tribals had earlier enjoyed much freedom to use the forest and hunt their animals. They are emotionally attached to the forests for they believe that their gods, spirits live in forests. The tribals who are "deprived" of their rights to the land and forest have reacted sharply to the restrictions imposed by the government on their traditional rights.

4. **Unemployment and Underemployment:** A large number of tribal young men and women are either unemployed or underemployed. They are unhappy for they are not able to get jobs that can keep them occupied throughout they year. They need to be helped in finding secondary source of income by developing animal husbandry, poultry farming, handicrafts, handloom weaving, etc.
5. **Non-Availability of Banking Facilities:** Banking facilities in the tribal areas are so inadequate that the triabals have mainly to depend on the money-lenders. The triabls, therefore, demand that "Agricultural Indebtedness Relief Acts" Should be enacted so that they may get back their mortgaged land.

Most Indian tribes are concentrated in heavily forested areas that combine inaccessibility with limited political or economic significance. Historically, the economy of most tribes was subsistence agriculture or hunting and gathering. Tribal members traded with outsiders for the few necessities they lacked, such as salt and iron. A few local Hindu craftsmen might provide such items as cooking utensils. The twentieth century, however, has seen far-reaching changes in the relationship between tribals in India and the larger society and, by extension, traditional tribal economies. Improved transportation and communications have brought ever deeper intrusions into tribal lands; merchants and a variety of government policies have involved tribal peoples more thoroughly in the cash economy, although by no means on the most favorable of terms. Large areas fell into the hands of nontribals around 1900, when many regions were opened by the government to homestead-style settlement. Immigrants received free land in return for cultivating it.

Tribal people, too, could apply for land titles, although even title to the portion of land they happened to be planting that season could not guarantee their ability to continue swidden cultivation. More important, the notion of permanent, individual ownership of land was foreign to most tribals. Land, if seen in terms of ownership at all, was viewed as a communal resource, free to whoever needed it. By the time tribals accepted the necessity of obtaining formal land titles, they had lost the opportunity to lay claim to lands that might rightfully have been considered theirs. Generally, tribals were severely disadvantaged in dealing with government officials who granted land titles. Albeit belatedly, the colonial regime realized the necessity of protecting tribals of India from the predations of outsiders and prohibited the sale of tribal lands. Although an important loophole in the form of land leases was left open, tribes made some gains in the mid-twentieth century. Despite considerable obstruction by local police and land officials, who were slow to delineate tribal holdings and slower still to offer police protection, some land was returned to tribal peoples.

In the 1970s, the gains tribal peoples had made in earlier decades were eroded in many regions, especially in central India. Migration into tribal lands increased dramatically, and the deadly combination of constabulary and revenue officers uninterested in tribal welfare and sophisticated nontribals willing and able to bribe local officials was sufficient to deprive many tribals of their landholdings. The means of subverting protective legislation were legion: local officials could be persuaded to ignore land acquisition by nontribal people, alter land registry records, lease plots of land for short periods and then simply refuse to relinquish them, or induce tribal members to become indebted and attach their lands. Whatever the means, the result was that many tribal members became landless labourers in the 1960s and 1970s, and regions that a few years earlier had been the exclusive domain of tribes had an increasingly heterogeneous population. Unlike previous eras in which tribal people were shunted into more remote forests, by the 1960s relatively little unoccupied land was available. Government efforts to evict nontribal members from illegal occupation have proceeded slowly; when evictions occur at all, those ejected are usually members of poor, lower castes. In a 1985 publication, anthropologist Christoph von Fürer-Haimendorf describes this process in Andhra Pradesh: on average only 25 to 33 per cent of the tribal families in such villages had managed to keep even a portion of their holdings. Outsiders had paid about 5 per cent of the market value of the lands they took.

Improved communications, roads with motorized traffic, and more frequent government intervention figured in the increased contact that tribal peoples had with outsiders. Tribes fared best where there was little to induce nontribals to settle; cash crops and commercial highways frequently signaled the dismemberment of the tribes. Merchants have long been a link to the outside world, but in the past they were generally petty traders, and the contact they had with tribal people was transient. By the 1960s and 1970s, the resident nontribal shopkeeper was a permanent feature of many villages. Shopkeepers often sold liquor on credit, enticing tribal members into debt and into mortgaging their land. In the past, tribes made up shortages before harvest by foraging from the surrounding forest. More recently shopkeepers have offered ready credit—with the proviso that loans be repaid in kind with 50 to 100 per cent interest after harvest. Repaying one bag of millet with two bags has set up a cycle of indebtedness from which many have been unable to break loose.

The possibility of cultivators growing a profitable cash crop, such as cotton or castor-oil plants, continues to draw merchants into tribal areas. Nontribal traders frequently establish an extensive network of relatives and associates as shopkeepers to serve as agents in a number of villages. Cultivators who grow a cash crop often sell to the same merchants, who provide consumption credit throughout the year. The credit carries a high-interest price tag, whereas the tribal peoples' crops are bought at a fraction of the market rate. Cash crops offer a further disadvantage in that they decrease the supply of available foodstuffs and increase tribal dependence on economic forces beyond their control. This transformation has meant a decline in both the tribes' security and their standard of living.

In previous generations, families might have purchased silver jewelry as a form of security; contemporary tribal people are more likely to buy minor consumer goods. Whereas jewelry could serve as collateral in critical emergencies, current purchases simply increase indebtedness. In areas where gathering forest products is remunerative, merchants exchange their products for tribal labour. Indebtedness is so extensive that although such transactions are illegal, traders sometimes "sell" their debtors to other merchants, much like indentured servants.

In some instances, tribes have managed to hold their own in contacts with outsiders. Some Chenchus, a hunting and gathering tribe of the central hill regions of Andhra Pradesh, have continued to specialize in collecting forest products for sale. Caste Hindus living among them rent land from the Chenchus and pay a portion of the harvest. The Chenchus themselves have responded unenthusiastically to government efforts to induce them to take up farming. Their relationship to nontribal people has been one of symbiosis, although there were indications in the early 1980s that other groups were beginning to compete with the Chenchus in gathering forest products. A large paper mill was cutting bamboo in their territory in a manner that did not allow regeneration, and two groups had begun to collect for sale the same products the Chenchus sell. Dalits settled among them with the help of the Chenchus and learned agriculture from them. The nomadic Banjara herders who graze their cattle in the forest also have been allotted land there. The Chenchus have a certain advantage in dealing with caste Hindus; because of their long association with Hindu hermits and their refusal to eat beef, they are considered an unpolluted caste. Other tribes, particularly in South India, have cultural practices that are offensive to Hindus and, when they are assimilated, are often considered Dalits (Sharma.K Yougendra, 2001).

Tribal Development in Tamil Nadu

The post-colonial government plans for development of tribes in Tamil Nadu may be reviewed in two phases: the first is the pre-Sub-Plan period from 1947 to 1978, and the second is during the sub-plan period from 1978 to 2000. Before 1978, when the Tribal Sub-Plan (TSP) was introduced, the government had neither come up with any major strategy nor initiated a development scheme for tribal development in Tamil Nadu. After the sub-plan, this laissez-faire policy was withdrawn and the intervention strategy got a momentum.

Till independence there was no separate department for tribal welfare in Tamil Nadu. The Commissioner of Labour was in charge of this subject. The Department of Adi-Dravidar and Tribal Welfare was established in 1949 on the recommendations of the Ministry of Adi-Dravidar Welfare, made in 1947 (Government of Tamil Nadu 1989:1). In 1976 the 'Directorate of Harijan and Tribal Welfare' was established, following the recommendations of the 'Committee on Welfare of Scheduled Tribes' under the Chairmanship of V.Karthikeyan. This has been the chief body in the government to formulate and implement welfare programmes for the tribes of Tamil Nadu.

The budgetary allocation for tribal development decreased over the years and no separated schemes were formulated and implemented for tribal development during the first decade of the five-year plans. All the welfare measures that the government then proposed were implemented under the Community Development Programmes in a limited way. In 1961, two separated Block Development Offices were established in the hill areas, in the Shervaroy and Kolli hills, which were converted into Tribal Development Blocks (TDB) in 1963. The strategy of 'Tribal Five-Year Plan. Under this plan, nine Integrated Tribal Development Project (ITDP) areas were identified in six districts of northern and north-western Tamil Nadu: Kolli hills of Namakkal district; Shervaroy hills, Kalrayan hills and Pachamalai hills of Salem District; Kalrayan hills of South Arcot district; Jawadhi-Elagiri hills of North Arcot district; Pachamalai hils of Tiruchi district, and Sitteri hills of Dharmapuri District. During the first five Five-Year

Plan, the government had spent only a meager amount for tribal development. Even after that, the state government had failed to initiate any constructive scheme for their development.

Tribal Welfare of Tamil Nadu

A separate Directorate for the Welfare of Tribals was formed in April 2000. The Directorate pays special attention to the districts where Tribal concentration is more. Out of the 36 Tribal communities in the State, 6 Tribal Communities (i.e) Toda, Kota, Kurumbas, Irular, Paniyan and Kattunayakan have been identified as Primitive Tribal Groups. The other Tribals living in scattered areas are classified as Dispersed Tribes. The areas where the population of Scheduled Tribes exceeds 50 per cent of the total population is declared as "Integrated Tribal Development Programme" area, which exists in 7 districts viz. Salem, Namakkal, Villupuram, Tiruvannamalai, Thiruchirapalli, Dharmapuri and Vellore.

Grands Under Article 275(1) of Constitution of India

Under Article 275 (1) of the Constitution of India, infrastructure facilities for Tribals are taken up. "Eklavya" Model Residential Higher Secondary School was opened in the year 1998 under this scheme in Vellimalai of Kalrayan Hills in Villupuram District. One more Eklavya Model Residential Higher Secondary School was opened in Salem district during the year 2006-07 and the Government of India have released a sum of Rs. 150.00 lakhs for non-recurring and Rs. 30.00 lakhs for recurring expenditure for the above School. Now this school is functioning in a rented building. The school building is under construction through "Kattidamaiyam" at Abinavam village in Attur Taluk. A proposal has been sent to Government of India for enhancement of recurring expenditure for Rs.62.14 lakhs to Vellimalai Eklavya School for the year 2007-08. Further proposals have also been sent to Government of India for starting two more Eklavya Schools, in Vellore and Namakkal districts during the year 2008-09. The results of X and XII in the Eklavya Model Residential School, Vellimalai are as follows:

Year	Standard	Percentage of Pass
2006	X	100%
	XII	71%
2007	X	100%
	XII	97%

A sum of Rs. 360.00 lakhs has been provided for the year 2008-09 pending release of funds from Government of India.

Tamil Nadu Tribal Welfare Board

The Tamil Nadu Tribal Welfare Board has been constituted under the Chairmanship of the Minister for Adi Dravidar Welfare from 20.04.2007 for the overall development of the Tribals in the fields of education, economic development and social welfare. 6 official members and 13 Non-official Members have been nominated and the first meeting was held. A sum of Rs.1.00 crore was sanctioned for implementing various welfare measures to the members to be enrolled.

Tamil Nadu Tribes Advisory Council

The Tamil Nadu Tribes Advisory Council has now been reconstituted w.e.f 25.10.2007 under the Chairmanship of Minister for Adi Dravidar Welfare. This Council consists of 2 official members, 3 MLAs and 12 Non-officials belonging to the Tribal Communities and 2 Non-Tribals members.

Hill Area Development Programme (HADP)

For the welfare of Tribals residing in the Nilgiris district, the Hill Area Development Programme is being implemented by the Collector. A sum of Rs. 659.55 lakhs has been earmarked for this scheme for the year 2007-08. Under this scheme, various works like construction of houses for Tribals, construction of Kitchen/dining halls and other infrastructure facilities to GTR schools are undertaken. Similar works are also undertaken for Scheduled Castes/Scheduled Tribes habitations. During the year 2008-09, a proposal to the tune of Rs. 673.70 lakhs have been sent to Government of India (www.tribal.nic).

Government's Policy Towards the Tribals

The Govt. of India for the purpose of its governance administratively defined the Adivasis or tribals as "Scheduled Tribes". But it has not been able to resolve the ethnic relations between the tribal society and the caste Hindu society. The secular government is not much bothered about it also. Ethnographers like Hutton, for example, maintained that "Caste system and many cultural traditions of Hindusim have organic links with the tribal cultures". Ghurye who called the Indian triabls "backward Hindus", also held more or less the same view. The Government, instead, wants that the tribals should be given benefits of development and protective safeguards. There are necessary because the tribals have suffered enough from exploitation, discrimination and oppression by the rest of the society. They remained poor, illiterate, ignorant and backward. (www.tn.gov.in).

Before independence, the policy of the British government was to let the tribals live in isolation. The Administration was, therefore, regulatory in character and dealt with such matters as revenue, regulation of land, and law and order. People had to go to the administrators in order to find solutions to their problems. After independence, through the introduction of various welfare measures, the government expressed its great concern in the development and progress of the tribals. Now the administrators are required to go to the tribal areas to meet the tribals in order to find out their problems. The government expects the administrators to be honest and humane in their approach towards the tribals. It is unfortunate that such a change in the attitude of the bureaucrats has not taken place. Hence, expected progress has not taken place in the tribal word. Still, the gap between the tribals and non-tribals is not bridged. The gap between the rich tribals and the poor tribals is also not minimized. Much is to be done in this regard. "Nevertheless, at the all India level, it cannot be denied that the tribal development schemes have broken the stagnation of tribal societies and have initiated the process of tribal transformation" (www.aptribes.gov.in).

The Indian Education Commission on Tribal Education

The Indian Education Commission examined the problem of education of the tribals in some detail and made several recommendations. They suggested that tribal children might be exempted from payment of fess and also that additional grants might be given to private schools on account of the tribal children attending them. In view of the fact that the missionaries were doing useful work for education of the tribals, the commissions suggested that bodies willing to undertake the work of education on among aboriginal tribes be liberally assisted on the basis of abstention from any interference with religious teaching. They also recommended that educated tribes should however, possible, be appointed as teachers in special schools established within or on the border or the tribal areas (Rath Govind Chandra, 2006).

Eklavya Residential Schools, Tribal Activisory Council, HADP and various plans through develop the Tribal community functioned by our Government. The monitory facilities also allotted by State and Central Government to Tribal community. In future we are see the development tribes.

REFERENCES

Rath Govind Chandra, (2006), Tribal Development in India, Sage Publications.

Sharma.k.yougendra, 2001, History and Problem of Education Vol. 2 Kanisha Publication and Distributors, New Delhi.

www.tribal.nic/index.html

www.tribal.nic.in

Sharma.k.youngendra.2001.

www.tribaledu.com

www.tribaledu.com.

www.tribal.nic.

www.tn.gov.in

www.aptribes.gov.in

22

Radio Lessons in Primary Schools in Tribal Areas

A Study in Visakhapatnam District Andhra Pradesh

– K. John Babu

As the formal school is not provided with entertainment, Primary School Radio programme is aimed at educating the children through entertainment programme. So much of priority is given to make children happy to the last possible limit of human happiness. Childhood is a period of information seeking, when the child's central concern lies in defining a different picture of the world. For the 21st century child, the picture is apt to be broad and complex. The mass media expose him to the world far beyond the limits of his immediate experience.

Since 1940s, radio has been utilized in educational broadcasting and it has got a widespread acceptance as an enrichment source in the teaching of subjects such as music and social studies (Thompson, 1969). Radio has become a dynamic force in schools both in urban and rural (Willey and Young 1948). Further, radio is a low-cost technology that can improve the quality of instructions in primary schools (Fried, Searle, and Suppes, 1980). Since, radio broadcasts bestow greater benefits both on teachers and students through various programmes it provides opportunity for students to participate in the various programmes such as quiz, travel, talks, plays, stories, development of lessons etc. It can also provide minute information by bringing together a variety of things, people and places which is not possible in the classroom. The teacher can improve their standards by presenting and receiving these broadcast programmes. Though sometimes overshadowed by television, 'radio represents a medium capable of reaching a wide geographic audience at a low production cost with proven educational results' (Couch 1997). 'Studies by the United Kingdom Open University have demonstrated that radio has a greater value for weak students who benefit from radio as a supplementary learning tool. The Agency for International Development has shown that radio is more cost-effective and results in a greater learning effect than textbooks or teacher education' (Tripp and Roby, 1996). Radio has the advantage of teaching subjects in which classroom teachers are deficient or untrained. An added benefit for multi-grade classrooms is that it provides instruction for one group of students while the teacher works with another group. Radio can also bring new or unavailable resources into the classroom (Muller, 1985). In his book, The *death of distance*, Cairncross (1997) points out that 'the death of the distance as a determinant of the cost of communicating will probably be the single most important force shaping society in the first half of the next century. Communities will of course practice and long distance education programmes will help people to find mentors and acquire new skills". Thus, Baruah (1983) commented on the role of All India Radio in respect of education.

All India Radio's education broadcasts for schools are mainly designed as a support to the curricular organisation in the schools of various states and union territories of the country. The scope of the programme is both of the enrichment and direct teaching types. The objective is to reinforce and consolidate the learning-teaching situation in the class room by means of new techniques, help of specialists, and approaches which are normally beyond the capacity of an average school. Besides giving a support, the programme also gives a lead by updating, filling curricular gaps and bringing contemporary development into the scope of the programmes and thereby closing the gap between the class room and the outside world".

Devgan (1996) expressed in his strategy paper that, 'the radio (and TV) undoubtedly could serve as a powerful reinforcement medium particularly in a situation where good motivation already exists'. Educational broadcasting facilitates qualitative improvement of education and as an inexpensive medium of communication. Radio brings into the class room the voice of the experts, giving firsthand experience. Radio adds variety to the class room procedure. Radio broadcasts those topics which normally are not covered in the school curriculum with a view to widening the mental horizon of students, or to discuss the subjects which cannot be adequately dealt within an average institution. The radio in the class room provides enrichment courses and has a definite appeal to the students. It operates as a stimulus to learning.

Further, in an elaborate statement, Satyanarayana and Sesharatnam (2000: 95-96) observed that "radio was useful in providing remedial tutorials, or some other forms of tutorial based feedback, providing corrections, alterations or updating of material, where print re-make budgets are limited, or where print cannot reach students quickly enough, recordings of naturally occurring events, e.g. political speech, children talking, concerts or performances, talks previously recorded, historical events presenting material in a dramatized form, enabling students to identify with the emotions and viewpoints of the main participants providing an alternative view to that presented in the correspondence text and or television programmes and enabling students to perceive the different points of view that exist, and observe ideas being challenged, through discussion and interviews". Radio can be used as an effective and interesting tool in education both for formal and non-formal education. In the words of Vyas, Sharma, Kumar (2002), 'the educational radio programmes indicate that radio can be an effective medium in reaching out quality education and training to the needy ones'. Das (2009) said that "radio is a powerful mass medium used in education for disseminating information, imparting instruction and giving entertainment".

Educational Broadcasting in India

As far back as 1927, the Madras Corporation had a transmitter and put out, for primary schools educational programmes in Tamil. The Indian Broadcasting Company too, occasionally put out informal broadcasts to schools in 1929. The Calcutta station put out broadcasts to schools in 1932. However soon after their inception, they were abandoned. In 1936, the demand for the revival of broadcasts to schools reappeared. In 1937, the University of Calcutta and the Department of Education, Bengal jointly approached All India Radio to resume broadcasts to schools, and in November of that year, Calcutta station started a half-hour programme for schools for two days in the week (Kapur 1961). Before Independence, school programme was broadcast by as large as 30 AIR centers. Lionel Fielden, then controller of AIR, wrote in his report on the progress of broadcasting in India (March 1939), that:

> "it was therefore decided to embark upon school broadcasting forthwith instead of insisting on an extensive installation of receiving sets as a condition prior to such broadcasts, since it was felt that the radiation of school programmes would in itself be the best means of stimulating interest and persuading educational institutions to equip themselves with the means of benefiting from them' (cited in Baruah, 1983: 12).

All stations had therefore instructed to draw up school programmes for October 1938 - March 1939 in consultation with educational authorities in the provinces. Regular school broadcasting thus began in October-December 1938 from Bombay, Calcutta, Delhi and Madras (Baruah 1983). It became a principle that the educational broadcasts should not attempt to replace the teacher but to supplement his work. The emphasis in AIR's broadcast to primary schools is education through entertainment.

Educational Broadcasting in Andhra Pradesh

In Andhra Pradesh, the Hyderabad All India Radio station was set up on 5th July 1954 and started transmitting the school programmes from the same year. Since then, AIR Hyderabad started producing school programmes for the students. Visakhapatnam station of AIR was formally inaugurated on the 4th August 1963. This was initially started as an auxiliary center to Hyderabad station with evening transmission only. Later on, three transmissions were introduced from March 1971 the power of transmitter was enhanced on the 29August 1976.

Introducing educational broadcasting of All India Radio, Hyderabad 21 June 1965, Bullayya (1973) the then vice-chancellor of Andhra University said, "I am glad to introduce the schedule of educational broadcasts for the year 1965-66, prepared by All India Radio. I find the schedule of school broadcasts for middle and high schools have been carefully planned. The talks are programmed to be broadcast through three media, English, Telugu, and Urdu. They include topics on English language, Indian History, Civics and Telugu Language. Notes on each unit lesson will be sent to the listening schools. It will also contain questions for the pupils to answer at the end of each broadcast".

As part of the educational broadcasts, AIR, Hyderabad introduced some school broadcasts for the benefit of school going children in Andhra Pradesh. Details of two programmes that have been broadcast by AIR are:

1. ***Vindham Nerchukundam* (listen and learn) a radio programme for primary school students**

As a source of distance education, All India Radio, Hyderabad and the District Primary Educational Project (DPEP) initiated the radio school programme *'Vindam Nerchukundam'* as a pilot project from All India Radio

Visakhapatnam from 18th March to 4th April 2002 and 3rd July to 28th August 2002. In the first stage, the programmes that contained 46 radio lessons for the students of Grade III were broadcast. It covered neighboring districts, Srikakulam Vijayanagaram, Visakhapatnam, East Godawari. With the inspiration given by the students and teachers, District Primary Educational Project took the help of Distance Education Project, New Delhi, and broadcast radio lessons for the students of Grades III and IV in all the costal districts from 25th November 2002 to 11th February 2003 (Malakondaiah, 2000).

Now Sarva Sikha Abhiyan (SSA) has been continuing this radio programme and enhanced to all the schools run by the state government such as primary, upper primary and high schools. All India Radio Hyderabad brings out the programme titled *"Vindham Nerchukundam"* along with the programme schedule for the students and teachers of primary and upper primary Grades in Telugu and Urdu medium from Monday to Friday.

2. ***Vidya Tharangalu*** **(waves of education) a radio programme for secondary school students**

Students of Grades VIII to X of schools following the state syllabus get radio lessons under the *'Vidya Tharangalu'* programme aired from 1, July 2008. An initiative of the Department of School Education, it is expected to reach out to an estimated 19 lakh students across the state through 12 All India Radio (AIR) stations - Hyderabad, Vijayawada, Visakhapatnam, Kadapa, Warangal, Tirupati, Adilabad, Nizamabad, Markapuram, Anantapur, Kurnool and Kothagudem at 6.25 P.M. daily. AIR and State Council for Education, Research and Training (SCERT), launched the lessons in an interactive format to make them appealing to students and supplement the classroom teaching. The 30-minute capsules will be broadcast twice a week for students of each Grade - Monday and Tuesday (IX Grade), Wednesday and Thursday (X Grade) and Friday and Saturday (VIII Grade). A teacher-educator's programme to improve teaching methodology would be aired every Friday from 12.40 PM. to 1.40 PM. The production work of the programme is being handled by radio producers from AIR stations at Hyderabad, Vijayawada and Visakhapatnam. State Council for Educational Research and Training (SCERT) Director D. Ravindranatham, who released the material, said the programme was revived in 2007 for students of IX and X and this year VIII standard was included. The SCERT would pay Rs. 43 lakh a year to *Prasar Bharati* for the broadcast (All India Radio, 2008).

Method

The present study aims at measuring effectiveness of a major and age old broadcast medium, Radio, in terms of its educational impact on the target audience. According to Gloria D. Feliciano (1996), Communication research in Asia started in the late 1950's and early 1960's by the researchers who introduced readability studies, Content analyses, and readership and listenership surveys. This study adopts a field study experimental design that is of quasi-experimental nature. Quasi-experiments always correspond to certain natural settings in which the experimenter can approximate experimental procedures for data collection, even though she lacks full control over the delivery of treatment. (Ricken Henry and Robert Boruch, 1974).

Objectives of the Study

In order to evaluate the programme, the objectives of the study are as follows:

1. To study the effectiveness of radio programmes on the primary and upper primary school children.
2. To study the achievement levels of the pupils comparatively in urban, rural and tribal localities.
3. To study the suitability of language and the format used in the radio broadcasts in terms of comprehension of primary and upper primary level radio programmes.
4. To ascertain the perceptions of students and teachers about the radio programmes.

Table 22.1: Selection of the Schools

Area	No. of Mandals	Mandal Name	Control Group		Experimental Group		Total
			MP UPS	MP ES	MP UPS	MP ES	
Tribal	1	Paderu	GUPS Thum pada	MP ES Madiga banda	MP UPS Bangaru-Metta	MP ES Geddam-puttu	4
Rural	2	Anandapuram	MP UPS Ananda-puram	MP ES Boipalem	MP UPS Bodda-palem	MP ES Garipeta	4
		Padmanabam	MPUPS Korada	MP ES Sankara peta	MP UPS Pandrangi	MP ES Revidi	4
Urban	1	Bhimunipatnam	MFC UPS Bhimili	CM ES Bhimili	GM UPS Bhimili	PNM ES Bhimili	4
Total	4	4	4	4	4	4	16

Note: *MP UPS = Mandal Parishad Upper Primary schools, MPES= Mandal Parishad Elementary Schools. MFC UPS= Mahatma Gandhi Fishermen Colony Upper Primary School, CMES= Central Municipal Elementary School, GMUPS=Government Modal Upper Primary School, PNMES=Pandit Nehru Municipal Elementary School.*

Table 22.2: Selection of the Subject for the Study

Area	Treatment	Grade V	Grade VI	Grade VII	Students Total	Teachers Total
Urban	Experimental	5	5	5	15	10
	Control	5	5	5	15	–
Rural	Experimental	10	10	10	30	20
	Control	10	10	10	30	–
Tribal	Experimental	5	5	5	15	10
	Control	5	5	5	15	–
Total	Experimental	20	20	20	60	40
	Control	20	20	20	60	–
	Exp & Con	40	40	40	120	40

Hypotheses

In view of these objectives, the following hypotheses have been formulated for examination:

H_1. There is a positive and effective impact of the radio programmes both at primary and upper primary level.

H_2. There is no difference in the achievement levels in both experimental and control groups.

$H_{3.}$ There is no difference in the achievement levels of students basing on their locality.

$H_{4.}$ There is a positive significant opinion of the students and teachers towards radio programmes.

Selection of the Sample

Sample for the study was drawn from upper primary and primary schools located in urban, rural, and tribal areas of Visakhapatnam district on the basis of their exposure of radio programmes. The schools in which radio programmes were played back were regarded as experimental group schools and others were treated as the control group schools in urban, rural and tribal areas. The investigator for this study selected randomly 4 mandals out of 43 in the district: 1 urban, 2 rural and 1 tribal areas, in which 16 schools were selected (4 urban, 8 rural and 4 tribal areas). In these, 8 schools were experimental, (2 urban, 4 rural and 2 tribal areas) and 8 schools were control, (2 urban, 4 rural and 2 tribal areas).

Selection of the Subjects

The researcher selected a sample of 120 students from the sampled schools. As the strength of the students ranged from 5 to 50, the researcher listed the selection of the students only 5 from each Grade of selected schools. In some of these schools, boys and girls together were higher than five and lower than ten. Hence, the researcher confined to only five students from each school basing on the geographical locality and ratio of the school/Grade and made a list of 120 subjects in 4 mandals. The students both boys and girls of urban, rural and tribal schools were treated as control and experimental groups. In the same way, the teachers were selected from primary and upper primary schools in only experimental settings and made a list of forty. Like that, the investigator selected a total of 120 pupils (60 control and 60 experimental) and 40 teacher (experimental only) by using a random sample population method.

Content: Cent per cent of the students from urban and rural areas feel that they have acquired their knowledge through radio lessons but 88 per cent of the tribal school children felt that they have gained knowledge through radio lessons.

Language: It was observed that despite different variations in accent, the language in radio maintained standard of the state and is up to the mark. But in tribal area, due to linguistic and biological problems, students expected little difficulty towards language of Telugu and English than urban and rural area.

Novelty: Radio lessons through songs, music, and different characters in the story are attractive and 93 per cent of the students from urban and rural area expressed their view that the radio lessons are novel, but it is 87 per cent by tribal students.

Style of presentation: 95 per cent rural area students 93 per cent of urban and 89 per cent of tribal area students expressed their view that the style of presentation in teaching language, mathematics, science, and social in radio is interesting. It was observed that the presentation in radio lessons for different classes with various formats was appealing.

Duration: 97 per cent of rural students feel more convenient with the present time and duration of broadcasting radio lessons 30 minutes for primary Grades (9: 30 AM to 10: 00 AM) and 15 minutes for upper primary Grades (10:00AM to 10:15 AM) than urban and tribal with 80 per cent equally. 68 per cent of the students are of the view that the narration of radio lessons is done speedily as the time is not sufficient to learn and imitate. 63 per cent of the students felt that songs, music, and advertisements were much used in radio lessons and 87 per cent of students expressed that the time is not allotted more on subject knowledge.

Table 22.3: Perceptions of Students towards Radio Lessons

Dimension	S.No.	Item No.	Statements	Urban	Rural	Tribal	Total
1	2	3	4	5	6	7	8
Content	1	4	The knowledge gained by the students could be improved more by listening to radio lessons	15100%	30100%	15100%	60100%
	2	6	The subject learned through radio lessons is very useful	15100%	30100%	1493%	5998%
	3	7	Students can learn more about a particular subject through listening to radio lessons	15100%	30100%	1173%	5693%
	4	8	It is very easy to learn the subject matter through radio lessons	15100%	30100%	1386%	5388%
			Content Total	**60100%**	**120100%**	**5388%**	**23397%**
Language	5	2	The language used in radio lessons is very clear and understandable.	15100%	30100%	15100%	5897%
	6	15	The questions on lessons which are listened through radio are easy to answer.	15100%	30100%	1386%	5897%
	7	18	Rhymes and word clarity in teaching English language in radio is interesting.	1386%	2687%	1173%	5083%
	8	21	The clarity of the words in teaching Telugu language through radio is interesting.	15100%	30100%	1280%	5795%
			Language Total	**5897%**	**11697%**	**4982%**	**22393%**

(Contd…)

1	2	3	4	5	6	7	8
Novelty	9	3	The songs and music used in radio lessons are very interesting.	1493%	2893%	1386%	5592%
	10	24	The characters in the story and drama, which are presented for the radio lessons, are attractive.	1493%	2893%	1386%	5592%
			Novelty Total	**2893%**	**5693%**	**2687%**	**11092%**
Presentation	11	9	Generally, the class teacher sometimes tries to imitate radio teaching method in the classroom.	1173%	2997%	1386%	5388%
	12	10	The teaching of the class teacher is good but the teaching through radio is still better.	15100%	2997%	15100%	5998%
	13	17	The way of teaching mathematics in radio in some cases is understandable and interesting.	1493%	2790%	1493%	5592%
	14	19	Teaching environmental science-1 (social studies) through drama and discussion in radio is interesting and understandable.	15100%	2893%	1386%	5693%
	15	20	Teaching environmental science –II (science) through song and drama in radio is interesting.	15100%	2997%	1280%	5693%
			Presentation Total	**7093%**	**14295%**	**6789%**	**27993%**

(Contd…)

1	2	3	4	5	6	7	8
Duration	16	5	Present times of the broadcasting radio lessons, 30 minutes for primary school (9:30 AM to 10:00 AM) and 15 minutes for upper primary school (10:00AM to 10:15AM) is convenient.	1280%	2997%	1280%	5388%
	17	11	Generally the radios are at speed, so the time is not sufficient to learn and imitate the radio lessons.	1386%	2687%	1280%	4168%
	18	16	Songs, music and advertisements are much used in the radio lessons. So the time is not allotted more on subject knowledge.	1067%	2170%	747%	3863%
	19	22	The lessons that heard through radio are remembered for a long period.	1173%	2893%	1386%	5083%
	20	23	The songs that heard in a radio are remembered for a long time.	1173%	2893%	1280%1	4778%
	21	25	Sufficient time has not been allotted to the subject matter in the Radio lessons.	1493%	2687%	1280%	5287%
			Duration Total	**7179%**	**14681%**	**6673%**	**28379%**

(Contd...)

1	2	3	4	5	6	7	8
Usefulness	22	1	It is very much useful to listen radio lessons.	15100%	30100%	15100%	60100%
	23	12	Before the radio lessons, the activities on the lesson conducted by the class teacher are good.	1386%	2687%	1493%	5388%
	24	13	After the radio lessons the activities conducted by the class teacher which are related to the lessons are very useful for developing learning in students.	1280%	30100%	1493%	5287%
	25	14	Before and after the radio lessons, the activities conducted by the teacher can possibly develop the subject knowledge among the students.	1386%	2687%	1386%	4880%
			Usefulness Total	**5388%**	**11293%**	**5592%**	**21392%**

Note: S. No= Serial Number, Item No= Statement Number.

It was observed that radio lessons were prepared up to 25-26 minutes out of 30 for primary classes, and 11-12 minutes were used for upper primary classes out of 15 minutes. Remaining time was used for advertisement, address and sponsorship of the broadcasters, and name of the participants.

Usefulness: 92 per cent of the students perceived that radio lessons were very useful to the students from three Grades and three areas. 80 per cent of the students feel that before and after the radio lessons, the activities conducted by the teacher could possible develop the subject knowledge. Students feel that it is an additional source of acquiring knowledge along with teaching of the class teacher.

Observation

Observations on school radio utilization were done on-the spot in a randomly drawn sample of eight experimental schools in urban, rural and tribal areas and content observation was carried out by the researcher through CD player individually in a room.

Class room atmosphere: In urban schools, on an average thirty to forty students sit together at a common class room for the purpose of listening to a broadcast. Because of this large number, it was not always easy to maintain minimum discipline as it would enable everyone to listen attentively. Lot of disturbance has been experienced by some students and also noise by the vehicles nearby the road, while the radio programmes were going on. So the class room for radio listening was not in a healthy atmosphere.

In rural schools, as the class rooms were filled with students belong to multi-grades, it was somewhat difficult to listen to the radio lessons peacefully. Almost all the experimental schools in rural areas were having one or two rooms filled students from five Grades. There is no provision separately for radio listening in rural schools. *Waranda* (extension part of the building) of the school has been used for the purpose of radio programme.

Whereas in tribal schools, class room atmosphere is calm to listen to the radio programmes. Pupils were obedient and sat according to the instructions given by the teacher. Children in tribal schools were also very few in number.

Sitting position of the pupils: Though most of the time the children were instructed to sit in a half circle, due to lack of healthy atmosphere in rural schools, pupils were allowed to sit according to their own convenience to listen to the radio lessons peacefully. In urban schools also, due to heavy crowd and lack of calm atmosphere, pupils were allowed to sit according to their own convenience to listen to the radio lessons. In tribal school, children sat in a half circle and constantly heard radio programmes.

Pre and post activities: Pupils in the tribal area have participated interestingly in the pre and post activities given by the teachers such as sitting in a hemi-spherical, while writing down difficult words used in the radio, listening carefully, preparing to answer the questions, and discussing on topics etc. It was observed that in rural schools, pre broadcasting discussion was inadequate as a result of which, students were not properly prepared for receiving the programme. It was also observed that in urban schools, the post activities were only limited to the questions. Post broadcasting discussion was not properly organised and adequate scope was not given for stimulating interest and curiosity of students in the radio programmes.

Student's response: Students of the urban schools responded very well to the clarity of voice of the radio teacher and easy language used by the various characters in different formats in the radio programmes. Some students in urban schools tried to write on the note books the points which they feel important. Students from rural area also responded by gestures and followed the commands of the radio teacher. It was observed that the tribal school children showed annoyance in their face on language used in radio lessons and felt difficulty in understanding some of the words of the radio teacher especially scientific Telugu and English words.

Attention of the students: It was observed that the students who sat in the front rows paid more attention as compared to the students sitting in the back rows. Further, the students sitting in the back rows were found to be restive and inattentive in all the experimental groups belonging to urban, rural and tribal settings.

Behavior of the students: In urban schools, students were over active and behaved dominantly. While the radio programme is going on, the teachers have faced difficulty to bring them into control. In rural schools, while the radio programme is going on, students used to come and go without taking permission of the class teacher or researcher. It was observed that students did not maintain proper discipline in rural schools. Some girl students sitting in the back rows were disturbed by their friends sitting beside them. In tribal schools, students were very quiet and obedient. They followed the instructions of the researcher and teacher.

Singing songs: At the time of songs on particular subject, children belonging to urban, rural and tribal were alert and paid much interest on the melodious music and mellifluous voice of the songs. They sang the songs enthusiastically along with the radio teacher at the time of repetition in the radio. The researcher observed that some students in urban schools tried to dance to the tunes of the radio lessons by moving their shoulders and body. A song *Bale Bale* ...... composed with music on 'Skin diseases', a Science programme for the Grade V was really enjoyed by the students. Another song *Jo achutananda jo jo mukhunda* ...... A melodious lullaby, a well known composition of 'Annamayya' for the Grade VII was remembered for a long time.

Replying questions: Students from urban, rural and tribal areas, tried to give proper answers to the questions asked by the radio teacher and class teachers as well. Most of the students in urban areas raised their voice while giving reply to the questions. It shows their interest and enthusiasm towards radio programmes.

***Merits of the study*:** Though the magnitude of the study is quite limited, it has few meritorious features that can be utilized in planning and production of programmes for primary school children.

1. The objectives of the findings of the present study have their credible root in the selection of an appropriate and up-to-date study design.
2. A comparative analysis of the gain in knowledge and perception across many dimensions, have provided the scope for looking into the state of art of educational broadcasting in Andhra Pradesh, more critically.
3. The analysis of the perceptions of the teachers, in particular have provided additional testimony of the effectiveness of educational broadcasting.
4. The use of test of significance of difference has provided an exact and precise picture of radio's influence.

It is conclusively proved that radio broadcasts enhance the knowledge level of students. Thus, the present study agrees with the earlier studies done in India that the radio lessons lead to knowledge gain of the students (Mohanty, 1992; Sudame, et al 1982). The findings of the present study are similar to the earlier study done in the tribal setting of Visakhapatnam district (Suryanarayana, 2006). The present study too found that the experimental groups in tribal areas scored more than the urban and rural settings.

REFERENCES

All India Radio (2008): 'Radio Lessons for School Students', *All India Radio Internet News* dated 1 July 2008, http://www.air.org.in, Accessed on 25 March 2009.

Baruah U.L. (1983): *This is All India Radio*, Publication Division, Ministry of I & B, Govt. of India, New Delhi.

Bullayya Lankapalli (1973): *On Education: Occasional Speeches.* 82-84, Andhra University Press & Publications, Waltair.

Cairncross, Frances (1997): *The Death of Distance*, Harvard Business School Press, Boston, Massachusetts.Couch, L. (1997): 'Digital and Analog Communication Systems' *Upper Saddle River*, NJ: Prentice-Hall quoted at http://www.telecommunications.msu.edu. Accessed on 17 March 2009.

Das J.K. (2009): 'Educational Broadcasting Through Radio' *Turkish online Journal of Distance of Education,* -TOJDE July 2002 ISSN 1302-6488 3 (3), Accessed on 13, March 2009.

Devagan A. K. (1996): 'Communication Strategies for Non-Radio, TV Areas' *Communicator* A Quarterly Magazine for Journalism and Mass Communication, 1 - XXXI (3), July-September, New Delhi.

Friend, Jamesine, Barbara Searle, and Patrick Suppes, Eds. (1980): *Radio Mathematics in Nicaragua, Stanford, California.* The Institute for Mathematical Studies in the Social Sciences, Stanford University.

Gloria D. Feliciano (1973): 'An Overview of Communication Research in Asia: Status Problems and Needs', *Papers of East-West Communication Institute*, 6, June 1973, Honolulu.

Kapur C. L. (1961): *Radio in School Education,* Ministry of Education, Government of India, Government of India Press, New Delhi.

Minti K. Mohanty (1992): *School Radio Programme, Their Effectiveness for Pupils growth*, 78-81, Deep & Deep Publications, New Delhi.

Muller, J. (1985): *Radio for Literacy. A Reader on the Use of Radio in Literacy Programmes.* Bonn, Germany: German Foundation for International Development. (ERIC Document Reproduction Service No. ED 265 372), cited at All India Radio: growth and development at http://www.air.org.in. Accessed on 20, March 2009.

Poonam Malakondaiah (2002): *'Vindaam Nerchukondam' Radio kaaryakrama karadeepika,* (SPD) DPEP, Directorate of School Education, Hyderabad, AP.

Ricken Henry W. and Robert F. Boruch (1974): *Social Experimentation: A Method for planning and Evaluating Social Intervention*, New York: Academic Press.

Satyanarayana , P. and Sesharatnam, C. (2000): *Distance Education : What? Why? How?* , 95-96, Booklinks Corporation , Hyderabad, India.

Sudame, G.R. et al., (1977): 'Planning and Administration of the Educational Broadcast from All India Radio Cuttack', *EPA Bulletin,* 1(4), January 1977.

Surya Narayana V.V. (2006): 'A Study on the Impact of Radio Lessons at the Primary School Level in the Tribal Area of Visakhapatnam Dist'. Unpublished *Small Scale Research* Submitted to the State Project Director, Sarva Shikha Abhiyan, Hyderabad, AP.

Tripp, S., and Roby, W. (1996): 'Auditory Presentations in Language Laboratories', D. H. Jonassen Ed., *Handbook of Research for*

Educational Communications and Technology, 821-850, New York: Simon & Schuster Macmillan.

Vyas R.V, Sharma R.C, Ashwini Kumar (2002): 'Educational Radio in India', *Turkish online Journal of Distance Education*, ISSN 1302-6488, 3 (3), Tojde, July 2002. Accessed on 17 March 2009.

Willey Roy De Verl and Young Helen Ann (1948): *Radio in Elementary Education*, DC Heath and Co, Boston.

Index